25 GREATEST SPEECHES of SWAMI VIVEKANANDA

Swami Vivekananda, born Narendranath Datta on 12 January 1863, in erstwhile Calcutta, was a Hindu spiritual leader and reformer in India who strove to reconcile Indian spirituality with western practical advancement, arguing that the two mutually reinforced and complemented each other. Influenced by western esotericism, Vivekananda played a pivotal role in introducing the Indian darsanas, or teachings, of Vedanta and Yoga to the western world, and is credited with promoting interfaith harmony and elevating Hinduism to the status of a major world religion in the late nineteenth century. He eventually rose to prominence as the most illustrious disciple of the Hindu mystic, Ramakrishna, demonstrating the inherent unity of all religions. He was a pioneering figure of modern Hindu reform movements in colonial India.

25 GREATEST SPEECHES *of* SWAMI VIVEKANANDA

RUPA

Published by
Rupa Publications India Pvt. Ltd 2022
7/16, Ansari Road, Daryaganj
New Delhi 110002

Sales Centres:
Allahabad Bengaluru Chennai
Hyderabad Jaipur Kathmandu
Kolkata Mumbai

Edition copyright © Rupa Publications India Pvt. Ltd 2022

The views and opinions expressed in this book are the author's own and the facts
are as reported by him which have been verified to the extent possible,
and the publishers are not in any way liable for the same.

All rights reserved.
No part of this publication may be reproduced, transmitted,
or stored in a retrieval system, in any form or by any means, electronic,
mechanical, photocopying, recording or otherwise,
without the prior permission of the publisher.

ISBN: 978-93-5520-371-7

First impression 2022

10 9 8 7 6 5 4 3 2 1

This book is sold subject to the condition that it shall not, by way of
trade or otherwise, be lent, resold, hired out, or otherwise circulated,
without the publisher's prior consent, in any form of binding or
cover other than that in which it is published.

CONTENTS

1. Response to the Welcome	1
2. Paper on Hinduism	3
3. Address at the Final Session	18
4. The Spirit and Influence of Vedanta	20
5. The Soul and God	26
6. Practical Religion: Breathing and Meditation	40
7. One Existence Appearing as Many	48
8. Bhakti	58
9. The Ideal of a Universal Religion	68
10. The Free Soul	90
11. The Ramayana	104
12. The Mahabharata	119
13. The Gita I	144
14. The Gita II	157
15. The Gita III	164
16. Christ, the Messenger	177
17. Krishna	193
18. Mohammed	201
19. On Lord Buddha	205
20. Buddha's Message to the World	208
21. Women of India	222

22. The Powers of the Mind	242
23. The Great Teachers of the World	257
24. My Life and Mission	273
25. The Sages of India	292

1

RESPONSE TO THE WELCOME

Delivered on 11 September 1893, at Parliament of the World's Religions, Chicago

Sisters and brothers of America, it fills my heart with joy unspeakable to rise in response to the warm and cordial welcome which you have given us. I thank you in the name of the most ancient order of monks in the world; I thank you in the name of the mother of religions; and I thank you in the name of millions and millions of Hindu people of all classes and sects.

My thanks, also, to some of the speakers on this platform who, referring to the delegates from the Orient, have told you that these men from far-off nations may well claim the honour of bearing to different lands the idea of toleration. I am proud to belong to a religion which has taught the world both tolerance and universal acceptance. We believe not only in universal toleration, but we accept all religions as true. I am proud to belong to a nation which has sheltered the persecuted and refugees of all religions and all nations of the Earth. I am proud to tell you that we have gathered in our bosom the purest remnant of the Israelites, who came to Southern India and took refuge with us in the very year in which their holy temple was shattered to pieces by Roman tyranny. I am proud to belong to the religion which has sheltered and is still fostering the remnant of the grand Zoroastrian nation. I will quote to you, brethren, a few lines from a hymn which I remember to have repeated from my earliest boyhood, which is every day repeated by millions of human beings: 'As the different streams having their sources in different places all mingle their water in the sea, so, O Lord, the different paths which men take through different tendencies, various though they appear, crooked or straight, all lead to Thee.'

The present convention, which is one of the most august assemblies ever held, is in itself a vindication, a declaration to the world of the wonderful doctrine preached in the Gita: 'Whosoever comes to Me, through whatsoever form, I reach him; all men are struggling through paths which in the end lead to me.' Sectarianism, bigotry and its horrible descendant, fanaticism, have long possessed this beautiful Earth. They have filled the Earth with violence, drenched it often with human blood, destroyed civilization and sent whole nations to despair. Had it not been for these horrible demons, human society would be far more advanced than it is now. But their time is come; and I fervently hope that the bell that tolled this morning in honour of this convention may be the death-knell of all fanaticism, of all persecutions with the sword or with the pen and of all uncharitable feelings between persons wending their way to the same goal.

2

PAPER ON HINDUISM

Delivered on 19 September 1893, at Parliament of the World's Religions, Chicago

Three religions now stand in the world which have come down to us from prehistoric times—Hinduism, Zoroastrianism and Judaism. They have all received tremendous shocks and all of them prove by their survival their internal strength. But while Judaism failed to absorb Christianity and was driven out of its place of birth by its all-conquering daughter, and a handful of Parsees is all that remains to tell the tale of their grand religion, sect after sect arose in India and seemed to shake the religion of the Vedas to its very foundations, but like the waters of the seashore in a tremendous earthquake, it receded only for a while, only to return in an all-absorbing flood, a thousand times more vigorous. And when the tumult of the rush was over, these sects were all sucked in, absorbed and assimilated into the immense body of the mother faith.

From the high spiritual flights of the Vedanta philosophy, of which the latest discoveries of science seem like echoes, to the low ideas of idolatry with its multifarious mythology, the agnosticism of the Buddhists and the atheism of the Jains, each and all have a place in Hindu's religion.

Where then, the question arises, where is the common centre to which all these widely diverging radii converge? Where is the common basis upon which all these seemingly hopeless contradictions rest? And this is the question I shall attempt to answer.

The Hindus have received their religion through revelation, the Vedas. They hold that the Vedas are without beginning and without end. It may sound ludicrous to this audience, how can a book be without beginning or end. But by the Vedas no books are meant. They mean the accumulated treasury of spiritual laws discovered by different persons in different times. Just as the law of gravitation existed before its discovery and would exist if all humanity forgot it, so is it with the laws that govern the spiritual world. The moral, ethical and spiritual relations between souls and between individual spirits and the Father of all spirits were there before their discovery and would remain even if we forget them.

The discoverers of these laws are called rishis and we honour them as perfected beings. I am glad to tell this audience that some of the very greatest of them were women. Here it may be said that these laws as laws may be without end, but they must have had a beginning. The Vedas teach us that creation is without beginning or end. Science is said to have proved that the sum total of cosmic energy is always the same. Then, if there was a time when nothing existed, where was all this manifested energy? Some say it was in a potential form in God. In that case, God is sometimes potential and sometimes kinetic, which would make Him mutable. Everything mutable is a compound and everything compound must undergo that change which is called destruction. So God would die, which is absurd. Therefore there never was a time when there was no creation.

If I may be allowed to use a simile, creation and creator are two lines, without beginning and without end, running parallel to each other. God is the ever-active providence, by

Paper on Hinduism ♦ 5

whose power systems after systems are being evolved out of chaos, made to run for a time and again destroyed. This is what the Brahmin boy repeats every day: 'The sun and the moon, the Lord created like the suns and moons of previous cycles.' And this agrees with modern science.

Here I stand, and if I shut my eyes and try to conceive my existence, 'I', 'I', 'I', what is the idea before me? The idea of a body. Am I, then, nothing but a combination of material substances? The vedas declare, 'No'. I am a spirit living in a body. I am not the body. The body will die, but I shall not die. Here am I in this body; it will fall, but I shall go on living. I had also a past. The soul was not created, for creation means a combination which means a certain future dissolution. If the soul was created, it must die. Some are born happy, enjoy perfect health, with beautiful body, mental vigour and all wants supplied. Others are born miserable, some are without hands or feet, others again are idiots and only drag on a wretched existence. Why, if they are all created, why does a just and merciful God create one happy and another unhappy, why is He so partial? Nor would it mend matters in the least to hold that those who are miserable in this life will be happy in a future one. Why should a man be miserable even here in the reign of a just and merciful God?

In the second place, the idea of a creator God does not explain the anomaly, but simply expresses the cruel fiat of an all-powerful being. There must have been causes, then, before his birth, to make a man miserable or happy and those were his past actions.

Are not all the tendencies of the mind and the body accounted for by inherited aptitude? Here are two parallel lines of existence—one of the mind, the other of the matter. If matter and its transformations answer for all that we have, there is no necessity for supposing the existence of a soul. But it cannot be proved that thought has been evolved out of matter, and if a philosophical monism is inevitable, spiritual monism is certainly logical and no less desirable than a materialistic monism. But neither of these are necessary here.

We cannot deny that bodies acquire certain tendencies from heredity, but those tendencies only mean the physical configuration, through which a peculiar mind alone can act in a peculiar way. There are other tendencies peculiar to a soul caused by its past actions. And a soul with a certain tendency would by the laws of affinity take birth in a body which is the fittest instrument for the display of that tendency. This is in accord with science, for science wants to explain everything by habit, and habit is formed through repetitions. So repetitions are necessary to explain the natural habits of a new-born soul. And since they were not obtained in this present life, they must have come down from past lives.

There is another suggestion. Taking all these for granted, how is it that I do not remember anything of my past life? This can be easily explained. I am now speaking English. It is not my mother tongue, in fact no words of my mother tongue are now present in my consciousness, but let me try to bring them up, and they rush in. That shows that consciousness is only the surface of the mental ocean and within its depths are stored all our experiences. Try and struggle, they would come up and you would be conscious even of your past life.

This is direct and demonstrative evidence. Verification is the perfect proof of a theory, and here is the challenge thrown to the world by the rishis. We have discovered the secret by which the very depths of the ocean of memory can be stirred up—try it and you would get a complete reminiscence of your past life.

So then the Hindu believes that he is a spirit. Him the

sword cannot pierce—him the fire cannot burn—him the water cannot melt—him the air cannot dry. The Hindu believes that every soul is a circle whose circumference is nowhere, but whose centre is located in the body, and that death means the change of this centre from body to body. Nor is the soul bound by the conditions of matter. In its very essence it is free, unbounded, holy, pure and perfect. But somehow or the other, it finds itself tied down to matter and thinks of itself as matter.

Why should the free, perfect and pure being be thus under the thraldom of matter, is the next question. How can the perfect soul be deluded into the belief that it is imperfect? We have been told that the Hindus shirk the question and say that no such question can be there. Some thinkers want to answer it by positing one or more quasi-perfect beings and use big scientific names to fill up the gap. But naming is not explaining. The question remains the same. How can the perfect become the quasi-perfect; how can the pure, the absolute change even a microscopic particle of its nature? But the Hindu is sincere. He does not want to take shelter under sophistry. He is brave enough to face the question in a manly fashion, and his answer is: 'I do not know. I do not know how the perfect being, the soul, came to think of itself as imperfect, as joined to and conditioned by matter.' But the fact is a fact for all that. It is a fact in everybody's consciousness that one thinks of oneself as the body. The Hindu does not attempt to explain why one thinks one is the body. The answer that it is the will of God is no explanation. This is nothing more than what the Hindu says, 'I do not know.'

Well, then, the human soul is eternal and immortal, perfect and infinite, and death means only a change of centre from one body to another. The present is determined by our past actions and the future by the present. The soul will go on evolving upwards or reverting back from birth to birth and death to death. But here is another question: Is man a tiny boat in a tempest, raised one moment on the foamy crest of a billow and dashed down into a yawning chasm the next, rolling to and fro at the mercy of good and bad actions—a powerless, helpless wreck in an ever-raging, ever-rushing, uncompromising current of cause and effect; a little moth placed under the wheel of causation which rolls on crushing everything in its way and waits not for the widow's tears or the orphan's cry? The heart sinks at the idea, yet this is the law of nature. Is there no hope? Is there no escape?—was the cry that went up from the bottom of the heart of despair. It reached the throne of mercy and words of hope and consolation came down and inspired a Vedic sage, and he stood up before the world and in trumpet voice proclaimed the glad tidings: 'Hear, ye children of immortal bliss! Even ye that reside in higher spheres! I have found the Ancient One who is beyond all darkness, all delusion: knowing Him alone you shall be saved from death over again.'

'Children of immortal bliss'—what a sweet, what a hopeful name! Allow me to call you, brethren, by that sweet name—heirs of immortal bliss—yea, the Hindu refuses to call you sinners. Ye are the Children of God, the sharers of immortal bliss, holy and perfect beings. Ye divinities on earth—sinners! It is a sin to call a man so; it is a standing libel on human nature. Come up, O lions, and shake off the delusion that you are sheep; you are souls immortal, spirits free, blest and eternal; ye are not matter, ye are not bodies; matter is your servant, not you the servant of matter.

Thus it is that the vedas proclaim not a dreadful combination of unforgiving laws, not an endless prison of cause and effect, but that at the head of all these laws, in and through every particle of matter and force stands One 'by whose command the wind blows, the fire burns, the clouds rain and death stalks upon the earth.'

And what is His nature?

He is everywhere, the pure and formless One, the Almighty and the All-merciful. 'Thou art our father, Thou art our mother, Thou art our beloved friend, Thou art the source of all strength; give us strength. Thou art He that beareth the burdens of the universe; help me bear the little burden of this life.' Thus sang the rishis of the vedas. And how to worship Him? Through love. 'He is to be worshipped as the one beloved, dearer than everything in this and the next life.'

This is the doctrine of love declared in the vedas, and let us see how it is fully developed and taught by Krishna, who the Hindus believe to have been God incarnate on earth.

He taught that a man ought to live in this world like a lotus leaf, which grows in water but is never moistened by water; so a man ought to live in the world—his heart to God and his hands to work.

It is good to love God for hope of reward in this or the next world, but it is better to love God for love's sake, and the prayer goes: 'Lord, I do not want wealth, nor children, nor learning. If it be Thy will, I shall go from birth to birth, but grant me this, that I may love Thee without the hope of reward—love unselfishly for love's sake.' One of the disciples of Krishna, the then Emperor of India, was driven away from his kingdom by his enemies and had to take shelter with his queen in a forest in the Himalayas, and there one day the queen asked him how it was that he, the most virtuous of men, should suffer so much misery. Yudhishthira answered, 'Behold, my queen, the Himalayas, how grand and beautiful they are, I love them. They do not give me anything, but my nature is to love the grand, the beautiful, therefore I love them. Similarly,

I love the Lord. He is the source of all beauty, of all sublimity. He is the only object to be loved; my nature is to love Him and therefore I love. I do not pray for anything; I do not ask for anything. Let Him place me wherever He likes. I must love Him for love's sake. I cannot trade in love.'

The vedas teach that the soul is divine, only held in the bondage of matter; perfection will be reached when this bond will burst, and the word they use for it is *mukti*—freedom, freedom from the bonds of imperfection, freedom from death and misery.

And this bondage can only fall off through the mercy of God and this mercy comes on the pure. So purity is the condition of His mercy. How does that mercy act? He reveals Himself to the pure heart; the pure and the stainless see God, even in this life. Then and then only all the crookedness of the heart is made straight. Then all doubt ceases. He is no more the freak of a terrible law of causation. This is the very centre, the very vital conception of Hinduism. The Hindu does not want to live upon words and theories. If there are existences beyond the ordinary sensuous existence, he wants to come face to face with them. If there is a soul in him which is not matter, if there is an all-merciful universal soul, he will go to Him direct. He must see Him and that alone can destroy all doubts. So the best proof a Hindu sage gives about the soul, about God, is: 'I have seen the soul; I have seen God.' And that is the only condition of perfection. The Hindu religion does not consist in struggles and attempts to believe a certain doctrine or dogma, but in realizing—not in believing, but in being and becoming.

Thus the whole object of their system is, by constant struggle, to become perfect, to become divine, to reach God and see God, and this reaching God, seeing God, becoming perfect even as the Father in Heaven is perfect, constitutes the religion of the Hindus.

And what becomes of a man when he attains perfection? He lives a life of infinite bliss. He enjoys infinite and perfect bliss, having obtained the only thing in which man ought to have pleasure, namely God and enjoys the bliss with God.

So far all the Hindus have agreed. This is the common religion of all the sects of India, but then, perfection is absolute and the absolute cannot be two or three. It cannot have any qualities. It cannot be an individual. And so when a soul becomes perfect and absolute, it must become one with Brahman, and it would only realize the Lord as the perfection, the reality of its own nature and existence, the existence absolute, knowledge absolute and bliss absolute. We have often read this as the losing of individuality and becoming a stock or a stone.

'He jests at scars that never felt a wound.'

I tell you it is nothing of the kind. If it is happiness to enjoy the consciousness of this small body, it must be greater happiness to enjoy the consciousness of two bodies, the measure of happiness increasing with the consciousness of an increasing number of bodies, the aim, the ultimate happiness being reached when it would become a universal consciousness.

Therefore, to gain this infinite universal individuality, this miserable little prison-individuality must go. Then alone can death cease when I am alone with life, then alone can misery cease when I am one with happiness itself, then alone can all errors cease when I am one with knowledge itself; and this is the necessary scientific conclusion. Science has proved to me that physical individuality is a delusion, that my body is one little continuously changing body in an unbroken ocean of matter; and *advaita* (unity) is the necessary conclusion with my other counterpart, soul.

Science is nothing but the finding of unity. As soon as science would reach perfect unity, it would stop from further progress, because it would reach the goal. Thus, Chemistry could not progress further when it would discover one element out of which all other could be made. Physics would stop progressing when it would be able to fulfil its services in discovering the one energy of which all others are but manifestations, and the science of religion become perfect when it would discover Him who is the one life in a universe of death, Him who is the constant basis of an ever-changing world, one who is the only soul of which all souls are but delusive manifestations. Thus, it is through multiplicity and duality that the ultimate unity is reached. Religion can go no further. This is the goal of all science.

All science is bound to come to this conclusion in the long run. Manifestation, and not creation, is the word of science today, and the Hindu is only glad that what he has been cherishing in his bosom for ages is going to be taught in more forcible languages and with further light from the latest conclusions of science.

Descend we now from the aspirations of philosophy to the religion of the ignorant. At the very outset, I may tell you that there is no polytheism in India. In every temple, if one stands by and listens, one will find the worshippers applying all the attributes of God, including omnipresence, to the images. It is not polytheism, nor would the name henotheism explain the situation. 'The rose called by any other name would smell as sweet.' Names are not explanations.

I remember, as a boy, hearing a Christian missionary preach to a crowd in India. Among other sweet things he was telling them was that if he gave a blow to their idol with his stick, what could it do? One of his hearers sharply answered, 'If I abuse your God, what can He do?' 'You would be punished,' said the preacher, 'when you die.' 'So my idol will punish you when you die,' retorted the Hindu.

The tree is known by its fruits. When I have seen amongst them that are called idolaters, men, the like of whom in morality and spirituality and love I have never seen anywhere, I stop and ask myself, 'Can sin beget holiness?'

Superstition is a great enemy of man, but bigotry is worse. Why does a Christian go to church? Why is the cross holy? Why is the face turned toward the sky in prayer? Why are there so many images in the Catholic Church? Why are there so many images in the minds of Protestants when they pray? My brethren, we can no more think about anything without a mental image than we can live without breathing. By the law of association, the material image calls up the mental idea and vice versa. This is why the Hindu uses an external symbol when he worships. He will tell you, it helps to keep his mind fixed on the Being to whom he prays. He knows as well as you do that the image is not God, it is not omnipresent. After all, how much does omnipresence mean to almost the whole world? It stands merely as a word, a symbol. Has God superficial area? If not, when we repeat that word 'omnipresent', we think of the extended sky or of space, that is all.

As we find that somehow or the other, by the laws of our mental constitution, we have to associate our ideas of infinity with the image of the blue sky, or of the sea, so we naturally connect our idea of holiness with the image of a church, a mosque, or a cross. The Hindus have associated the idea of holiness, purity, truth, omnipresence and such other ideas with different images and forms. While some people devote their whole lives to their idol of a church and never rise higher, because with them religion means an intellectual assent to certain doctrines and doing good to their fellows, the whole religion of the Hindu is centred on realization. Man is to become divine by realizing the divine. Idols or temples or churches or books are only the supports, the helps, of his spiritual childhood, but on and on he must progress.

He must not stop anywhere. 'External worship, material worship,' say the scriptures, 'is the lowest stage; struggling to rise high, mental prayer is the next stage, but the highest stage is when the Lord has been realized.' Mark, the same earnest man who is kneeling before the idol tells you, 'Him the sun cannot express, nor the moon, nor the stars, the lightning cannot express Him, nor what we speak of as fire; through Him they shine.' But he does not abuse anyone's idol or call its worship sin. He recognizes in it a necessary stage of life. 'The child is father of the man.' Would it be right for an old man to say that childhood is a sin or youth a sin?

If a man can realize his divine nature with the help of an image, would it be right to call that a sin? Nor even when he has passed that stage, should he call it an error. To the Hindu, man is not travelling from error to truth, but from truth to truth, from lower to higher truth. To him all the religions, from the lowest fetishism to the highest absolutism, mean so many attempts of the human soul to grasp and realize the infinite, each determined by the conditions of its birth and association, and each of these marks a stage of progress; and every soul is a young eagle soaring higher and higher, gathering more and more strength, till it reaches the glorious sun.

Unity in variety is the plan of nature and the Hindu has recognized it. Every other religion lays down certain fixed dogmas and tries to force society to adopt them. It places before society only one coat which must fit Jack and John and Henry, all alike. If it does not fit John or Henry, he must go without a coat to cover his body. The Hindus have discovered that the absolute can only be realized, or thought of, or stated, through the relative, and the images, crosses and crescents are simply so many symbols, so many pegs to hang the spiritual ideas on. It is not that this help is necessary for everyone, but those that do not need it have no right to say that it is wrong. Nor is it compulsory in Hinduism.

One thing I must tell you. Idolatry in India does not mean anything horrible. It is not the mother of harlots. On the other hand, it is the attempt of undeveloped minds to grasp high spiritual truths. The Hindus have their faults, they sometimes have their exceptions, but mark this: they are always for punishing their own bodies and never for cutting the throats of their neighbours. If the Hindu fanatic burns himself on the pyre, he never lights the fire of inquisition. And even this cannot be laid at the door of his religion any more than the burning of witches can be laid at the door of Christianity.

To the Hindu, then, the whole world of religions is only a travelling, a coming up, of different men and women, through various conditions and circumstances, to the same goal. Every religion is only evolving a God out of the material man, and the same God is the inspirer of all of them. Why, then, are there so many contradictions? They are only apparent, says the Hindu. The contradictions come from the same truth adapting itself to the varying circumstances of different natures.

It is the same light coming through glasses of different colours. And these little variations are necessary for purposes of adaptation. But in the heart of everything the same truth reigns. The Lord has declared to the Hindu in His incarnation as Krishna, 'I am in every religion as the thread through a string of pearls. Wherever thou seest extraordinary holiness and extraordinary power rising and purifying humanity, know thou that I am there.' And what has been the result? I challenge the world to find, throughout the whole system of Sanskrit philosophy, any such expression as that the Hindu alone will be saved and not others. Says Vyasa, 'We find perfect men even beyond the pale of our caste and creed.' One thing more. How, then, can the Hindu, whose whole fabric of thought centres on God, believe in Buddhism which is agnostic, or in Jainism which is atheistic?

The Buddhists or the Jains do not depend upon God, but the whole force of their religion is directed towards the great central truth in every religion, to evolve a God out of man. They have not seen the Father, but they have seen the Son. And he that hath seen the Son hath seen the Father also.

This, brethren, is a short sketch of the religious ideas of the Hindus. The Hindu may have failed to carry out all his plans, but if there is ever to be a universal religion, it must be one which will have no location in place or time, which will be infinite like the God it will preach, and whose sun will shine upon the followers of Krishna and of Christ, on saints and sinners alike; which will not be Brahminic or Buddhistic, Christian or Mohammedan, but the sum total of all these, and still have infinite space for development; which in its catholicity will embrace in its infinite arms and find a place for every human being, from the lowest groveling savage not far removed from the brute, to the highest man towering by the virtues of his head and heart almost above humanity, making society stand in awe of him and doubt his human nature. It will be a religion which will have no place for persecution or intolerance in its polity, which will recognize divinity in every man and woman, and whose whole scope, whose whole force, will be created in aiding humanity to realize its own true, divine nature.

Offer such a religion, and all the nations will follow you.

Asoka's council was a council of the Buddhist faith. Akbar's, though more to the purpose, was only a parlour-meeting. It was reserved for America to proclaim to all quarters of the globe that the Lord is in every religion.

May He who is the Brahman of the Hindus, the Ahura Mazda of the Zoroastrians, the Buddha of the Buddhists, the Jehovah of the Jews, the Father in Heaven of the Christians, give strength to you to carry out your noble idea! The star arose in the east, it travelled steadily towards the west, sometimes dimmed and sometimes effulgent, till it made a circuit of the world; and now it is again rising on the very horizon of the east, the borders of the Sanpo, a thousandfold more effulgent than it ever was before.

Hail, Columbia, motherland of liberty! It has been given to thee, who never dipped her hand in her neighbour's blood, who never found out that the shortest way of becoming rich was by robbing one's neighbours, it has been given to thee to march at the vanguard of civilization with the flag of harmony.

3

ADDRESS AT THE FINAL SESSION

Delivered on 27 September 1893, at Parliament of the World's Religions, Chicago

The Parliament of World's Religions has become an accomplished fact, and the merciful Father has helped those who laboured to bring it into existence and crowned with success their most unselfish labour.

My thanks to those noble souls whose large hearts and love of truth first dreamt this wonderful dream and then realized it. My thanks to the shower of liberal sentiments that has overflowed this platform. My thanks to his enlightened audience for their uniform kindness to me and for their appreciation of every thought that tends to smooth the friction of religions. A few jarring notes were heard from time to time in this harmony. My special thanks to them, for they have, by their striking contrast, made general harmony the sweeter.

Much has been said of the common ground of religious unity. I am not going just now to venture my own theory. But if anyone here hopes that this unity will come by the triumph of any one of the religions and the destruction of the others, to him I say, 'Brother, yours is an impossible hope.' Do I wish that the Christian would become Hindu? God forbid. Do I wish that the Hindu or Buddhist would become Christian? God forbid.

The seed is put in the ground, and earth and air and water are placed around it. Does the seed become the earth, or the air, or the water? No. It becomes a plant, it develops after the law of its own growth, assimilates the air, the earth and the water, converts them into plant substance and grows into one.

Similar is the case with religion. The Christian is not to become a Hindu or a Buddhist, nor a Hindu or a Buddhist to become a Christian. But each must assimilate the spirit of the others and yet preserve his individuality and grow according to his own law of growth.

If the Parliament of the World's Religions has shown anything to the world, it is this: it has proved to the world that holiness, purity and charity are not the exclusive possessions of any church in the world, and that every system has produced men and women of the most exalted character. In the face of this evidence, if anybody dreams of the exclusive survival of his own religion and the destruction of the others, I pity him from the bottom of my heart and point out to him that upon the banner of every religion will soon be written, in spite of resistance: 'Help and not fight', 'Assimilation and not destruction,' 'Harmony and peace and not dissension.'

4

THE SPIRIT AND INFLUENCE OF VEDANTA

Delivered at Twentieth Century Club, Boston

Before going into the subject of this afternoon, will you allow me to say a few words of thanks, now that I have the opportunity? I have lived three years amongst you. I have travelled over nearly the whole of America, and as I am going back from here to my own country, it is meet that I should take this opportunity of expressing my gratitude in this Athens of America. When I first came to this country, after a few days I thought I would be able to write a book on the nation. But after three years' stay here, I find I am not able to write even a page. On the other hand, I find on travelling in various countries that beneath the surface differences that we find in dress and food and little details of manners, man is man all the world over; the same wonderful human nature is everywhere represented. Yet there are certain characteristics and in a few words I would like to sum up all my experiences here. In this land of America, no question is asked about a man's peculiarities. If a man is a man, that is enough, and they take him into their hearts, and that is one thing I have never seen in any other country in the world.

I came here to represent a philosophy of India, which is called the Vedanta philosophy. This philosophy is very, very ancient; it is the outcome of that mass of ancient Aryan literature known by the name of the vedas. It is, as it were, the very flower of all the speculations and experiences and analyses, embodied in that mass of literature collected and culled through centuries. This Vedanta philosophy has certain peculiarities. In the first place, it is perfectly impersonal; it does not owe its origin to any person or prophet: it does not build itself around one man as a centre. Yet it has nothing to say against philosophies which do build themselves around certain persons. In later days in India, other philosophies and systems arose, built around certain persons—such as Buddhism, or many of our present sects. They each have a certain leader to whom they owe allegiance, just as the Christians and Mohammedans have. But the Vedanta philosophy stands at the background of all these various sects, and there is no fight and no antagonism between the Vedanta and any other system in the world.

One principle it lays down—and that, the Vedanta claims, is to be found in every religion in the world—that man is divine, that all this which we see around us is the outcome of that consciousness of the divine. Everything that is strong and good and powerful in human nature is the outcome of that divinity, and though potential in many, there is no difference between man and man essentially, all being alike divine. There is, as it were, an infinite ocean behind, and you and I are so many waves, coming out of that infinite ocean; each one of us is trying his best to manifest that infinite outside. So, potentially, each one of us has that infinite ocean of existence, knowledge and bliss as our birthright, our real nature. The difference between us is caused by the greater or lesser power to manifest that divine. Therefore the Vedanta lays down that each man should be treated not as what he manifests, but as what he stands for. Each human being stands for the divine, and, therefore, every teacher should be helpful, not by condemning man, but by helping him to call forth the divinity that is within him.

It also teaches that all the vast mass of energy that we see displayed in society and in every plane of action is really from inside out; and, therefore, what is called inspiration by other sects, the Vedantist begs the liberty to call the expiration of man. At the same time, it does not quarrel with other sects; the Vedanta has no quarrel with those who do not understand this divinity of man. Consciously or unconsciously, every man is trying to unfold that divinity.

Man is like an infinite spring, coiled up in a small box, and that spring is trying to unfold itself; all the social phenomena that we see is the result of this trying to unfold. All the competitions, struggles and evils that we see around us are neither the causes of these unfoldments, nor the effects. As one of our great philosophers says—in the case of the irrigation of a field, the tank is somewhere upon a higher level, the water is trying to rush into the field and is barred by a gate. But as soon as the gate is opened, the water rushes in by its own nature; and if there is dust and dirt in the way, the water rolls over them. But dust and dirt are neither the result, nor the cause of this unfolding of the divine nature of man. They are coexistent circumstances, and, therefore, can be remedied.

Now, this idea, claims the Vedanta, is to be found in all religions, whether in India or outside of it; only, in some of them, the idea is expressed through mythology, and in others through symbology. The Vedanta claims that there has not been one religious inspiration, one manifestation of the divine man, however great, but it has been the expression of that infinite oneness in human nature; and all that we call ethics and morality and doing good to others is also but the manifestation of this oneness. There are moments when every man feels that he is one with the universe and he rushes forth to express it, whether he knows it or not. This expression of oneness is what we call love and sympathy, and it is the basis of all our ethics and morality. This is summed up in the Vedanta philosophy by the celebrated aphorism, '*Tat Tvam Asi* (Thou art That)'.

To every man, this is taught: thou art one with this universal Being, and, as such, every soul that exists is your soul; and everybody that exists is your body; and in hurting anyone, you hurt yourself, in loving anyone, you love yourself. As soon as a current of hatred is thrown outside, whomsoever else it hurts, it also hurts yourself; and if love comes out from you, it is bound to come back to you. For I am the universe, this universe is my body. I am the Infinite, only I am not conscious of it now, but I am struggling to get this consciousness of the infinite, and perfection will be reached when full consciousness of this infinite comes.

Another peculiar idea of the Vedanta is that we must allow this infinite variation in religious thought, and not try to bring everybody to the same opinion, because the goal is the same. As the Vedantist says in his poetical language, 'As so many rivers, having their source in different mountains, roll down, crooked or straight, and at last come into the ocean—so, all these various creeds and religions, taking their start from different standpoints and running through crooked or straight courses, at last come unto THEE.'

As a manifestation of that, we find that this most ancient philosophy has, through its influence, directly inspired Buddhism, the first missionary religion of the world, and indirectly, it has also influenced Christianity, through the Alexandrians, the Gnostics and the European philosophers of the middle ages. And later, influencing German thought, it has produced almost a revolution in the regions of philosophy and psychology. Yet all this mass of influence has been given to the world almost unperceived. As the gentle falling of the dew at night brings support to all vegetable life, so, slowly and imperceptibly, this divine philosophy has been spread through the world for the good of mankind. No march of armies has been used to preach this religion. In Buddhism, one of the most missionary religions of the world, we find inscriptions remaining of the great Emperor Asoka—recording how missionaries were sent to Alexandria, to Antioch, to Persia, to China and to various other countries of the then civilized world. Three hundred years before Christ, instructions were given them not to revile other religions: 'The basis of all religions is the same, wherever they are; try to help them all you can, teach them all you can, but do not try to injure them.'

Thus in India, there never was any religious persecution by the Hindus, but only that wonderful reverence, which they have for all the religions of the world. They sheltered a portion of the Hebrews, when they were driven out of their own country; and the Malabar Jews remain as a result. They received at another time the remnant of the Persians, when they were almost annihilated and they remain to this day as a part of us and loved by us, as the modern Parsees of Bombay. There were Christians who claimed to have come with St Thomas, the disciple of Jesus Christ, and they were allowed to settle in India and hold their own opinions; and a colony of them is even now in existence in India. And this spirit of toleration has not died out. It will not and cannot die there.

This is one of the great lessons that the Vedanta has to teach. Knowing that, consciously or unconsciously, we are struggling to reach the same goal, why should we be impatient? If one man is slower than another, we need not be impatient, we need not curse him, or revile him. When our eyes are opened and the heart is purified, the work of the same divine influence, the unfolding of the same divinity in every human heart will manifest and then alone we shall be in a position to claim the brotherhood of man.

When a man has reached the highest, when he sees neither man nor woman, neither sect nor creed, nor colour, nor birth, nor any of these differentiations, but goes beyond and finds that divinity which is the real man behind every human being—then alone he has reached the universal brotherhood, and that man alone is a Vedantist.

Such are some of the practical historical results of the Vedanta.

5

THE SOUL AND GOD

Delivered on 23 March 1900, in San Francisco

Whether it was fear or mere inquisitiveness which first led man to think of powers superior to himself, we need not discuss…These raised in the mind peculiar worship tendencies and so on. There never have been [times in the history of mankind] without [some ideal] of worship. Why? What makes us all struggle for something beyond what we see—whether it be a beautiful morning or a fear of dead spirits?…We need not go back into prehistoric times, for it is a fact present today as it was two thousand years ago. We do not find satisfaction here. Whatever our station in life—[even if we are] powerful and wealthy—we cannot find satisfaction.

Desire is infinite. Its fulfilment is very limited. There is no end to our desires, but when we go to fulfil them, the difficulty comes. It has been so with the most primitive minds, when their desires were [few]. Even [these] could not be accomplished. Now, with our arts and sciences improved and multiplied, our desires cannot be fulfilled [either]. On the other hand, we are struggling to perfect means for the fulfilment of desires and the desires are increasing…

The most primitive man naturally wanted help from outside for things which he could not accomplish… He desired something and it could not be obtained. He wanted help from other powers. The most ignorant primitive man and the most cultivated man today, each appealing to God, and asking for the fulfilment of some desire, are exactly the same. What difference? Some people find a great deal of difference. We are always finding many differences in things when there is no difference at all. Both [the primitive man and the cultivated man] plead to the same [power]. You may call it God or Allah or Jehovah. Human beings want something and cannot get it by their own powers and are after someone who will help them. This is primitive and it is still present with us... We are all born savages and gradually civilize ourselves... All of us here, if we search, will find the same fact. Even now this fear does not leave us. We may talk big, become philosophers and all that, but when the blow comes, we find that we must beg for help. We believe in all the superstitions that ever existed. [But] there is no superstition in the world [that does not have some basis of truth]. If I cover my face and only the tip of my nose is showing, still it is a bit of my face. So [with] the superstitions—the little bits are true.

You see, the lowest sort of manifestation of religion came with the burial of the departed... First they wrapped them up and put them in mounds and the spirits of the departed came and lived in the [mounds, at night]... Then they began to bury them... At the gate stands a terrible goddess with a thousand teeth... Then [came] the burning of the body and the flames bore the spirit up... The Egyptians brought food and water for the departed.

The next great idea was that of the tribal gods. This tribe had one god and that tribe another. The Jews had their God Jehovah, who was their own tribal god and fought against all the other gods and tribes. That god would do anything to please his own people. If he killed a whole tribe not protected by him, that was all right, quite good. A little love was given, but that love was confined to a small section.

Gradually, higher ideals came. The chief of the conquering tribe was the Chief of chiefs, God of gods...So with the Persians when they conquered Egypt. The Persian emperor was the Lord of [lords], and before the emperor nobody could stand. Death was the penalty for anyone who looked at the Persian emperor.

Then came the ideal of God Almighty and All-powerful, the omnipotent, omniscient Ruler of the universe: He lives in heaven and man pays special tribute to his Most Beloved, who creates everything for man. The whole world is for man. The sun and moon and stars are [for him]. All who have those ideas are primitive men, not civilized and not cultivated at all. All the superior religions had their growth between the Ganga and the Euphrates... Outside of India we will find no further development [of religion beyond this idea of God in heaven]. That was the highest knowledge ever obtained outside of India. There is the local heaven where he is and [where] the faithful shall go when they die...As far as I have seen, we should call it a very primitive idea... Mumbo Jumbo in Africa [and] God in heaven—the same. He moves the world and of course his will is being done everywhere...

The old Hebrew people did not care for any heaven. That is one of the reasons they opposed Jesus of Nazareth—because he taught life after death. Paradise in Sanskrit means land beyond this life. So the paradise was to make up for all this evil. The primitive man does not care about evil... He never questions why there should be any...

...The word devil is a Persian word... The Persians and Hindus share the Aryan ancestry upon religious grounds and... they spoke the same language, only the words one sect uses for good the other uses for bad. The word 'deva' is an old Sanskrit word for God, the same word in the Aryan languages. Here the word means the devil...

Later on, when man developed [his inner life], he began to question and to say that God is good. The Persians said that there were two gods—one was bad and one was good. [Their idea was that] everything in this life was good: beautiful country, where there was spring almost the whole year round and nobody died; there was no disease, everything was fine. Then came this Wicked One and he touched the land, and then came death and disease and mosquitoes and tigers and lions. Then the Aryans left their fatherland and migrated southward. The old Aryans must have lived way to the north. The Jews learnt it [the idea of the devil] from the Persians. The Persians also taught that there will come a day when this wicked god will be killed, and it is our duty to stay with the good god and add our force with him in this eternal struggle between him and the Wicked One...The whole world will be burnt out and everyone will get a new body.

The Persian idea was that even the wicked will be purified and not be bad any more. The nature of the Aryan was love and poetry. They cannot think of their being burnt [for eternity]. They will all receive new bodies. Then no more death. So that is the best about [religious] ideas outside of India...

Along with that is the ethical strain. All that man has to do is to take care of three things: good thought, good word and good deed. That is all. It is a practical, wise religion. Already there has come a little poetry in it. But there is higher poetry and higher thought.

In India, we see this Satan in the most ancient part of the vedas. He just (appears) and immediately disappears... In the vedas, the bad god got a blow and disappeared. He is gone, the Persians took him. We are trying to make him leave the world [al]together. Taking the Persian idea, we are going to make a decent gentleman of him; give him a new body. There was the end of the idea of Satan in India.

The idea of God went on, but mind you, here comes another fact. The idea of God grew side by side with the idea of [materialism] until you have traced it up to the emperor of Persia. But on the other hand comes in metaphysics, philosophy. There is another line of thought, the idea of [the non-dual *atman*, man's] own soul. That also grows. So, outside of India ideas about God had to remain in that concrete form until India came to help them out a bit... The other nations stopped with that old concrete idea. In this country [America], there are millions who believe that God is [has?] a body... Whole sects say it. [They believe that] He rules the world, but there is a place where He has a body. He sits upon a throne. They light candles and sing songs just as they do in our temples.

But in India they are sensible enough never to make [their God a physical being]. You never see in India a temple of Brahma. Why? Because the idea of the soul always existed. The Hebrew race never questioned about the soul. There is no soul idea in the Old Testament at all. The first is in the New Testament. The Persians, they became so practical—wonderfully practical people—a fighting, conquering race. They were the English people of the old time, always fighting and destroying their neighbours—too much engaged in that sort of thing to think about the soul...

The oldest idea of [the] soul [was that of] a fine body inside this gross one. The gross one disappears and the fine one appears. In Egypt that fine one also dies, and as soon as the gross body disintegrates, the fine one also disintegrates. That is why they built those pyramids [and embalmed the dead bodies of their ancestors, thus hoping to secure immortality for the departed]...

The Indian people have no regard for the dead body at all.

[Their attitude is:] 'Let us take it and burn it.' The son has to set fire to his father's body...

There are two sorts of races, the divine and the demonic. The divine think that they are soul and spirit. The demonic think that they are bodies. The old Indian philosophers tried to insist that the body is nothing. 'As a man emits his old garment and takes a new one, even so the old body is [shed] and he takes a new one.' In my case, all my surrounding and education were trying to [make me] the other way. I was always associated with Mohammedans and Christians, who take more care of the body...

It is only one step from [the body] to the spirit... [In India] they became insistent on this ideal of the soul. It became [synonymous with] the idea of God... If the idea of the soul begins to expand, [man must arrive at the conclusion that it is beyond name and form]... The Indian idea is that the soul is formless. Whatever is formed must break some time or the other. There cannot be any form unless it is the result of force and matter, and all combinations must dissolve. If such is the case, [if] your soul is [made of name and form, it disintegrates], and you die, and you are no more immortal. If it is double, it has form and it belongs to nature and it obeys nature's laws of birth and death... They find that this [soul] is not the mind... neither a double...

Thoughts can be guided and controlled... [The yogis of India] practiced to see how far the thoughts can be guided and controlled. By dint of hard work, thoughts may be silenced altogether. If thoughts were [the real man], as soon as thought ceases, he ought to die. Thought ceases in meditation; even the mind's elements are quite quiet. Blood circulation stops. His breath stops, but he is not dead. If thought were he, the whole thing ought to go, but they find it does not go. That is practical [proof]. They came to the conclusion that even mind and thought were not the real man. Then speculation showed that it could not be.

I come, I think and talk. In the midst of all [this activity is] this unity [of the Self]. My thought and action are varied, many [fold]...but in and through them runs...that one unchangeable One. It cannot be the body. That is changing every minute. It cannot be the mind; new and fresh thoughts [come] all the time. It is neither the body, nor the mind. Both body and mind belong to nature and must obey nature's laws. A free mind never will...

Now, therefore, this real man does not belong to nature. It is the person whose mind and body belong to nature. So much of nature we are using. Just as you come to use the pen and ink and chair, so he uses so much of nature in fine and in gross form; gross form, the body, and fine form, the mind. If it is simple, it must be formless. In nature alone are forms. That which is not of nature cannot have any forms, fine or gross. It must be formless. It must be omnipresent. Understand this. [Take] this glass on the table. The glass is form and the table is form. So much of the glass-ness goes off, so much of table-ness [when they break]...

The soul...is nameless because it is formless. It will neither go to heaven nor [to hell] any more than it will enter this glass. It takes the form of the vessel it fills. If it is not in space, either of two things is possible. Either the [soul permeates] space or space is in [it]. You are in space and must have a form. Space limits us, binds us, and makes a form of us. If you are not in space, space is in you. All the heavens and the world are in the person...

So it must be with God. God is omnipresent. 'Without hands [he grasps] everything; without feet he can move...' He [is] the formless, the deathless, the eternal. The idea of God came... He is the Lord of souls, just as my soul is the [lord] of my body. If my soul left the body, the body would not be for a moment. If He left my soul, the soul would not exist. He is the creator of the universe; of everything that dies He is the destroyer. His shadow is death; His shadow is life.

[The ancient Indian philosophers] thought: This filthy world is not fit for man's attention. There is nothing in the universe that is [permanent—neither good nor evil]...

I told you...Satan...did not have much chance [in India]. Why? Because they were very bold in religion. They were not babies. Have you seen that characteristic of children? They are always trying to throw the blame on someone else. Baby minds [are] trying, when they make a mistake, to throw the blame upon someone [else]. On the one hand, we say, 'Give me this, give me that.' On the other hand, we say, 'I did not do this, the devil tempted me. The devil did it.' That is the history of mankind, weak mankind...

Why is evil? Why is [the world] the filthy, dirty hole? We have made it. Nobody is to blame. We put our hand in the fire. The Lord bless us, [man gets] just what he deserves. Only He is merciful. If we pray to Him, He helps us. He gives Himself to us.

That is their idea. They are [of a] poetic nature. They go crazy over poetry. Their philosophy is poetry. This philosophy is a poem...All [high thought] in the Sanskrit is written in poetry, metaphysics, astronomy—all in poetry.

We are responsible and how do we come to mischief? [You may say], 'I was born poor and miserable. I remembered the hard struggle all my life.' Philosophers say that you are to blame. You do not mean to say that all this sprang up without any cause whatever? You are a rational being. Your life is not without cause and you are the cause. You manufacture your own life all the time… You make and mould your own life. You are responsible for yourself. Do not lay the blame upon anybody, any Satan. You will only get punished a little more…

[A man] is brought up before God and He says, 'Thirty-one stripes for you,' …when comes another man, He says, 'Thirty stripes: 15 for that fellow and 15 for the teacher—that awful man who taught him.' That is the awful thing in teaching. I do not know what I am going to get. I go all over the world. If I have to get 15 for each one I have taught!…

We have to come to this idea: 'This My Maya is divine.' It is My activity, [My] divinity. ' [My Maya] is hard to cross, but those that take refuge in me [go beyond Maya].' But you find out that it is very difficult to cross this ocean [of Maya by] yourself. You cannot. It is the old question of hen and egg. If you do any work, that work becomes the cause and produces the effect. That effect [again] becomes the cause and produces the effect. And so on. If you push this down, it never stops. Once you set a thing in motion, there is no more stopping. I do some work, good or bad, [and it sets up a chain reaction]… I cannot stop now.

It is impossible for us to get out from this bondage [by ourselves]. It is only possible if there is someone more powerful than this law of causation and if he takes mercy on us and drags us out.

And we declare that there is such a one, God. There is such a being, all merciful… If there is a God, then it is possible for me to be saved. How can you be saved by your own will? Do you see the philosophy of the doctrine of salvation by grace? You Western people are wonderfully clever, but when you undertake to explain philosophy, you are so wonderfully complicated. How can you save yourself by work, if by salvation you mean that you will be taken out of all this nature? Salvation means just standing upon God, but if you understand what is meant by salvation, then you are the Self...you are not nature. You are the only thing outside of souls and gods and nature. These are the external existences, and God [is] interpenetrating both nature and soul.

Therefore, just as my soul is [to] my body, we, as it were, are the bodies of God. God—souls—nature—it is one, the One, because, as I say, I mean the body, soul and mind. But, we have seen, the law of causation pervades every bit of nature and once you have got caught you cannot get out. When once you get into the meshes of law, a possible way of escape is not [through work done] by you. You can build hospitals for every fly and flea that ever lived...All this you may do, but it would never lead to salvation... [Hospitals] go up and they come down again. [Salvation] is only possible if there is some being whom nature never caught, who is the Ruler of nature. He rules nature instead of being ruled by nature. He wills law instead of being downed by law... He exists and he is all merciful. The moment you seek Him, He will save you.

Why has He not taken us out? You do not want Him. You want everything but Him. The moment you want Him, that moment you get Him. We never want Him. We say, 'Lord, give me a fine house.' We want the house, not Him. 'Give me health! Save me from this difficulty!' When a man wants nothing but Him, [he gets Him]. 'The same love which wealthy men have for gold and silver and possessions, Lord, may I have the same love for Thee. I want neither earth, nor heaven, nor beauty, nor learning. I do not want salvation. Let me go to hell again and again. But one thing I want: to love Thee, and for love's sake—not even for heaven.'

Whatever man desires, he gets. If you always dream of having a body, [you will get another body]. When this body goes away, he wants another and goes on begetting body after body. Love matter and you become matter. You first become animals. When I see a dog gnawing a bone, I say, 'Lord help us!' Love body until you become dogs and cats! Still degenerate, until you become minerals—all body and nothing else...

There are other people, who would have no compromise. The road to salvation is through truth. That was another watchword...

[Man began to progress spiritually] when he kicked the devil out. He stood up and took the responsibility of the misery of the world upon his own shoulders. But whenever he looked [at the] past and future and [at the] law of causation, he knelt down and said, 'Lord, save me, [thou] who [art] our creator, our father and dearest friend.' That is poetry, but not very good poetry, I think. Why not? It is the painting of the infinite [no doubt]. You have it in every language how they paint the infinite. [But] it is the infinite of the senses, of the muscles...

'[Him] the sun [does not illumine], nor the moon, nor the stars, [nor] the flash of lightning.' That is another painting of the infinite, by negative language... And the last infinite is painted in [the] spirituality of the Upanishads. Not only is Vedanta the highest philosophy in the world, but it is the greatest poem...

Mark today, this is the...difference between the first part of the vedas and the second. In the first, it is all in [the domain of] sense. But all religions are only [concerned with the] infinite of the external world—nature and nature's God... [Not so Vedanta]. This is the first light that the human mind throws back [of] all that. No satisfaction [comes] of the infinite [in] space. ' [The] Self-existent [One] has [created] the [senses as turned]...to the outer world. Those therefore who [seek] outside will never find that [which is within]. There are the few who, wanting to know the truth, turn their eyes inward and in their own souls behold the glory [of the Self].'

It is not the infinite of space, but the real infinite, beyond space, beyond time... Such is the world missed by the Occident... Their minds have been turned to external nature and nature's God. Look within yourself and find the truth that you had [forgotten]. Is it possible for the mind to come out of this dream without the help of the gods? Once you start the action, there is no help unless the merciful Father takes us out.

That would not be freedom, [even] at the hands of the merciful God. Slavery is slavery. The chain of gold is quite as bad as the chain of iron. Is there a way out?

You are not bound. No one was ever bound. [The Self] is beyond. It is the all. You are the One; there are no two. God was your own reflection cast upon the screen of Maya. The real God [is the Self]. He [whom man] ignorantly worships is that reflection. [They say that] the Father in heaven is God. Why God? [It is because He is] your own reflection that [He] is God. Do you see how you are seeing God all the time? As you unfold yourself, the reflection grows [clearer].

'Two beautiful birds are there sitting upon the same tree. The one [is] calm, silent, majestic; the one below [the individual self], is eating the fruits, sweet and bitter, and becoming happy and sad. [But when the individual self beholds the worshipful Lord as his own true Self, he grieves no more.]'

...Do not say 'God'. Do not say 'Thou'. Say 'I' The language of [dualism] says, 'God, Thou, my Father.' The language of [non-dualism] says, 'Dearer unto me than I am myself. I would have no name for Thee. The nearest I can use is I...'

'God is true. The universe is a dream. Blessed am I that I know this moment that I [have been and] shall be free all eternity; ...that I know that I am worshipping only myself; that no nature, no delusion had any hold on me. Vanish nature from me, vanish [these] gods; vanish worship; …vanish superstitions, for I know myself. I am the infinite. All these—Mrs So-and-so, Mr So-and-so, responsibility, happiness, misery—have vanished. I am the infinite. How can there be death for me, or birth? Whom shall I fear? I am the One. Shall I be afraid of myself? Who is to be afraid of [whom]? I am the one Existence. Nothing else exists. I am everything.'

It is only the question of memory [of your true nature], not salvation by work. Do you *get* salvation? You are [already] free.

Go on saying, 'I am free'. Never mind if the next moment delusion comes and says, 'I am bound.' Dehypnotize the whole thing.

[This truth] is first to be heard. Hear it first. Think on it day and night. Fill the mind [with it] day and night: 'I am It. I am the Lord of the universe. Never was there any delusion…' Meditate upon it with all the strength of the mind till you actually see these walls, houses, everything, melt away—[until] body, everything vanishes. 'I will stand alone. I am the One.' Struggle on! 'Who cares! We want to be free; [we] do not want any powers. Worlds we renounce; heavens we renounce; hells we renounce. What do I care about all these powers, and this and that! What do I care if the mind is controlled or uncontrolled! Let it run on. What of that! I am not the mind, Let it go on!'

The sun [shines on the just and on the unjust]. Is he touched by the defective [character] of anyone? 'I am He. Whatever [my] mind does, I am not touched. The sun is not touched by shining on filthy places, I am Existence.'

This is the religion of [non-dual] philosophy. [It is] difficult. Struggle on! Down with all superstitions! Neither teachers nor scriptures nor gods [exist]. Down with temples, with priests, with gods, with incarnations, with God himself! I am the God that ever existed! There, stand up philosophers! No fear! Speak no more of God and [the] superstition of the world. Truth alone triumphs and this is true. I am the infinite.

All religious superstitions are vain imaginations... This society, that I see you before me, and [that] I am talking to you—this is all superstition; all must be given up. Just see what it takes to become a philosopher! This is the [path] of [Jnana-] Yoga, the way through knowledge. The other [paths] are easy, slow...but this is pure strength of mind. No weakling [can follow this path of knowledge. You must be able to say:] 'I am the Soul, the ever free; [I] never was bound. Time is in me, not I in time. God was born in my mind. God the Father, Father of the universe—he is created by me in my own mind...'

Do you call yourselves philosophers? Show it! Think of this, talk [of] this, and [help] each other in this path and give up all superstition!

6

PRACTICAL RELIGION: BREATHING AND MEDITATION

Delivered on 5 April 1900, in San Francisco

Everyone's idea of practical religion is according to his theory of practicality and the standpoint he starts from. There is work. There is the system of worship. There is knowledge.

The philosopher thinks...the difference between bondage and freedom is only caused by knowledge and ignorance. To him, knowledge is the goal, and his practicality is gaining that knowledge... The worshipper's practical religion is the power of love and devotion. The worker's practical religion consists in doing good works. And so, as in every other thing, we are always trying to ignore the standard of another, trying to bind the whole world to our standard.

Doing good to his fellow beings is the practical religion of the man full of love. If men do not help to build hospitals, they think that they have no religion at all. But there is no reason why everyone should do that. The philosopher, in the same way, may denounce every man who does not have knowledge. People may build 20,000 hospitals and the philosopher declares they are but...the beasts of burden of the gods. The worshipper has his own idea and standard: men who cannot love God are no good, whatever work they do. The [yogi believes in] psychic [control and] the conquest of [internal] nature. 'How much have you gained towards that? How much control over your senses, over your body?'—that is all the yogi asks. And, as we said, each one judges the others by his own standard. Men may have given millions of dollars and fed rats and cats, as some do in India. They say that men can take care of themselves, but the poor animals cannot. That is their idea. But to the yogi the goal is conquest of [internal] nature, and he judges man by that standard...

We are always talking [about] practical religion. But it must be practical in our sense. Especially [so] in the Western countries. The Protestants' ideal is good works. They do not care much for devotion and philosophy. They think there is not much in it. 'What is your knowledge!' [they say]. 'Man has to do something!' ...A little humanitarianism! The churches rail day and night against callous agnosticism. Yet they seem to be veering rapidly towards just that. Callous slaves! Religion of utility! That is the spirit just now. And that is why some Buddhists have become so popular in the West. People do not know whether there is a God or not, whether there is a soul or not. [They think:] this world is full of misery. Try to help this world.

The Yoga doctrine, which we are having our lecture on, is not from that standpoint. [It teaches that] there is the soul, and inside this soul is all power. It is already there, and if we can master this body, all the power will be unfolded. All knowledge is in the soul. Why are people struggling? To lessen the misery... All unhappiness is caused by us not having mastery over the body... We are all putting the cart before the horse... Take the system of work, for instance. We are trying to do good by... comforting the poor. We do not get to the cause which created the misery. It is like taking a bucket to empty out the ocean and more [water] comes all the time. The yogi sees that this is nonsense. [He says that] the way out of misery is to know the cause of misery first... We try to do the good we can. What for? If there is an incurable disease, why should we struggle and take care of ourselves? If the utilitarians say: 'Do not bother about soul and God!' What is that to the yogi and what is it to the world? The world does not derive any good [from such an attitude]. More and more misery is going on all the time...

The yogi says you are to go to the root of all this. Why is there misery in the world? He answers: 'It is all our own foolishness, not having proper mastery of our own bodies. That is all.' He advises the means by which this misery can be [overcome]. If you can thus get mastery of your body, all the misery of the world will vanish. Every hospital is praying that more and more sick people will come there. Every time you think of doing some charity, you think there is some beggar to take your charity. If you say, 'O Lord, let the world be full of charitable people!'—you mean, let the world be full of beggars also. Let the world be full of good works—let the world be full of misery. This is out-and-out slavishness!

...The yogi says religion is practical if you know first why misery exists. All the misery in the world is in the senses. Is there any ailment in the sun, moon and stars? The same fire that cooks your meal burns the child. Is it the fault of the fire? Blessed be the fire! Blessed be this electricity! It gives light... Where can you lay the blame? Not on the elements. The world is neither good, nor bad; the world is the world. The fire is the fire. If you burn your finger in it, you are a fool. If you [cook your meal and with it satisfy your hunger,] you are a wise man. That is all the difference. Circumstances can never be good or bad. Only the individual man can be good or bad. What is meant by the world being good or bad? Misery and happiness can only belong to the sensuous individual man.

The yogis say that nature is the enjoyed, the soul is the

enjoyer. All misery and happiness—where is it? In the senses. It is the touch of the senses that causes pleasure and pain, heat and cold. If we can control the senses and order what they shall feel—not let them order us about as they are doing now—if they can obey our commands, become our servants, the problem is solved at once. We are bound by the senses; they play upon us, make fools of us all the time.

Here is a bad odour. It will bring me unhappiness as soon as it touches my nose. I am the slave of my nose. If I am not its slave, I do not care. A man curses me. His curses enter my ears and are retained in my mind and body. If I am the master, I shall say: 'Let these things go; they are nothing to me. I am not miserable. I do not bother.' This is the outright, pure, simple, clear-cut truth.

The other problem to be solved is—is it practical? Can man attain the power of mastery of the body? …Yoga says it is practical… Supposing it is not—suppose there are doubts in your mind. You have got to try it. There is no other way out…

You may do good works all the time. All the same, you will be the slave of your senses, you will be miserable and unhappy. You may study the philosophy of every religion. Men in this country carry loads and loads of books on their backs. They are mere scholars, slaves of the senses, and therefore happy and unhappy. They read 2,000 books and that is all right but as soon as a little misery comes, they are worried, anxious… You call yourselves men! You stand up…and build hospitals. You are fools!

What is the difference between men and animals?… 'Food and [sleep], procreation of the species and fear exist in common with the animals. There is one difference: man can control all these and become God, the master.' Animals cannot do it. Animals can do charitable work. Ants do it. Dogs do it. What is the difference then? Men can be masters of themselves. They can resist the reaction to anything… The animal cannot resist anything. He is held…by the string of nature everywhere. That is all the distinction. One is the master of nature, the other the slave of nature. What is nature? The five senses…

[The conquest of internal nature] is the only way out, according to Yoga… The thirst for God is religion… Good works and all that [merely] make the mind a little quiet. To practice this—to be perfect—depends upon our past. I have been studying [Yoga] all my life and have made very little progress yet. But I have got enough [result] to believe that this is the only true way. The day will come when I will be master of myself. If not in this life, [in another life]. I will struggle and never let go. Nothing is lost. If I die this moment, all my past struggles [will come to my help]. Have you not seen what makes the difference between one man and another? It is their past. The past habits make one man a genius and another man a fool. You may have the power of the past and can succeed in five minutes. None can predict the moment of time. We all have to attain [perfection] some time or the other.

The greater part of the practical lessons which the yogi gives us is in the mind, the power of concentration and meditation… We have become so materialistic. When we think of ourselves, we find only the body. The body has become the ideal, nothing else. Therefore a little physical help is necessary…

First, to sit in the posture in which you can sit still for a long time. All the nerve currents which are working pass along the spine. The spine is not intended to support the weight of the body. Therefore the posture must be such that the weight of the body is not on the spine. Let it be free from all pressure.

There are some other preliminary things. There is the great question of food and exercise…

The food must be simple and taken several times [a day] instead of once or twice. Never get very hungry. 'He who eats too much cannot be a yogi. He who fasts too much cannot be a yogi. He who sleeps too much cannot be a yogi, nor he who stays awake too much.' He who does not do any work and he who works too hard cannot succeed. Proper food, proper exercise, proper sleep, proper wakefulness—these are necessary for any success.

What the proper food is, what kind, we have to determine ourselves. Nobody can determine that [for us]. As a general practice, we have to shun exciting food... We do not know how to vary our diet with our occupation. We always forget that it is the food out of which we manufacture everything we have. So the amount and kind of energy that we want, the food must determine...

Violent exercises are not all necessary... If you want to be muscular, yoga is not for you. You have to manufacture a finer organism than you have now. Violent exercises are positively hurtful... Live amongst those who do not do too much exercise. If you do not do violent exercise, you will live longer. You do not want to burn out your lamp in the muscles! People who work with their brains are the longest-lived people... Do not burn the lamp quickly. Let it burn slowly and gently... Every anxiety, every violent exercise—physical and mental—[means] you are burning the lamp.

The proper diet means, generally, simply do not eat highly spiced foods. There are three sorts of mind, says the yogi, according to the elements of nature. One is the dull mind, which covers the luminosity of the soul. Then there is that which makes people active and lastly that which makes them calm and peaceful.

Now there are persons born with the tendency to sleep all

the time. Their taste will be towards that type of food which is rotting—crawling cheese. They will eat cheese that fairly jumps off the table. It is a natural tendency with them.

Then come active people. Their taste is for everything hot and pungent, strong alcohol…

Sattvika people are very thoughtful, quiet and patient. They take food in small quantities and never anything bad.

I am always asked the question: 'Shall I give up meat?' My master said, 'Why should you give up anything? It will give you up.' Do not give up anything in nature. Make it so hot for nature that she will give you up. There will come a time when you cannot possibly eat meat. The very sight of it will disgust you. There will come a time when many things you are struggling to give up will be distasteful, positively loathsome.

Then there are various sorts of breathing exercises. One consists of three parts: the drawing in of the breath, the holding of the breath—stopping still without breathing—and throwing the breath out. [Some breathing exercises] are rather difficult, and some of the complicated ones are attended with great danger if done without proper diet. I would not advise you to go through any one of these except the very simple ones.

Take a deep breath and fill the lungs. Slowly throw the breath out. Take it through one nostril and fill the lungs, and throw it out slowly through the other nostril. Some of us do not breathe deeply enough. Others cannot fill the lungs enough. These breathings will correct that very much. Half an hour in the morning and half an hour in the evening will make you another person. This sort of breathing is never dangerous. The other exercises should be practiced very slowly. And measure your strength. If 10 minutes are a drain, only take five.

The yogi is expected to keep his own body well. These various breathing exercises are a great help in regulating the different parts of the body. All the different parts are inundated with breath. It is through breath that we gain control of them all. Disharmony in parts of the body is controlled by more flow of the nerve currents towards them. The yogi ought to be able to tell when in any part pain is caused by less vitality or more. He has to equalize that...

Another condition [for success in yoga] is chastity. It is the corner-stone of all practice. Married or unmarried—perfect chastity. It is a long subject, of course, but I want to tell you: public discussions of this subject are not to the taste of this country. These Western countries are full of the most degraded beings in the shape of teachers who teach men and women that if they are chaste they will be hurt. How do they gather all this?... People come to me—thousands come every year—with this one question. Someone has told them that if they are chaste and pure they will be hurt physically... How do these teachers know it? Have they been chaste? Those unchaste, impure fools, lustful creatures, want to drag the whole world down to their [level]!...

Nothing is gained except by sacrifice... The holiest function of our human consciousness, the noblest do not make it unclean! Do not degrade it to the level of the brutes... Make yourselves decent men!... Be chaste and pure!... There is no other way. Did Christ find any other way?... If you can conserve and use the energy properly, it leads you to God. Inverted, it is hell itself...

It is much easier to do anything upon the external plane, but the greatest conqueror in the world finds himself a mere child when he tries to control his own mind. This is the world he has to conquer—the greater and more difficult world to conquer. Do not despair! Awake, arise and stop not until the goal is reached!...

7

ONE EXISTENCE APPEARING AS MANY

Delivered in 1896, New York.

Vairagya or renunciation is the turning point in all the various yogas. The *karmi* (worker) renounces the fruits of his work. The *bhakta* (devotee) renounces all little loves for the almighty and omnipresent love. The yogi renounces his experiences, because his philosophy is that the whole nature, although it is for the experience of the soul, at last brings him to know that he is not in nature, but eternally separate from nature. The *jnani* (philosopher) renounces everything because his philosophy is that nature never existed, neither in the past, nor present, nor will it in the future. The question of utility cannot be asked in these higher themes.

It is very absurd to ask it; and even if it be asked, after a proper analysis, what do we find in this question of utility? The ideal of happiness, that which brings man more happiness, is of greater utility to him than these higher things which do not improve his material conditions or bring him such great happiness. All the sciences are for this one end, to bring happiness to humanity; and that which brings the larger amount of happiness, man takes and gives up that which brings a lesser amount of happiness. We have seen how happiness is either in the body, or in the mind, or in the atman. With animals, and in the lowest human beings who are very much like animals, happiness is all in the body. No man can eat with the same pleasure as a famished dog or a wolf; so in the dog and the wolf the happiness is entirely in the body. In men, we find a higher plane of happiness, that of thought; and in the jnani there is the highest plane of happiness in the Self, the atman. So to the philosopher this knowledge of the Self is of the highest utility because it gives him the highest happiness possible. Sense-gratifications or physical things cannot be of the highest utility to him because he does not find in them the same pleasure that he finds in knowledge itself; and after all, knowledge is the one goal and is really the highest happiness that we know. All who work in ignorance are, as it were, the draught animals of the devas. The word 'deva' is here used in the sense of a wise man. All the people that work and toil and labour like machines do not really enjoy life, but it is the wise man who enjoys. A rich man buys a picture at a cost of a hundred thousand dollars perhaps, but it is the man who understands art that enjoys it; and if the rich man is without knowledge of art, it is useless to him, he is only the owner. All over the world, it is the wise man who enjoys the happiness of the world. The ignorant man never enjoys, he has to work for others unconsciously.

Thus far we have seen the theories of these Advaitist philosophers, how there is but one atman, there cannot be two. We have seen how in the whole of this universe there is but one existence; and that one existence when seen through the senses is called the world, the world of matter. When it is seen through the mind, it is called the world of thoughts and ideas; and when it is seen as it is, then it is the one infinite being. You must bear this in mind: it is not that there is a soul in man, although I had to take that for granted in order to explain it at first, but that there is only one existence and that one the atman, the Self; and when this is perceived through the senses, through sense-imageries, it is called the body. When it is perceived through thought, it is called the mind. When it is perceived in its own nature, it is the atman, the one only existence. So it is not that there are three things in one, the body and the mind and the Self, although that was a convenient way of putting it in the course of explanation. But all that is atman, and that one being is sometimes called the body, sometimes the mind and sometimes the Self, according to different vision. There is but one being which the ignorant call the world. When a man goes higher in knowledge, he calls the very same being the world of thought. Again, when knowledge itself comes, all illusions vanish, man finds it is all nothing but atman. I am that one existence. This is the last conclusion. There are neither three, nor two in the universe; it is all one. That one, under the illusion of Maya, is seen as many, just as a rope is seen as a snake. It is the very rope that is seen as a snake. There are not two things there, a rope separate and a snake separate. No man sees these two things there at the same time.

Dualism and non-dualism are very good philosophic terms, but in perfect perception we never perceive the real and the false at the same time. We are all born monists, we cannot help it. We always perceive the one. When we perceive the rope, we do not perceive the snake at all; and when we see the snake, we do not see the rope at all—it has vanished. When you see illusion, you do not see reality. Suppose you see one of your friends coming at a distance in the street. You know him very well, but through the haze and mist that is before you, you think it is another man. When you see your friend as another man, you do not see your friend at all, he has vanished. You are perceiving only one. Suppose your friend is Mr A, but when you perceive Mr A as Mr B, you do not see Mr A at all. In each case you perceive only one. When you see yourself as a body, you are body and nothing else, and that is the perception of the vast majority of mankind. They may talk of soul and mind and all these things, but what they perceive is the physical form, the touch, taste, vision and so on. Again, with certain men in certain states of consciousness, they perceive themselves as thought. You know, of course, the story told of Sir Humphrey Davy, who was making experiments before his class with laughing-gas and suddenly one of the tubes broke, and with the gas escaping, he breathed it in. For some moments he remained like a statue. Afterwards he told his class that when he was in that state, he actually perceived that the whole world is made up of ideas. The gas, for a time, made him forget the consciousness of the body, and that very thing which he was seeing as the body, he began to perceive as ideas. When the consciousness rises still higher, when this little puny consciousness is gone forever, that which is the reality behind shines, and we see it as the one existence-knowledge-bliss, the one atman, the universal. 'One that is only knowledge itself, one that is bliss itself, beyond all comparison, beyond all limit, ever free, never bound, infinite as the sky, unchangeable as the sky. Such a one will manifest Himself in your heart in meditation.'

How does the Advaitist theory explain these various phases of heaven and hells and these various ideas we find in all religions? When a man dies, it is said that he goes to heaven or hell, goes here or there, or that when a man dies, he is born again in another body either in heaven or in another world or somewhere. These are all hallucinations. Really speaking nobody is ever born or dies. There is neither heaven, nor hell, nor this world; all three never really existed. Tell a child a lot of ghost stories and let him go out into the street in the evening. There is a little stump of a tree. What does the child see? A ghost, with hands stretched out, ready to grab him. Suppose a man comes from the corner of the street, wanting to meet his sweetheart, he sees that stump of the tree as the girl. A policeman coming from the street corner sees the stump as a thief. The thief sees it as a policeman. It is the same stump of a tree that was seen in various ways. The stump is the reality and the visions of the stump are the projections of the various minds. There is one being, this Self; it neither comes, nor goes. When a man is ignorant, he wants to go to heaven or some place, and all his life he has been thinking and thinking of this; and when this earth dream vanishes, he sees this world as a heaven with devas and angels flying about and all such things. If a man all his life desires to meet his forefathers, he gets them all from Adam downwards, because he creates them. If a man is still more ignorant and has always been frightened by fanatics with ideas of hell, with all sorts of punishments, when he dies, he will see this very world as hell. All that is meant by dying or being born is simply changes in the plane of vision. Neither do you move, nor does that move upon which you project your vision.

You are the permanent, the unchangeable. How can you come and go? It is impossible; you are omnipresent. The sky never moves, but the clouds move over the surface of the sky and we may think that the sky itself moves, just as when you are in a railway train, you think the land is moving. It is not so, as it is the train which is moving. You are where you are; these dreams, these various clouds move. One dream follows another without connection. There is no such thing as law or connection in this world, but we are thinking that there is a great deal of connection. All of you have probably read *Alice in Wonderland*. It is the most wonderful book for children written in this century. When I read it, I was delighted; it was always in my head to write that sort of a book for children. What pleased me most in it was what you think most incongruous, that there is no connection there. One idea comes and jumps into another, without any connection. When you were children, you thought that as the most wonderful connection. So this man brought back his thoughts of childhood, which were perfectly connected to him as a child and composed this book for children. And all these books which men write, trying to make children swallow their own ideas as men, are nonsense. We too are grown-up children, that is all. The world is the same unconnected thing—*Alice in Wonderland*—with no connection whatever. When we see things happen a number of times in a certain sequence, we call it cause and effect and say that the thing will happen again. When this dream changes, another dream will seem quite as connected as this. When we dream, the things we see all seem to be connected; during the dream we never think they are incongruous; it is only when we wake up that we see the want of connection. When we wake from this dream of the world and compare it with the reality, it will be found all incongruous nonsense, a mass of incongruity passing before us, we do not know whence or whither, but we know it will end; this is called Maya and is like masses of fleeting fleecy clouds. They represent all this changing existence, and the sun itself, the unchanging, is you. When you look at that unchanging existence from the outside, you call it God; and when you look at it from the inside, you call it yourself. It is but one. There is no God separate from you, no God higher than you, the real 'you'. All the gods are little beings to you, all the ideas of God and Father in heaven are but your own reflection. God Himself is your image. 'God created man after His own image.' That is wrong. Man creates God after his own image. That is right. Throughout the universe we are creating gods after our own image. We create the god and fall down at his feet and worship him; and when this dream comes, we love it!

This is a good point to understand—that the sum and substance of this lecture is that there is but one existence, and that one-existence seen through different constitutions appears either as the earth, or heaven, or hell, or gods, or ghosts, or men, or demons, or world, or all these things. But among these many, 'He who sees that one in this ocean of death, he who sees that one life in this floating universe, who realizes that one who never changes, unto him belongs eternal peace; unto none else, unto none else.' This one existence has to be realized. How, is the next question. How is it to be realized? How is this dream to be broken, how shall we wake up from this dream that we are little men and women, and all such things? We are the infinite being of the universe and have become materialized into these little beings, men and women, depending upon the sweet word of one man, or the angry word of another and so forth. What a terrible dependence, what a terrible slavery!

I who am beyond all pleasure and pain, whose reflection is the whole universe, little bits of whose life are the suns and moons and stars—I am held down as a terrible slave! If you pinch my body, I feel pain. If one says a kind word, I begin to rejoice. See my condition—slave of the body, slave of the mind, slave of the world, slave of a good word, slave of a bad word, slave of passion, slave of happiness, slave of life, slave of death, slave of everything! This slavery has to be broken. How? 'This atman has first to be heard, then reasoned upon and then meditated upon.' This is the method of the Advaita Jnani. The truth has to be heard, then reflected upon and then to be constantly asserted. Think always, 'I am Brahman'. Every other thought must be cast aside as weakening. Cast aside every thought that says that you are men or women. Let body go, mind go, gods go and ghosts go. Let everything go but that one existence. 'Where one hears another, where one sees another, that is small; where one does not hear another, where one does not see another, that is infinite.' That is the highest when the subject and the object become one. When I am the listener and I am the speaker, when I am the teacher and I am the taught, when I am the creator and I am the created—then alone fear ceases; there is not another to make us afraid. There is nothing but myself, what can frighten me? This is to be heard day after day. Get rid of all other thoughts. Everything else must be thrown aside, and this is to be repeated continually, poured through the ears until it reaches the heart, until every nerve and muscle, every drop of blood tingles with the idea that I am He, I am He. Even at the gate of death say, 'I am He'. There was a man in India, a sannyasin, who used to repeat 'Shivoham'—'I am bliss eternal'; a tiger jumped on him one day and dragged him away and killed him, but so long as he was living, the sound came, 'Shivoham, Shivoham'. Even at the gate of death, in the greatest danger, in the thick of the battlefield, at the bottom of the ocean, on the tops of the highest mountains, in the thickest of the forest, tell yourself, 'I am He, I am He'. Day and night say, 'I am He'. It is the greatest strength; it is religion. 'The weak will never reach the atman.' Never say, 'O Lord, I am a miserable sinner.' Who will help you? You are the help of the universe. What in this universe can help you? Where is the man, or the god, or the demon to help you? What can prevail over you? You are the God of the universe; where can you seek for help? Never help came from anywhere but from yourself. In your ignorance, every prayer that you made and that was answered, you thought was answered by some being, but you answered the prayer yourself unknowingly. The help came from yourself and you fondly imagined that someone was sending help to you. There is no help for you outside of yourself; you are the creator of the universe. Like the silkworm you have built a cocoon around yourself. Who will save you? Burst your own cocoon and come out as the beautiful butterfly, as the free soul. Then alone you will see truth. Ever tell yourself, 'I am He.' These are the words that will burn up the dross that is in the mind, words that will bring out the tremendous energy which is within you already, the infinite power which is sleeping in your heart. This is to be brought out by constantly hearing the truth and nothing else. Wherever there is thought of weakness, approach not the place. Avoid all weakness if you want to be a jnani.

Before you begin to practice, clear your mind of all doubts. Fight and reason and argue; and when you have established it in your mind that this and this alone can be the truth and nothing else, do not argue anymore; close your mouth. Hear not argumentation, neither argue yourself. What is the use of any more arguments? You have satisfied yourself, you have decided the question. What remains? The truth has now to be realized, therefore why waste valuable time in vain arguments? The truth has now to be meditated upon and every idea that strengthens you must be taken up and every thought that weakens you must be rejected. The bhakta meditates upon forms and images and all such things and upon God. This is the natural process, but a slower one. The yogi meditates upon various centres in his body and manipulates powers in his mind. The jnani says the mind does not exist, neither the body. This idea of the body and of the mind must go, must be driven off; therefore it is foolish to think of them. It would be like trying to cure one ailment by bringing in another. His meditation therefore is the most difficult one, the negative; he denies everything, and what is left is the Self. This is the most analytical way. The jnani wants to tear away the universe from the Self by the sheer force of analysis. It is very easy to say, 'I am a jnani', but very hard to be really one. 'The way is long', it is, as it were, walking on the sharp edge of a razor; yet despair not. 'Awake, arise, and stop not until the goal is reached,' say the vedas.

So what is the meditation of the jnani? He wants to rise above every idea of body or mind, to drive away the idea that he is the body. For instance, when I say, 'I Swami', immediately the idea of the body comes. What must I do then? I must give the mind a hard blow and say, 'No, I am not the body, I am the Self.' Who cares if disease comes or death in the most horrible form? I am not the body. Why make the body nice? To enjoy the illusion once more? To continue the slavery? Let it go, I am not the body. That is the way of the jnani. The bhakta says, 'The Lord has given me this body that I may safely cross the ocean of life, and I must cherish it until the journey is accomplished.' The yogi says, 'I must be careful of the body, so that I may go on steadily and finally attain liberation.' The jnani feels that he cannot wait, he must reach the goal this very moment. He says, 'I am free through eternity, I am never bound; I am the God of the universe through all eternity. Who shall make me perfect? I am perfect already.' When a man is perfect, he sees perfection in others. When he sees imperfection, it is his own mind projecting itself. How can he see imperfection if he has not got it in himself? So the jnani does not care for perfection or imperfection. None exists for him. As soon as he is free, he does not see good and evil. Who sees evil and good? He who has it in himself. Who sees the body? He who thinks he is the body. The moment you get rid of the idea that you are the body, you do not see the world at all; it vanishes forever. The jnani seeks to tear himself away from this bondage of matter by the force of intellectual conviction. This is the negative way—the 'Neti, neti'—'Not this, not this.'

8

BHAKTI

Delivered at Sialkot, Punjab

In response to invitations from Punjab and Kashmir, Swami Vivekananda travelled through those parts. He stayed in Kashmir for over a month and his work there was very much appreciated by the Maharaja and his brothers. He then spent a few days in visiting Murree, Rawalpindi and Jammu, and at each of these places he delivered lectures. Subsequently he visited Sialkot and lectured twice, once in English and once in Hindi. The subject of the Swamiji's Hindi lecture was bhakti, a summary of which, translated into English, is given below:

The various religions that exist in the world, although they differ in the form of worship they take, are really one. In some places, the people build temples and worship in them, in some they worship fire, in others they prostrate themselves before idols, while there are many who do not believe at all in God. All are true, for, if you look at the real spirit, the real religion and the truths in each of them, they are all alike. In some religions, God is not worshipped, nay, His existence is not believed in, but good and worthy men are worshipped as if they were Gods. The example worthy of citation in this case is Buddhism. Bhakti is everywhere, whether directed to God or to noble persons. Upasana in the form of bhakti is everywhere supreme and bhakti is more easily attained than jnana. The latter requires favourable circumstances and strenuous practice.

Yoga cannot be properly practiced unless a man is physically very healthy and free from all worldly attachments. But bhakti can be more easily practiced by persons in every condition of life. Shandilya Rishi, who wrote about bhakti, says that extreme love for God is bhakti. Prahlada speaks to the same effect. If a man does not get food one day, he is troubled; if his son dies, how agonizing it is to him! The true bhakta feels the same pangs in his heart when he yearns after God. The great quality of bhakti is that it cleanses the mind and the firmly established bhakti for the Supreme Lord is alone sufficient to purify the mind. 'O God, Thy names are innumerable, but in every name Thy power is manifest and every name is pregnant with deep and mighty significance.' We should think of God always and not consider a time and place for doing so.

The various names under which God is worshipped are apparently different. One thinks that his method of worshipping God is the most efficacious and another thinks that his is the more potent process of attaining salvation. But look at the true basis of all—it is one. The Shaivas call Shiva the most powerful; the Vaishnavas hold to their all-powerful Vishnu; the worshippers of Devi will not yield to any in their idea that their Devi is the most omnipotent power in the universe. Leave inimical thoughts aside if you want to have permanent bhakti. Hatred is a thing which greatly impedes the course of bhakti and the man who hates none reaches God. Even then the devotion for one's own ideal is necessary. Hanuman says, 'Vishnu and Rama, I know, are one and the same, but after all, the lotus-eyed Rama is my best treasure.' The peculiar tendencies with which a person is born must remain with him. That is the chief reason why the world cannot be of one religion—and God forbid that there should be one religion only—for the world would then be a chaos and not a cosmos. A man must follow the tendencies peculiar to himself; and if he gets a teacher to help him to advance along his own lines, he will progress. We should let a person go the way he intends to go, but if we try to force him into another path, he will lose what he has already attained and will become worthless. As the face of one person does not resemble that of another, so the nature of one differs from that of another, then why should he not be allowed to act accordingly? A river flows in a certain direction; if you direct the course into a regular channel, the current becomes more rapid and the force is increased, but try to divert it from its proper course and you will see the result; the volume as well as the force will be lessened. This life is very important, and it, therefore, ought to be guided in the way one's tendency prompts him. In India, there was no enmity and every religion was left unmolested; so religion has lived. It ought to be remembered that quarrels about religion arise from thinking that one alone has the truth and whoever does not believe as one does is a fool; while another thinks that the other is a hypocrite, for if he were not one, he would follow him.

If God wished that people should follow one religion, why have so many religions sprung up? Methods have been vainly tried to force one religion upon everyone. Even when the sword was lifted to make all people follow one religion, history tells us that 10 religions sprang up in its place. One religion cannot suit all. Man is the product of two forces, action and reaction, which make him think. If such forces did not exercise a man's mind, he would be incapable of thinking. Man is a creature who thinks; *manushya* (man) is a being with *manas* (mind); and as soon as his thinking power goes, he becomes no better than an animal. Who would like such a man? God forbid that any such state should come upon the people of India. Variety in unity is necessary to keep man as man. Variety ought to be preserved in everything; for as long as there is variety the world will exist. Of course variety does not merely mean that one is small and the other is great, but if all play their parts equally well in their respective position in life, the variety is still preserved. In every religion there have been men good and able, thus making the religion to which they belonged worthy of respect; and as there are such people in every religion, there ought to be no hatred for any sect whatsoever.

Then the question may be asked, should we respect that religion which advocates vice? The answer will be certainly in the negative and such a religion ought to be expelled at once because it is productive of harm. All religion is to be based upon morality and personal purity is to be counted superior to dharma. In this connection it ought to be known that *achara* means purity inside and outside. External purity can be attained by cleansing the body with water and other things which are recommended in the shastras. The internal man is to be purified by not speaking falsehood, by not drinking, by not doing immoral acts and by doing good to others. If you do not commit any sin, if you do not tell lies, if you do not drink, gamble, or commit theft, it is good. But that is only your duty and you cannot be applauded for it. Some service to others is also to be done. As you do good to yourself, so you must do good to others.

Here I shall say something about food regulations. All the old customs have faded away and nothing but a vague notion of not eating with this man, with that man has been left among our countrymen. Purity by touch is the only relic left of the good rules laid down hundreds of years ago. Three kinds of food are forbidden in the shastras. First, the food that is by its very nature defective, as garlic or onions. If a man eats too much of them it creates passion and he may be led to commit immoralities, hateful both to God and man. Secondly, food contaminated by external impurities. We ought to select some place quite neat and clean in which to keep our food. Thirdly, we should avoid eating food touched by a wicked man because contact with such produces bad ideas in us. Even if one be a son of a Brahmin, but is profligate and immoral in his habits, we should not eat food from his hands.

But the spirit of these observances is gone. What is left is this that we cannot eat from the hands of any man who is not of the highest caste, even though he be the most wise and holy person. The disregard of those old rules is ever to be found in the confectioner's shop. If you look there, you will find flies hovering all over the confectionery, the dust from the road blowing upon the sweetmeats and the confectioner himself in a dress that is not very clean and neat. Purchasers should declare with one voice that they will not buy sweets unless they are kept in glass-cases in the halwai's shop. That would have the salutary effect of preventing flies from conveying cholera and other plague germs to the sweets. We ought to improve, but instead of improving we have gone back. Manu says that we should not spit in water, but we throw all sorts of filth into the rivers. Considering all these things we find that the purification of one's outer self is very necessary.

The Shastrakaras knew that very well. But now the real spirit of this observance of purity about food is lost and the letter only remains. Thieves, drunkards and criminals can be our caste fellows, but if a good and noble man eats food with a person of a lower caste, who is quite as respectable as himself, he will be outcasted and lost forever. This custom has been the bane of our country. It ought, therefore, to be distinctly understood that sin is incurred by coming in contact with sinners and nobility in the company of good persons; keeping aloof from the wicked is the external purification.

The internal purification is a task much more severe. It consists in speaking the truth, sensing the poor, helping the needy, etc. Do we always speak the truth? What happens is often this. People go to the house of a rich person for some business of their own and flatter him by calling him benefactor of the poor and so forth, even though that man may cut the throat of a poor man coming to his house. What is this? Nothing, but falsehood. And it is this that pollutes the mind. It is therefore, truly said that whatever a man says who has purified his inner self for 12 years without entertaining a single vicious idea during that period is sure to come true. This is the power of truth, and one who has cleansed both the inner and the outer self is alone capable of bhakti. But the beauty is that bhakti itself cleanses the mind to a great extent.

Although the Jews, Mohammedans and Christians do not set so much importance upon the excessive external purification of the body as the Hindus do, still they have it in some form or other; they find that to a certain extent it is always required. Among the Jews, idol-worship is condemned, but they had a temple in which was kept a chest which they called an ark, in which the Tables of the Law were preserved and above the chest were two figures of angels with wings outstretched, between which the divine presence was supposed to manifest itself as a cloud. That temple has long since been destroyed, but the new temples are made exactly after the old fashion and in the chest religious books are kept. The Roman Catholics and the Greek Christians have idol-worship in certain forms. The image of Jesus and that of his mother are worshipped. Among Protestants there is no idol-worship, yet they worship God in a personal form, which may be called idol-worship in another form. Among Parsees and Iranians fire-worship is carried on to a great extent. Among Mohammedans, the prophets and great and noble persons are worshipped, and they turn their faces towards the Caaba when they pray. These things show that men at the first stage of religious development have to make use of something external, and when the inner self becomes purified they turn to more abstract conceptions. 'When the jiva is sought to be united with Brahman it is best, when meditation is practiced it is mediocre, repetition of names is the lowest form and external worship is the lowest of the low.' But it should be distinctly understood that even in practicing the last there is no sin. Everybody ought to do what he is able to do; and if he be dissuaded from that, he will do it in some other way in order to attain his end. So we should not speak ill of a man who worships idols. He is in that stage of growth, and, therefore, must have them; wise men should try to help forward such men and get them to do better. But there is no use in quarrelling about these various sorts of worship.

Some persons worship God for the sake of obtaining wealth, others because they want to have a son and they think themselves bhagavatas (devotees). This is no bhakti and they are not true bhagavatas. When a sadhu comes who professes that he can make gold, they run to him and they still consider themselves bhagavatas. It is not bhakti if we worship God with the desire for a son; it is not bhakti if we worship with the desire to be rich; it is not bhakti even if we have a desire for heaven; it is not bhakti if a man worships with the desire of being saved from the tortures of hell. Bhakti is not the outcome of fear or greediness. He is the true bhagavata who says, 'O God, I do not want a beautiful wife, I do not want knowledge or salvation. Let me be born and die hundreds of times. What I want is that I should be ever engaged in Thy service.' It is at this stage—and when a man sees God in everything and everything in God—that he attains perfect bhakti. It is then that he sees Vishnu incarnated in everything from the microbe to Brahma, and it is then that he sees God manifesting Himself in everything, it is then that he feels that there is nothing without God, and it is then and then alone that thinking himself to be the most insignificant of all beings he worships God with the true spirit of a bhakta. He then leaves tirthas and external forms of worship far behind him, he sees every man to be the most perfect temple.

Bhakti is described in several ways in the shastras. We say that God is our Father. In the same way we call Him Mother and so on. These relationships are conceived in order to strengthen bhakti in us and they make us feel nearer and dearer to God. Hence these names are justifiable in one way, and that is that the words are simply words of endearment, the outcome of the fond love which a true bhagavata feels for God.

Take the story of Radha and Krishna in Rasalila. The story simply exemplifies the true spirit of a bhakta because no love in the world exceeds that existing between a man and a woman. When there is such intense love, there is no fear, no other attachment save that one which binds that pair in an inseparable and all-absorbing bond. But with regard to parents, love is accompanied with fear due to the reverence we have for them. Why should we care whether God created anything or not, what have we to do with the fact that He is our preserver? He is only our beloved and we should adore Him devoid of all thoughts of fear. A man loves God only when he has no other desire, when he thinks of nothing else and when he is mad after Him. That love which a man has for his beloved can illustrate the love we ought to have for God. Krishna is the God and Radha loves Him; read those books which describe that story and then you can imagine the way you should love God. But how many understand this? How can people who are vicious to their very core and have no idea of what morality is understand all this? When people drive all sorts of worldly thoughts from their minds and live in a clear moral and spiritual atmosphere, it is then that they understand the most abstruse of thoughts even if they be uneducated. But how few are there of that nature!

There is not a single religion which cannot be perverted by man. For example, he may think that the atman is quite separate from the body, and so, when committing sins with the body his atman is unaffected. If religions were truly followed, there would not have been a single man, whether Hindu, Mohammedan, or Christian, who would not have been all pure. But men are guided by their own nature, whether good or bad; there is no gainsaying that. But in the world, there are always some who get intoxicated when they hear of Go and shed tears of joy when they read of God. Such men are true bhaktas.

At the initial stage of religious development, a man thinks of God as his master and himself as His servant. He feels indebted to Him for providing for his daily wants and so forth. Put such thoughts aside. There is but one attractive power and that is God; and it is in obedience to that attractive power that the sun and the moon and everything else move. Everything in this world, whether good or bad, belongs to God. Whatever occurs in our life, whether good or bad, is bringing us to Him. One man kills another because of some selfish purpose. But the motive behind is love, whether for himself or for anyone else. Whether we do good or evil, the propeller is love. When a tiger kills a buffalo, it is because he or his cubs are hungry.

God is love personified. He is apparent in everything. Everybody is being drawn to Him whether he knows it or not. When a woman loves her husband, she does not understand that it is the divine in her husband that is the great attractive power. The God of Love is the one thing to be worshipped. So long as we think of Him only as the creator and preserver, we can offer Him external worship, but when we get beyond all that and think Him to be love incarnate, seeing Him in all things and all things in Him, it is then that supreme bhakti is attained.

9

THE IDEAL OF A UNIVERSAL RELIGION

HOW IT MUST EMBRACE DIFFERENT TYPES OF MINDS AND METHODS

Delivered on 12 January 1896, at Hardman Hall

Wheresoever our senses reach, or whatsoever our minds imagine, we find therein the action and reaction of two forces, the one counteracting the other and causing the constant play of the mixed phenomena that we see around us and of those which we feel in our minds. In the external world, the action of these opposite forces is expressing itself as attraction and repulsion, or as centripetal and centrifugal forces; and in the internal, as love and hatred, good and evil. We repel some things, we attract others. We are attracted by one, we are repelled by another. Many times in our lives we find that without any reason whatsoever we are, as it were, we get attracted towards certain persons; at other times, similarly, we are repelled by others. This is patent to all, and the higher the field of action, the more potent, the more remarkable are the influences of these opposite forces. Religion is the highest plane of human thought and life, and herein we find that the workings of these two forces have been most marked. The most intense love that humanity has ever known has come from religion and the most diabolical hatred that humanity has known has also come from religion. The noblest words of peace that the world has ever heard have come from men on the religious plane and the bitterest denunciation that the world has ever known has been uttered by religious men. The higher the object of any religion and the finer its organization, the more remarkable are its activities. No other human motive has deluged the world with blood so much as religion; at the same time, nothing has brought into existence so many hospitals and asylums for the poor; no other human influence has taken such care, not only of humanity, but also of the lowest of animals, as religion has done. Nothing makes us so cruel as religion and nothing makes us so tender as religion. This has been so in the past and will also, in all probability, be so in the future. Yet out of the midst of this din and turmoil, this strife and struggle, this hatred and jealousy of religions and sects, there have arisen, from time to time, potent voices, drowning all this noise—making themselves heard from pole to pole, as it were—proclaiming peace and harmony. Will it ever come?

Is it possible that there should ever reign unbroken harmony in this plane of mighty religious struggle? The world is exercised in the latter part of this century by the question of harmony; in society, various plans are being proposed and attempts are made to carry them into practice, but we know how difficult it is to do so. People find that it is almost impossible to mitigate the fury of the struggle of life, to tone down the tremendous nervous tension that is in man. Now, if it is so difficult to bring harmony and peace to the physical plane of life—the external, gross and outward side of it—then a thousand times more difficult is it to bring peace and harmony to rule over the internal nature of man. I would ask you for the time being to come out of the network of words. We have all been hearing from childhood of such things as love, peace, charity, equality and universal brotherhood, but they have become to us mere words without meaning, words which we repeat like parrots and it has become quite natural for us to do so. We cannot help it. Great souls, who first felt these great ideas in their hearts, manufactured these words; and at that time many understood their meaning. Later on, ignorant people have taken up those words to play with them and made religion a mere play upon words and not a thing to be carried into practice. It becomes 'my father's religion', 'our nation's religion', 'our country's religion' and so forth. It becomes only a phase of patriotism to profess any religion and patriotism is always partial. To bring harmony into religion must always be difficult. Yet we will consider this problem of the harmony of religions.

We see that in every religion there are three parts—I mean in every great and recognized religion. First, there is the philosophy which presents the whole scope of that religion, setting forth its basic principles, the goal and the means of reaching it. The second part is mythology, which is philosophy made concrete. It consists of legends relating to the lives of men, or of supernatural beings and so forth. It is the abstractions of philosophy concretized in the more or less imaginary lives of men and supernatural beings. The third part is the ritual. This is still more concrete and is made up of forms and ceremonies, various physical attitudes, flowers, incense and many other things that appeal to the senses. In these consists the ritual. You will find that all recognized religions have these three elements. Some lay more stress on one, some on another. Let us now take into consideration the first part, philosophy. Is there one universal philosophy? Not yet. Each religion brings out its own doctrines and insists upon them as being the only true ones. And not only does it do that, but it thinks that he who does not believe in them must go to some horrible place. Some will even draw the sword to compel others to believe as they do. This is not through wickedness, but through a particular disease of the human brain called fanaticism. They are very sincere, these fanatics, the most sincere of human beings, but they are quite as irresponsible as other lunatics in the world. This disease of fanaticism is one of the most dangerous of all diseases. All the wickedness of human nature is roused by it. Anger is stirred up, nerves are strung high and human beings become like tigers.

Is there any mythological similarity, is there any mythological harmony, any universal mythology accepted by all religions? Certainly not. All religions have their own mythology, only each of them says, 'My stories are not mere myths.' Let us try to understand the question by illustration. I simply mean to illustrate, I do not mean criticism of any religion. The Christian believes that God took the shape of a dove and came down to earth; to him this is history and not mythology. The Hindu believes that God is manifested in the cow. Christians say that to believe so is mere mythology and not history—that it is superstition. The Jews think that if an image be made in the form of a box, or a chest, with an angel on either side, then it may be placed in the Holy of Holies; it is sacred to Jehovah. But if the image be made in the form of a beautiful man or woman, they say, 'This is a horrible idol, break it down!' This is our unity in mythology! If a man stands up and says, 'My prophet did such and such a wonderful thing,' others will say, 'That is only superstition,' but at the same time they say that their own prophet did still more wonderful things, which they hold to be historical. Nobody in the world, as far as I have seen, is able to make out the fine distinction between history and mythology, as it exists in the brains of these persons. All such stories, to whatever religion they may belong, are really mythological, mixed up occasionally, it may be with, a little history.

Next comes the rituals. One sect has one particular form of ritual and thinks that that is holy, while the rituals of another sect are simply arrant superstition. If one sect worships a peculiar sort of symbol, another sect says, 'Oh, it is horrible!' Take, for instance, a general form of symbol. The phallus symbol is certainly a sexual symbol, but gradually that aspect of it has been forgotten and it stands now as a symbol of the creator. Those nations which have this as their symbol never think of it as the phallus; it is just a symbol and there it ends. But a man from another race or creed sees in it nothing but the phallus and begins to condemn it; yet at the same time he may be doing something which to the so-called phallic worshippers appears most horrible. Let me take two points for illustration, the phallus symbol and the sacrament of the Christians. To the Christians, the phallus is horrible and to the Hindus, the Christian sacrament is horrible. They say that the Christian sacrament, the killing of a man and the eating of his flesh and the drinking of his blood to get the good qualities of that man is cannibalism. This is what some of the savage tribes do; if a man is brave, they kill him and eat his heart because they think that it will give them the qualities of courage and bravery possessed by that man. Even such a devout Christian as Sir John Lubbock admits this and says that the origin of this Christian symbol is in this savage idea. The Christians, of course, do not admit this view of its origin; what it may imply never comes to their mind. It stands for holy things and that is all they want to know. So even in rituals there is no universal symbol, which can command general recognition and acceptance. Where then is any universality? How is it possible then to have a universal form of religion? That, however, already exists. And let us see what it is.

We all hear about universal brotherhood and how societies

stand up especially to preach this. I remember an old story. In India, taking wine is considered very bad. There were two brothers who wished, one night, to drink wine secretly; their uncle, who was a very orthodox man, was sleeping in a room quite close to theirs. So, before they began to drink, they said to each other, 'We must be very silent, or uncle will wake up.' When they were drinking, they continued repeating to each other, 'Silence! Uncle will wake up,' each trying to shout the other down. And, as the shouting increased, the uncle woke up, came into the room and discovered the whole thing. Now, we all shout like these drunken men, 'Universal brotherhood! We are all equal, therefore let us make a sect.' As soon as you make a sect you protest against equality, and equality is no more. Mohammedans talk of universal brotherhood, but what comes out of that in reality? Why, anybody who is not a Mohammedan will not be admitted into the brotherhood; he will more likely have his throat cut. Christians talk of universal brotherhood, but anyone who is not a Christian must go to that place where he will be eternally barbecued.

And so we go on in this world in our search after universal brotherhood and equality. When you hear such talk in the world, I would ask you to be a little reticent, to take care of yourselves for behind all this talk is often the most intense selfishness. 'In the winter sometimes a thunder-cloud comes up; it roars and roars, but it does not rain. In the rainy season the clouds speak not, but deluge the world with water.' So those who are *really* workers, and *really* feel at heart the universal brotherhood of man, do not talk much, do not make little sects for universal brotherhood, but their acts, their movements, their whole life, show out clearly that they in truth possess the feeling of brotherhood for mankind, that they have love and sympathy for all. They do not speak, they *do* and they *live*.

This world is too full of blustering talk. We want a little more earnest work and less talk.

So far we see that it is hard to find any universal features in regard to religion and yet we know that they exist. We are all human beings, but are we all equal? Certainly not. Who says we are equal? Only the lunatic. Are we all equal in our brains, in our powers, in our bodies? One man is stronger than another, one man has more brain power than another. If we are all equal, why is there this inequality? Who made it? We. Because we have more or less powers, more or less brain, more or less physical strength, it must make a difference between us. Yet we know that the doctrine of equality appeals to our heart. We are all human beings, but some are men and some are women. Here is a black man, there is a white man, but all are men, all belong to one humanity. Various are our faces; I see no two alike, yet we are all human beings. Where is this one humanity? I find a man or a woman, either dark or fair; among all these faces I know that there is an abstract humanity which is common to all. I may not find it when I try to grasp it, to sense it and to actualize it, yet I know for certain that it is there. If I am sure of anything, it is of this humanity which is common to us all. It is through this generalized entity that I see you as a man or a woman. So it is with this universal religion, which runs through all the various religions of the world in the form of God; it must and does exist through eternity. 'I am the thread that runs through all these pearls,' and each pearl is a religion or even a sect thereof. Such are the different pearls and the Lord is the thread that runs through all of them; only the majority of mankind is entirely unconscious of it.

Unity in variety is the plan of the universe. We are all men and yet we are all distinct from one another. As a part of humanity, I am one with you, and as Mr So-and-so I am different from you. As a man you are separate from the woman; as a human being you are one with the woman. As a man you are separate from the animal, but as living beings, man, woman, animal and plant are all one; and as existence, you are one with the whole universe. That universal existence is God, the ultimate Unity in the universe. In Him we are all one. At the same time, in manifestation, these differences must always remain. In our work, in our energies, as they are being manifested outside, these differences must always remain. We find then that if by the idea of a universal religion it is meant that one set of doctrines should be believed in by all mankind it is wholly impossible. It can never be, there can never be a time when all faces will be the same. Again, if we expect that there will be one universal mythology, that is also impossible, it cannot be. Neither can there be one universal ritual. Such a state of things can never come into existence; if it ever did, the world would be destroyed because variety is the first principle of life. What makes us formed beings? Differentiation. Perfect balance would be our destruction. Suppose the amount of heat in this room, the tendency of which is towards equal and perfect diffusion, gets that kind of diffusion, then for all practical purposes that heat will cease to be. What makes motion possible in this universe? Lost balance. The unity of sameness can come only when this universe is destroyed, otherwise such a thing is impossible. Not only so, it would be dangerous to have it. We must not wish that all of us should think alike. There would then be no thought to think. We should be all alike, as the Egyptian mummies in a museum, looking at each other without a thought to think. It is this difference, this differentiation, this losing of the balance between us, which is the very soul of our progress, the soul of all our thoughts. This must always be.

What then do I mean by the idea of a universal religion? I

do not mean any one universal philosophy, or any one universal mythology, or any one universal ritual held alike by all for I know that this world must go on working, wheel within wheel, this intricate mass of machinery, most complex, most wonderful. What can *we* do then? We can make it run smoothly, we can lessen the friction, we can grease the wheels, as it were. How? By recognizing the natural necessity of variation. Just as we have recognized unity by our very nature, so we must also recognize variation. We must learn that truth may be expressed in a hundred thousand ways and that each of these ways is true as far as it goes. We must learn that the same thing can be viewed from a hundred different standpoints and yet be the same thing. Take for instance the sun. Suppose a man standing on the Earth looks at the sun when it rises in the morning; he sees a big ball. Suppose he starts on a journey towards the sun and takes a camera with him, taking photographs at every stage of his journey, until he reaches the sun. The photographs of each stage will be seen to be different from those of the other stages; in fact, when he gets back, he brings with him so many photographs of so many different suns, as it would appear; and yet we know that the same sun was photographed by the man at the different stages of his progress. Even so is it with the Lord. Through high philosophy or low, through the most exalted mythology or the grossest, through the most refined ritualism or arrant fetishism, every sect, every soul, every nation, every religion, consciously or unconsciously, is struggling upward, towards God; every vision of truth that man has, is a vision of Him and of none else.

Suppose we all go with vessels in our hands to fetch water from a lake. One has a cup, another a jar, another a bucket and so forth, and we all fill our vessels. The water in each case naturally takes the form of the vessel carried by each of us. He who brought the cup has the water in the form of a cup; he who brought the jar, his water is in the shape of a jar and so forth, but, in every case, water and nothing but water is in the vessel. So it is in the case of religion; our minds are like these vessels, and each one of us is trying to arrive at the realization of God. God is like that water filling these different vessels and in each vessel the vision of God comes in the form of the vessel. Yet He is one. He is God in every case. This is the only recognition of universality that we can get.

So far it is all right theoretically. But is there any way of practically working out this harmony in religions? We find that this recognition that all the various views of religion are true has been very old. Hundreds of attempts have been made in India, in Alexandria, in Europe, in China, in Japan, in Tibet and lastly in America, to formulate a harmonious religious creed, to make all religions come together in love. They have all failed because they did not adopt any practical plan. Many have admitted that all the religions of the world are right, but they show no practical way of bringing them together, so as to enable each of them to maintain its own individuality in the conflux. That plan alone is practical, which does not destroy the individuality of any man in religion and at the same time shows him a point of union with all others. But so far, all the plans of religious harmony that have been tried, while proposing to take in all the various views of religion, have, in practice, tried to bind them all down to a few doctrines and so have produced more new sects, fighting, struggling and pushing against each other.

I have also my little plan. I do not know whether it will work or not, but I want to present it to you for discussion. What is my plan? In the first place I would ask mankind to recognize this maxim, 'Do not destroy.' Iconoclastic reformers do no good to the world. Break not, pull not anything down, but build.

Help, if you can; if you cannot, fold your hands and stand by and see things go on. Do not injure, if you cannot render help. Say not a word against any man's convictions so far as they are sincere. Secondly, take man where he stands and from there give him a lift. If it be true that God is the centre of all religions and that each of us is moving towards Him along one of these radii, then it is certain that all of us *must* reach that centre. And at the centre, where all the radii meet, all our differences will cease, but until we reach there, differences there must be. All these radii converge to the same centre. One, according to his nature, travels along one of these lines and another along another; and if we all push onward along our own lines, we shall surely come to the centre because 'All roads lead to Rome.' Each of us is naturally growing and developing according to his own nature; each will in time come to know the highest truth for after all, men must teach themselves. What can you and I do? Do you think you can teach even a child? You cannot. The child teaches himself. Your duty is to afford opportunities and to remove obstacles. A plant grows. Do *you* make the plant grow? Your duty is to put a hedge round it and see that no animal eats up the plant and there your duty ends. The plant grows of itself. So it is in regard to the spiritual growth of every man. None can teach you, none can make a spiritual man of you. You have to teach yourself, your growth must come from inside.

What can an external teacher do? He can remove the obstructions a little and there his duty ends. Therefore help, if you can, but do not destroy. Give up all ideas that *you* can make men spiritual. It is impossible. There is no other teacher to you than your own soul. Recognize this. What comes of it? In society we see so many different natures. There are thousands and thousands of varieties of minds and inclinations. A thorough generalization of them is impossible, but for our

The Ideal of a Universal Religion

practical purpose it is sufficient to have them characterized into four classes. First, there is the active man, the worker; he wants to work and there is tremendous energy in his muscles and his nerves. His aim is to work—to build hospitals, do charitable deeds, make streets, to plan and to organize. Then there is the emotional man who loves the sublime and the beautiful to an excessive degree. He loves to think of the beautiful, to enjoy the aesthetic side of nature and adore love and the God of Love. He loves with his whole heart the great souls of all times, the prophets of religions and the incarnations of God on earth; he does not care whether reason can or cannot prove that Christ or Buddha existed; he does not care for the exact date when the Sermon on the Mount was preached, or for the exact moment of Krishna's birth; what he cares for is their personalities, their lovable figures. Such is his ideal. This is the nature of the lover, the emotional man. Then, there is the mystic whose mind wants to analyse its own self, to understand the workings of the human mind, what the forces are that are working inside, and how to know, manipulate and obtain control over them. This is the mystical mind. Then, there is the philosopher who wants to weigh everything and use his intellect even beyond the possibilities of all human philosophy.

Now a religion, to satisfy the largest proportion of mankind, must be able to supply food for all these various types of minds; and where this capability is wanting, the existing sects all become one-sided. Suppose you go to a sect, which preaches love and emotion. They sing and weep and preach love. But as soon as you say, 'My friend, that is all right, but I want something stronger than this—a little reason and philosophy; I want to understand things step by step and more rationally,' they say, 'Get out'; and they not only ask you to get out but would send you to the other place, if they could. The result is that that sect can only help people of an emotional turn of mind. They not only do not help others, but try to destroy them; and the most wicked part of the whole thing is that they will not only *not* help others, but do not believe in their sincerity. Again, there are philosophers who talk of the wisdom of India and the East and use big psychological terms, 50 syllables long, but if an ordinary man like me goes to them and says, 'Can you tell me anything to make me spiritual?', the first thing they would do would be to smile and say, 'Oh, you are too far below us in your reason. What can you understand about spirituality?' These are high-up philosophers. They simply show you the door. Then there are the mystical sects who speak all sorts of things about different planes of existence, different states of mind and what the power of the mind can do and so on; and if you are an ordinary man and say, 'Show me anything good that I can do; I am not much given to speculation; can you give me anything that will suit me?', they will smile and say, 'Listen to that fool; he knows nothing, his existence is for nothing.' And this is going on everywhere in the world. I would like to get extreme exponents of all these different sects, shut them up in a room and photograph their beautiful derisive smiles!

This is the existing condition of religion, the existing condition of things. What I want to propagate is a religion that will be equally acceptable to all minds; it must be equally philosophic, equally emotional, equally mystic and equally conducive to action. If professors from the colleges come, scientific men and physicists, they will court reason. Let them have it as much as they want. There will be a point beyond which they will think they cannot go, without breaking with reason. They will say, 'These ideas of God and salvation are superstitious, guise them up!' I say, 'Mr Philosopher, this body

The Ideal of a Universal Religion

of yours is a bigger superstition. Give *it* up, don't go home to dinner or to your philosophic chair. Give up the body and if you cannot, cry quarter and sit down.' For religion must be able to show how to realize the philosophy that teaches us that this world is one, that there is but one existence in the universe. Similarly, if the mystic comes, we must welcome him, be ready to give him the science of mental analysis and practically demonstrate it before him. And if emotional people come, we must sit, laugh and weep with them in the name of the Lord; we must 'drink the cup of love and become mad.' If the energetic worker comes, we must work with him, with all the energy that we have. And this combination will be the ideal of the nearest approach to a universal religion. Would to God that all men were so constituted that in their minds *all* these elements of philosophy, mysticism, emotion and of work were equally present in full! That is the ideal, my ideal of a perfect man. Everyone who has only one or two of these elements of character, I consider 'one-sided'; and this world is almost full of such 'one-sided' men, with knowledge of that one road only in which they move; and anything else is dangerous and horrible to them. To become harmoniously balanced in all these four directions is *my* ideal of religion. And this religion is attained by what we, in India, call yoga—union. To the worker, it is union between men and the whole of humanity; to the mystic, between his lower and higher self; to the lover, union between himself and the God of Love; and to the philosopher, it is the union of *all* existence. This is what is meant by yoga. This is a Sanskrit term, and these four divisions of yoga have in Sanskrit different names. The man who seeks after this kind of union is called a yogi. The worker is called the Karma Yogi. He who seeks the union through love is called the Bhakti Yogi. He who seeks it through mysticism is called the Raja Yogi. And he who seeks it through philosophy is called the Jnana Yogi So, this word Yogi comprises them all.

Now, first of all let me take up Raja Yoga. What is this Raja Yoga, this controlling of the mind? In this country, you are associating all sorts of hobgoblins with the word yoga, I am afraid. Therefore, I must start by telling you that it has nothing to do with such things. No one of these yogas gives up reason, no one of them asks you to be hoodwinked, or to deliver your reason into the hands of priests of any type whatsoever. No one of them asks that you should give your allegiance to any superhuman messenger. Each one of them tells you to *cling* to your reason to hold fast to it. We find in all beings three sorts of instruments of knowledge. The first is instinct, which you find most highly developed in animals; this is the lowest instrument of knowledge. What is the second instrument of knowledge? Reasoning. You find that most highly developed in man. Now in the first place, instinct is an inadequate instrument; to animals, the sphere of action is very limited and within that limit instinct acts. When you come to man, you see it is largely developed into reason. The sphere of action also has here become enlarged. Yet even reason is still very insufficient. Reason can go only a little way and then it stops, it cannot go any further; and if you try to push it, the result is helpless confusion, reason itself becomes unreasonable. Logic becomes argument in a circle. Take, for instance, the very basis of our perception, matter and force. What is matter? That which is acted upon by force. And force? That which acts upon matter. You see the complication, what the logicians call see-saw, one idea depending on the other and this again depending on that. You find a mighty barrier before reason, beyond which reasoning cannot go; yet it always feels impatient to get into the region of the infinite beyond. This world, this universe which our senses feel, or our mind thinks, is but one atom, so to say, of the infinite, projected on to the plane of consciousness; and within that narrow limit, defined by the network of consciousness, works our reason, and not beyond. Therefore, there must be some other instrument to take us beyond and that instrument is called inspiration. So instinct, reason and inspiration are the three instruments of knowledge. Instinct belongs to animals, reason to man and inspiration to God-men. But in all human beings are to be found, in a more or less developed condition, the germs of all these three instruments of knowledge. To have these mental instruments evolved, the germs must be there. And this must also be remembered that one instrument is a development of the other and, therefore, does not contradict it. It is reason that develops into inspiration and, therefore, inspiration does not contradict reason, but fulfils it.

Things which reason cannot get at are brought to light by inspiration; and they do not contradict reason. The old man does not contradict the child, but fulfils the child. Therefore you must always bear in mind that the great danger lies in mistaking the lower form of instrument to be the higher. Many times instinct is presented before the world as inspiration, and then come all the spurious claims for the gift of prophecy. A fool or a semi-lunatic thinks that the confusion going on in his brain is inspiration and he wants men to follow him. The most contradictory irrational nonsense that has been preached in the world is simply the instinctive jargon of confused lunatic brains trying to pass for the language of inspiration.

The first test of true teaching must be that the teaching should not contradict reason. And you may see that such is the basis of all these yogas. We take the Raja Yoga, the psychological yoga, the psychological way to union. It is a vast subject and I can only point out to you now the central idea of this yoga. We have but one method of acquiring knowledge. From the lowest man to the highest yogi, all have to use the same method and that method is what is called concentration. The chemist who works in his laboratory concentrates all the powers of his mind, brings them into one focus and throws them on the elements; the elements stand analysed and thus his knowledge comes. The astronomer has also concentrated the powers of his mind and brought them into one focus; and he throws them on to objects through his telescope; and stars and systems roll forward and give up their secrets to him. So it is in every case—with the professor in his chair, the student with his book—with every man who is working to know. You are hearing me, and if my words interest you, your mind will become concentrated on them; and then suppose a clock strikes, you will not hear it, on account of this concentration; and the more you are able to concentrate your mind, the better you will understand me; and the more I concentrate my love and powers, the better I shall be able to give expression to what I want to convey to you. The more this power of concentration, the more knowledge is acquired because this is the one and only method of acquiring knowledge. Even the lowest shoeblack, if he gives more concentration, will black shoes better; the cook with concentration will cook a meal all the better. In making money, or in worshipping God, or in doing anything, the stronger the power of concentration, the better will that thing be done. This is the one call, the one knock, which opens the gates of nature and lets out floods of light. This, the power of concentration, is the only key to the treasure-house of knowledge. The system of Raja Yoga deals almost exclusively with this. In the present state of our body, we are so much distracted and the mind is frittering away its energies upon a hundred sorts of things. As soon as I try to calm my thoughts and concentrate my mind upon any one object of knowledge, thousands of undesired impulses rush into the brain, thousands of thoughts rush into the mind and disturb it. How to check it and bring the mind under control is the whole subject of study in Raja Yoga.

Now take Karma Yoga, the attainment of God through work. It is evident that in society there are many persons who seem to be born for some sort of activity or other, whose minds cannot be concentrated on the plane of thought alone and who have but one idea, concretized in work, visible and tangible. There must be a science for this kind of life too. Each one of us is engaged in some work, but the majority of us fritter away the greater portion of our energies, because we do not know the secret of work. Karma Yoga explains this secret and teaches where and how to work, how to employ to the greatest advantage the largest part of our energies in the work that is before us. But with this secret, we must take into consideration the great objection against work, namely that it causes pain. All misery and pain come from attachment. I want to do work, I want to do good to a human being; and it is 90 to one that that human being whom I have helped will prove ungrateful and go against me; and the result to me will be pain. Such things deter mankind from working; and it spoils a good portion of the work and energy of mankind, this fear of pain and misery. Karma Yoga teaches us how to work for work's sake, unattached, without caring who is helped, and what for. The Karma Yogi works because it is his nature, because he *feels* that it is good for him to do so and he has no object beyond that. His position in this world is that of a giver, and he never cares to receive anything. He knows that he is giving and does not ask for anything in return and, therefore, he eludes the grasp of misery. The grasp of pain, whenever it comes, is the result of the reaction of 'attachment'.

There is then the Bhakti Yoga for the man of emotional nature, the lover. He wants to love God, he relies upon and uses all sorts of rituals, flowers, incense, beautiful buildings, forms and all such things. Do you mean to say they are wrong? One fact I must tell you. It is good for you to remember, in this country especially, that the world's great spiritual giants have all been produced only by those religious sects which have been in possession of very rich mythology and ritual. All sects that have attempted to worship God without any form or ceremony have crushed without mercy everything that is beautiful and sublime in religion. Their religion is a fanaticism at best, a dry thing. The history of the world is a standing witness to this fact. Therefore do not decry these rituals and mythologies. Let people have them; let those who so desire have them. Do not exhibit that unworthy derisive smile and say, 'They are fools; let them have it.' Not so; the greatest men I have seen in my life, the most wonderfully developed in spirituality, have all come through the discipline of these rituals. I do not hold myself worthy to sit at their feet and for *me* to criticize *them*! How do I know how these ideas act upon the human minds, which of them I am to accept and which to reject? We are apt to criticize everything in the world: without sufficient warrant. Let people have all the mythology they want, with its beautiful inspirations for you must always bear in mind that emotional natures do not care for abstract definitions of the truth. God to them is something tangible, the only thing that is real; they feel, hear, see Him and love Him. Let them have their God. Your rationalist seems to them to be like the fool who, when he saw a beautiful statue, wanted to break it to find out of what material it was made. Bhakti Yoga teaches them how to

The Ideal of a Universal Religion ♦ 87

love, without any ulterior motives, loving God and loving the good because it is good to do so, not for going to heaven, nor to get children, wealth, or anything else. It teaches them that love itself is the highest recompense of love—that God Himself is love. It teaches them to pay all kinds of tribute to God as the creator, the omnipresent, omniscient, almighty ruler, the father and the mother. The highest phrase that can express Him, the highest idea that the human mind can conceive of Him, is that He is the God of Love. Wherever there is love, it is He. 'Wherever there is any love, it is He, the Lord is present there.' Where the husband kisses the wife, He is there in the kiss; where the mother kisses the child, He is there in the kiss; where friends clasp hands, He, the Lord, is present as the God of Love. When a great man loves and wishes to help mankind, He is there giving freely His bounty out of His love to mankind. Wherever the heart expands, He is there manifested. This is what the Bhakti Yoga teaches.

We lastly come to the Jnana Yogi, the philosopher, the thinker, he who wants to go beyond the visible. He is the man who is not satisfied with the little things of this world. His idea is to go beyond the daily routine of eating, drinking and so on; not even the teaching of thousands of books will satisfy him. Not even all the sciences will satisfy him; at the best, they only bring this little world before him. What else will give him satisfaction? Not even myriads of systems of worlds will satisfy him; they are to him but a drop in the ocean of existence. His soul wants to go beyond all that into the very heart of being, by seeing reality as it is; by realizing it, by being it, by becoming one with that universal being. That is the philosopher. To say that God is the Father or the Mother, the creator of this universe, its protector and guide, is to him quite inadequate to express Him. To him, God is the life of his life, the soul of his soul. God is his own Self. Nothing else remains which is other than God. All the mortal parts of him become pounded by the weighty strokes of philosophy are brushed away. What at last truly remains is God Himself.

Upon the same tree there are two birds, one on the top, the other below. The one on the top is calm, silent and majestic, immersed in his own glory; the one on the lower branches, eating sweet and bitter fruits by turns, hopping from branch to branch, is becoming happy and miserable by turns. After a time the, lower bird eats an exceptionally bitter fruit and gets disgustful and looks up and sees the other bird, that wondrous one of golden plumage, who eats neither sweet nor bitter fruit, who is neither happy nor miserable, but calm, self-centred and sees nothing beyond his Self. The lower bird longs for this condition but soon forgets it and again begins to eat the fruits. In a little while, he eats another exceptionally bitter fruit, which makes him feel miserable, and he again looks up and tries to get nearer to the upper bird. Once more, he forgets and after a time he looks up, and so on he goes again and again, until he comes very near to the beautiful bird and sees the reflection of light from his plumage playing around his own body. He feels a change and seems to melt away; still nearer he comes, and everything about him melts away and at last he understands this wonderful change. The lower bird was, as it were, only the substantial-looking shadow, the reflection of the higher; he himself was in essence the upper bird all the time. This eating of fruits, sweet and bitter, this lower, little bird, weeping and happy by turns, was a vain chimera, a dream: all along, the real bird was there above, calm and silent, glorious and majestic, beyond grief, beyond sorrow. The upper bird is God, the Lord of this universe. The lower bird is the human soul, eating the sweet and bitter fruits of this world. Now and then comes a heavy blow to the soul. For a time, he stops the eating and goes towards the unknown God, and a flood of light comes. He thinks that this world is a vain show. Yet again the senses drag hint down and he begins as before to eat the sweet and bitter fruits of the world. Again an exceptionally hard blow comes. His heart becomes open again to the divine light; thus gradually he approaches God and as he gets nearer and nearer, he finds his old self melting away. When he has come near enough, he sees that he is no other than God and he exclaims, 'He whom I have described to you as the life of this universe, as present in the atom and in suns and moons—He is the basis of our own life, the soul of our soul. Nay, thou art That.' This is what this Jnana Yoga teaches. It tells man that he is essentially divine. It shows to mankind the real unity of being and that each one of us is the Lord God Himself, manifested on earth. All of us, from the lowest worm that crawls under our feet to the highest beings to whom we look up with wonder and awe—all are manifestations of the same Lord.

Lastly, it is imperative that all these various yogas should be carried out in practice; mere theories about them will not do any good. First we have to hear about them, then we have to think about them. We have to reason the thoughts out, impress them on our minds and we have to meditate on them, realize them, until at last they become our whole life. No longer will religion remain a bundle of ideas or theories, nor an intellectual assent; it will enter into our very self. By means of intellectual assent we may today subscribe to many foolish things and change our minds altogether tomorrow. But true religion never changes. Religion is realization; not talk, nor doctrine, nor theories, however beautiful they may be. It is being and becoming, not hearing or acknowledging; it is the whole soul becoming changed into what it believes. That is religion.

10

THE FREE SOUL

Delivered in 1896, New York

The analysis of the Sankhyas stops with the duality of existence—nature and souls. There are an infinite number of souls, which being simple cannot die and must therefore be separate from nature. Nature in itself changes and manifests all these phenomena; the soul according to the Sankhyas is inactive. It is a simple by itself and nature works out all these phenomena for the liberation of the soul; liberation consists in the soul discriminating that it is not nature. At the same time we have seen that the Sankhyas were bound to admit that every soul was omnipresent. Being a simple, the soul cannot be limited, because all limitation comes either through time, space, or causation. The soul being entirely beyond these cannot have any limitation. To have limitation one must be in space, which means the body, and that which is body must be in nature. If the soul had form, it would be identified with nature. Therefore, the soul is formless and that which is formless cannot be said to exist here, there, or anywhere. It must be omnipresent. Beyond this the Sankhya philosophy does not go.

The first argument of the Vedantists against this is that this analysis is not a perfect one. If their nature be absolute and the soul be also absolute, there will be two absolutes, and all the arguments that apply in the case of the soul to show that it is omnipresent will apply in the case of nature and nature too will be beyond all time, space and causation, and as the result there will be no change or manifestation. Then will come the difficulty of having two absolutes, which is impossible. What is the solution of the Vedantist? His solution is that just as the Sankhyas say it requires some sentient Being as the motive power behind, which makes the mind think and nature work because Nature in all its modifications, from gross matter up to *mahat* (intelligence), is simply insentient. Now, says the Vedantist, this sentient Being which is behind the whole universe is what we call *God*, and consequently this universe is not different from Him. It is He Himself who has become this universe. He not only is the instrumental cause of this universe, but also the material cause. Cause is never different from effect, the effect is but the cause reproduced in another form. We see that every day. So this Being is the cause of Nature. All the forms and phases of Vedanta, either dualistic, or qualified-monistic, or monistic, first take this position that God is not only the instrumental, but also the material cause of this universe, that everything which exists is He.

The second step in Vedanta is that these souls are also a part of God, one spark of that infinite fire. 'As from a mass of fire millions of small particles fly, even so from this ancient one have come all these souls.' So far so good, but it does not yet satisfy. What is meant by a part of the infinite? The infinite is indivisible; there cannot be parts of the infinite. The absolute cannot be divided. What is meant, therefore, by saying that all these sparks are from Him? The Advaitist, the non-dualistic Vedantist, solves the problem by maintaining that there is really no part, that each soul is really not a part of the infinite, but actually is the infinite Brahman. Then how can there be so many? The sun reflected from millions of globules of water appears to be millions of suns and in each globule is a miniature picture of the sun-form; so all these souls are but reflections and not real. They are not the real 'I' which is the God of this universe, the one undivided Being of the universe. And all these little different beings, men and animals etc., are but reflections and not real. They are simply illusory reflections upon nature. There is but one infinite Being in the universe, and that Being appears as you and as I, but this appearance of divisions is after all a delusion. He has not been divided, but only appears to be divided. This apparent division is caused by looking at Him through the network of time, space and causation. When I look at God through the network of time, space and causation, I see Him as the material world. When I look at Him from a little higher plane, yet through the same network, I see Him as an animal, a little higher as a man, a little higher as a god, but yet He is the one infinite Being of the universe and that Being we are. I am That and you are That. Not parts of it, but the whole of it.

'It is the eternal knower standing behind the whole phenomena; He Himself is the phenomena.' He is both the subject and the object, He is the 'I' and the 'You'. How is this? 'How to know the knower?' The knower cannot know Himself; I see everything but cannot see myself. The self, the knower, the Lord of all, the real Being, is the cause of all the vision that is in the universe, but it is impossible for Him to see Himself or know Himself, excepting through reflection. You cannot see your own face except in a mirror, and so the Self cannot see its own nature until it is reflected, and this whole universe therefore is the self trying to realize itself. This reflection is thrown back first from the protoplasm, then from plants and animals and so on and on from better and better reflectors, until the best reflector, the perfect man, is reached—just as a man who, wanting to see his face, looks first in a little pool of muddy water and sees just an outline; then he comes to clear water and sees a better image; then to a piece of shining metal and sees a still better image; and at last to a looking-glass and sees himself reflected as he is. Therefore the perfect man is the highest reflection of that Being who is both subject and object. You now find why man instinctively worships everything and how perfect men are instinctively worshipped as God in every country. You may talk as you like, but it is they who are bound to be worshipped. That is why men worship incarnations, such as Christ or Buddha. They are the most perfect manifestations of the eternal Self. They are much higher than all the conceptions of God that you or I can make. A perfect man is much higher than such conceptions. In him, the circle becomes complete; the subject and the object become one. In him, all delusions go away and in their place come the realization that he has always been that perfect Being. How came this bondage then? How was it possible for this perfect Being to degenerate into the imperfect? How was it possible that the free became bound?

The Advaitist says, he was never bound, but was always free. Various clouds of various colours come before the sky. They remain there a minute and then pass away. It is the same eternal blue sky stretching there forever. The sky never changes: it is the cloud that is changing. So you are always perfect, eternally perfect. Nothing ever changes your nature or ever will. All these ideas that I am imperfect, I am a man, or a woman, or a sinner, or I am the mind, I have thought, I will think—all are hallucinations; you never think, you never had a body; you never were imperfect. You are the blessed Lord of this universe, the one Almighty ruler of everything that is and ever will be, the one mighty ruler of these suns and stars and moons and earths and planets and all the little bits of our universe. It is through you that the sun shines and the stars shed their lustre and the earth becomes beautiful. It is through your blessedness that they all love and are attracted to each other. You are in all and you are all. Whom to avoid and whom to take? You are the all in all. When this knowledge comes, delusion immediately vanishes.

I was once travelling in the desert in India. I travelled for over a month and always found the most beautiful landscapes before me, beautiful lakes and all that. One day, I was very thirsty and I wanted to have a drink at one of these lakes, but when I approached that lake it vanished. Immediately with a blow came into my brain the idea that this was a mirage about which I had read all my life; then I remembered and smiled at my folly, that for the last month all the beautiful landscapes and lakes I had been seeing were this mirage, but I could not distinguish them then. The next morning, I again began my march; there was the lake and the landscape, but with it immediately came the idea, 'This is a mirage.' Once known it had lost its power of illusion. So this illusion of the universe will break one day. The whole of this will vanish, melt away. This is realization.

Philosophy is no joke or talk. It has to be realized; this body will vanish, this earth and everything will vanish, this idea that I am the body or the mind will for some time vanish, or if the karma is ended, it will disappear, never to come back. But if one part of the karma remains, then as a potter's wheel, after the potter has finished the pot, this will go on from the past momentum. So this body, when the delusion has vanished altogether, will go on for some time. Again this world will come, men and women and animals will come, just as the mirage came the next day, but not with the same force; along with it will come the idea that I know its nature now, and that it will cause no bondage, no more pain, nor grief, nor misery. Whenever anything miserable will come, the mind will be able to say, 'I know you as hallucination.' When a man has reached that state, he is called *jivanmukta*, living-free, free even while living.

The aim and end in this life for the Jnana Yogi is to become this jivanmukta, 'living-freee'. He is jivanmukta who can live in this world without being attached. He is like the lotus leaves in water, which are never wetted by the water. He is the highest of human beings, nay, the highest of all beings, for he has realized his identity with the absolute, he has realized that he is one with God. So long as you think you have the least difference from God, fear will seize you, but when you have known that you are He, that there is no difference, entirely no difference, that you are He, all of Him, and the whole of Him, all fear ceases. 'There, who sees whom? Who worships whom? Who talks to whom? Who hears whom? Where one sees another, where one talks to another, where one hears another, that is little. Where none sees none, where none speaks to none, that is the highest, that is the great, that is the Brahman.' Being That, you are always That. What will become of the world then? What good shall we do to the world? Such questions do not arise. 'What becomes of my gingerbread if I become old?' says the baby! 'What becomes of my marbles if I grow? So I will not grow,' says the boy! 'What will become of my dolls if I grow old?' says the little child! It is the same question in connection with this world, it has no existence in the past, present, or future.

If we have known the atman as it is, if we have known that there is nothing else, but this atman, that everything else is but a dream, with no existence in reality, then this world with its poverties, its miseries, its wickedness and its goodness will cease to disturb us. If they do not exist, for whom and for what shall we take trouble? This is what the Jnana Yogis teach. Therefore, dare to be free, dare to go as far as your thought lead and dare to carry that out in your life. It is very hard to come to jnana. It is for the bravest and most daring, who dare to smash all idols, not only intellectual, but in the senses. This body is not I; it must go. All sorts of curious things may come out of this. A man stands up and says, 'I am not the body, therefore my headache must be cured', but where is the headache if not in his body? Let a thousand headaches and a thousand bodies come and go. What is that to me? I have neither birth nor death; father or mother I never had; friends and foes I have none, because they are all I. I am my own friend and I am my own enemy. I am existence-knowledge-bliss absolute. I am He, I am He. If in a thousand bodies I am suffering from fever and other ills, in millions of bodies I am healthy. If in a thousand bodies I am starving, in other thousand bodies I am feasting. If in thousands of bodies I am suffering misery, in thousands of bodies I am happy. Who shall blame whom, who praise whom? Whom to seek, whom to avoid? I seek none, nor avoid any, for I am all the universe. I praise myself, I blame myself, I suffer for myself, I am happy at my own will, I am free. This is the jnani, the brave and daring. Let the whole universe tumble down; he smiles and says it never existed, it was all a hallucination. He sees the universe tumble down. Where was it! Where has it gone!

Before going into the practical part, we will take up one more intellectual question. So far the logic is tremendously rigorous. If man reasons, there is no place for him to stand until he comes to this, that there is but one existence, that everything else is nothing. There is no other way left for rational mankind but to take this view. But how is it that what is infinite, ever perfect, ever blessed, existence-knowledge-bliss absolute, has come under these delusions? It is the same question that has been asked all the world over. In the vulgar form, the question becomes, 'How did sin come into this world?' This is the most vulgar and sensuous form of the question and the other is the most philosophic form, but the answer is the same. The same question has been asked in various grades and fashions, but in its lower forms it finds no solution because the stories of apples and serpents and women do not give the explanation. In that state, the question is childish, and so is the answer. But the question has assumed very high proportions now: 'How did this illusion come?' And the answer is as fine. The answer is that we cannot expect any answer to an impossible question. The very question is impossible in terms. You have no right to ask that question. Why? What is perfection? That which is beyond time, space and causation—that is perfect. Then you ask how the perfect became imperfect. In logical language the question may be put in this form: 'How did that which is beyond causation become caused?' You contradict yourself. You first admit it is beyond causation and then ask what causes it. This question can only be asked within the limits of causation. As far as time and space and causation extend, so far can this question be asked. But beyond that it will be nonsense to ask it because the question is illogical. Within time, space and causation it can never be answered and what answer may lie beyond these limits can only be known when we have transcended them; therefore the wise will let this question rest. When a man is ill, he devotes himself to curing his disease without insisting that he must first learn how he came to have it.

There is another form of this question, a little lower, but more practical and illustrative: What produced this delusion? Can any reality produce delusion? Certainly not. We see that one delusion produces another and so on. It is delusion always that produces delusion. It is disease that produces disease and not health that produces disease. The wave is the same thing as the water, the effect is the cause in another form. The effect is delusion and therefore the cause must be delusion. What produced this delusion? Another delusion. And so on without beginning. The only question that remains for you to ask is: does not this break your monism because you get two existences in the universe, one yourself and the other the delusion? The answer is: delusion cannot be called an existence. Thousands of dreams come into your life, but do not form any part of your life. Dreams come and go; they have no existence. To call delusion existence will be sophistry. Therefore there is only one individual existence in the universe, ever free, and ever blessed; and that is what you are. This is the last conclusion reached by the Advaitists.

It may then be asked: what becomes of all these various forms of worship? They will remain; they are simply groping in the dark for light and through this groping light will come. We have just seen that the Self cannot see itself. Our knowledge is within the network of Maya (unreality) and beyond that is freedom. Within the network, there is slavery, it is all under law; beyond that there is no law. So far as the universe is concerned, existence is ruled by law, and beyond that is freedom. As long as you are in the network of time, space and causation, to say you are free is nonsense because in that network all is under rigorous law, sequence and consequence. Every thought that you think is caused, every feeling has been caused; to say that the will is free is sheer nonsense. It is only when the infinite existence comes, as it were, into this network of Maya that it takes the form of will. Will is a portion of that being, caught in the network of Maya, and therefore 'free will' is a misnomer. It means nothing—sheer nonsense. So is all this talk about freedom. There is no freedom in Maya.

Everyone is as much bound in thought, word, deed and

mind as a piece of stone or this table. That I talk to you now is as rigorous in causation as that you listen to me. There is no freedom until you go beyond Maya. That is the real freedom of the soul. Men, however sharp and intellectual, however clearly they see the force of the logic that nothing here can be free, are all compelled to think they are free; they cannot help it. No work can go on until we begin to say we are free. It means that the freedom we talk about is the glimpse of the blue sky through the clouds and that the real freedom—the blue sky itself—is behind. True freedom cannot exist in the midst of this delusion, this hallucination, this nonsense of the world, this universe of the senses, body and mind. All these dreams, without beginning or end, uncontrolled and uncontrollable, ill-adjusted, broken, inharmonious, form our idea of this universe. In a dream, when you see a giant with 20 heads chasing you, and you are flying from him, you do not think it is inharmonious; you think it is proper and right. So is this law. All that you call law is simply chance without meaning. In this dream state you call it law. Within Maya, so far as this law of time, space and causation exists, there is no freedom; and all these various forms of worship are within this Maya. The idea of God and the ideas of brute and of man are within this Maya and as such are equally hallucinations; all of them are dreams. But you must take care not to argue like some extraordinary men of whom we hear at the present time. They say the idea of God is a delusion, but the idea of this world is true. Both ideas stand or fall by the same logic. He alone has the right to be an atheist who denies this world, as well as the other. The same argument is for both. The same mass of delusion extends from God to the lowest animal, from a blade of grass to the creator. They stand or fall by the same logic. The same person who sees falsity in the idea of God ought also to see it in the idea of his own body or his own mind. When God vanishes, then also vanish the body and mind; and when both vanish, that which is the real existence remains forever. 'There the eyes cannot go, nor the speech, nor the mind. We cannot see it, neither know it.' And we now understand that so far as speech and thought and knowledge and intellect go, it is all within this Maya within bondage. Beyond that is reality. There neither thought, nor mind, nor speech can reach.

So far it is intellectually all right, but then comes the practice. The real work is in the practice. Are any practices necessary to realize this oneness? Most decidedly. It is not that you become this Brahman. You are already that. It is not that you are going to become God or perfect; you are already perfect; and whenever you think you are not, it is a delusion. This delusion which says that you are Mr So-and-so or Mrs So-and-so can be got rid of by another delusion, and that is practice. Fire will eat fire, and you can use one delusion to conquer another delusion. One cloud will come and brush away another cloud and then both will go away. What are these practices then? We must always bear in mind that we are not going to be free, but are free already. Every idea that we are bound by is a delusion. Every idea that we are happy or unhappy is a tremendous delusion; and another delusion will come—that we have got to work and worship and struggle to be free—and this will chase out the first delusion and then both will stop.

The fox is considered very unholy by the Mohammedans and by the Hindus. Also, if a dog touches any bit of food, it has to be thrown out, it cannot be eaten by any man. In a certain Mohammedan house, a fox entered and took a little bit of food from the table, ate it up and fled. The man was a poor man and had prepared a very nice feast for himself; that feast was made unholy and now he could not eat it. So he went to a Mulla, a priest, and said, 'This has happened to me; a fox came and took a mouthful out of my meal. What can be done? I had prepared a feast and wanted so much to eat it, and now comes this fox and destroys the whole affair.' The Mulla thought for a minute and then found only one solution and said, 'The only way for you is to get a dog and make him eat a bit out of the same plate because dogs and foxes are eternally quarrelling. The food that was left by the fox will go into your stomach and that left by the dog will go there too, and both will be purified.' We are very much in the same predicament. This is a hallucination that we are imperfect; and we take up another, that we have to practice to become perfect. Then one will chase the other as we can use one thorn to extract another and then throw both away. There are people for whom it is sufficient knowledge to hear, 'Thou art That.' With a flash, this universe goes away and the real nature shines, but others have to struggle hard to get rid of this idea of bondage.

The first question is: who are fit to become Jnana Yogis? Those who are equipped with these requisites: first, renunciation of all fruits of work and of all enjoyments in this life or another life. If you are the creator of this universe, whatever you desire you will have because you will create it for yourself. It is only a question of time. Some get it immediately; with others the past *samskaras* (impressions) stand in the way of getting their desires. We give the first place to desires for enjoyment, either in this or another life. Deny that there is any life at all because life is only another name for death. Deny that you are a living being. Who cares for life? Life is one of these hallucinations and death is its counterpart. Joy is one part of these hallucinations and misery the other part and so on. What have you to do with life or death? These are all creations of the mind. This is called giving up desires of enjoyment either in this life or another.

Then comes controlling the mind, calming it so that it will not break into waves and have all sorts of desires, holding the mind steady, not allowing it to get into waves from external or internal causes, controlling the mind perfectly, just by the power of will. The Jnana Yogi does not take any one of these physical helps or mental helps: simply philosophic reasoning, knowledge and his own will, these are the instrumentalities he believes in. Next comes Titiksha, forbearance, bearing all miseries without murmuring, without complaining. When an injury comes, do not mind it. If a tiger comes, stand there. Who flies? There are men who practice Titiksha and succeed in it. There are men who sleep on the banks of the Ganga in the midsummer sun of India and in winter float in the waters of the Ganga for a whole day, they do not care. Men sit in the snow of the Himalayas and do not care to wear any garment. What is heat? What is cold? Let things come and go, what is that to me, I am not the body. It is hard to believe this in these Western countries, but it is better to know that it is done. Just as your people are brave to jump at the mouth of a cannon, or into the midst of the battlefield, so our people are brave to think and act out their philosophy. They give up their lives for it. 'I am existence-knowledge-bliss absolute; I am He, I am He.' Just as the Western ideal is to keep up luxury in practical life, so ours is to keep up the highest form of spirituality, to demonstrate that religion is not merely frothy words, but can be carried out, every bit of it, in this life. This is Titiksha, to bear everything, not to complain of anything. I myself have seen men who say, 'I am the soul; what is the universe to me? Neither pleasure nor pain, nor virtue, nor vice, nor heat, nor cold is anything to me.' That is Titiksha, not running after the enjoyments of the body. What is religion? To pray, 'Give me this and that'?

Foolish ideas of religion! Those who believe them have no true idea of God and soul.

My master used to say, 'The vulture rise higher and higher until he becomes a speck, but his eye is always on the piece of rotten carrion on the Earth.' After all, what is the result of your ideas of religion? To cleanse the streets and have more bread and clothes? Who cares for bread and clothes? Millions come and go every minute. Who cares? Why care for the joys and vicissitudes of this little world? Go beyond that if you dare; go beyond law, let the whole universe vanish and stand alone. 'I am existence-absolute, knowledge-absolute, bliss-absolute; I am He, I am He.'

11

THE RAMAYANA

Delivered on 31 January 1900, at Shakespeare Club, Pasadena, California

There are two great epics in the Sanskrit language, which are very ancient. Of course, there are hundreds of other epic poems. The Sanskrit language and literature have been continued down to the present day, although, for more than 2,000 years, it has ceased to be a spoken language. I am now going to speak to you of the two most ancient epics, called the Ramayana and the Mahabharata. They embody the manners and customs, the state of society, civilization, etc., of the ancient Indians. The oldest of these epics is called Ramayana, 'The Life of Rama'. There was some poetical literature before this—most of the vedas, the sacred books of the Hindus, are written in a sort of metre—but this book is held by common consent in India as the very beginning of poetry.

The name of the poet or sage was Valmiki. Later on, a great many poetical stories were fastened upon that ancient poet; subsequently, it became a very general practice to attribute to his authorship very many verses that were not his. Notwithstanding all these interpolations, it comes down to us as a very beautiful arrangement, without equal in the literatures of the world.

There was a young man that could not in any way support his family. He was strong and vigorous and, finally, became a highway robber; he attacked persons in the street and robbed them, and with that money he supported his father, mother, wife and children. This went on continually, until one day a great saint called Narada was passing by, and the robber attacked him.

The sage asked the robber, 'Why are you going to rob me? It is a great sin to rob human beings and kill them. What do you incur all this sin for?'

The robber said, 'Why, I want to support my family with this money.'

'Now,' said the sage, 'do you think that they take a share of your sin also?'

'Certainly, they do,' replied the robber.

'Very good,' said the sage, 'make me safe by tying me up here, while you go home and ask your people whether they will share your sin in the same way as they share the money you make.'

The man accordingly went to his father and asked, 'Father, do you know how I support you?'

He answered, 'No, I do not.'

'I am a robber, and I kill persons and rob them.'

'What! You do that, my son? Get away! You outcast!'

He then went to his mother and asked her, 'Mother, do you know how I support you?'

'No,' she replied.

'Through robbery and murder.'

'How horrible it is!' cried the mother.

'But, do you partake in my sin?' asked the son.

'Why should I? I never committed a robbery,' answered the mother.

Then, he went to his wife and questioned her, 'Do you know how I maintain you all?'

'No,' she responded.

'Why, I am a highwayman,' he rejoined, 'and for years have

been robbing people; that is how I support and maintain you all. And what I now want to know is, whether you are ready to share in my sin.'

'By no means. You are my husband and it is your duty to support me.'

The eyes of the robber were opened. 'That is the way of the world—even my nearest relatives, for whom I have been robbing, will not share in my destiny.' He came back to the place where he had bound the sage, unfastened his bonds, fell at his feet, recounted everything and said, 'Save me! What can I do?'

The sage said, 'Give up your present course of life. You see that none of your family really loves you, so give up all these delusions. They will share your prosperity, but the moment you have nothing, they will desert you. There is none who will share in your evil, but they will all share in your good. Therefore worship Him who alone stands by us whether we are doing good or evil. He never leaves us, for love never drags down, knows no barter, no selfishness.'

Then the sage taught him how to worship. And this man left everything and went into a forest. There he went on praying and meditating until he forgot himself so entirely that the ants came and built ant-hills around him and he was quite unconscious of it. After many years had passed, a voice came saying, 'Arise, O sage!'

Thus aroused, he exclaimed, 'Sage? I am a robber!'

'No more a "robber",' answered the voice, 'a purified sage art thou. Thine old name is gone. But now, since thy meditation was so deep and great that thou didst not remark even the ant-hills which surrounded thee, henceforth, thy name shall be Valmiki, "he that was born in the ant-hill".' So, he became a sage.

And this is how he became a poet. One day as this sage, Valmiki, was going to bathe in the holy river Ganga, he saw a pair of doves wheeling round and round, and kissing each other. The sage looked up and was pleased at the sight, but in a second an arrow whisked past him and killed the male dove. As the dove fell down on the ground, the female dove went on whirling round and round the dead body of its companion in grief. In a moment the poet became miserable and looking round, he saw the hunter. 'Thou art a wretch,' he cried, 'without the smallest mercy! Thy slaying hand would not even stop for love!' 'What is this? What am I saying?' the poet thought to himself, 'I have never spoken in this sort of way before.' And then a voice came: 'Be not afraid. This is poetry that is coming out of your mouth. Write the life of Rama in poetic language for the benefit of the world.' And that is how the poem first began. The first verse sprang out of pits from the mouth of Valmiki, the first poet. And it was after that, that he wrote the beautiful Ramayana, 'The Life of Rama'.

There was an ancient Indian town called Ayodhya—and it exists even in modern times. The province in which it is still located is called Oudh[1], and most of you may have noticed it in the map of India. That was the ancient Ayodhya. There, in ancient times, reigned a king called Dasharatha. He had three queens, but the king had not any children by them. And like good Hindus, the king and the queens, all went on pilgrimages fasting and praying that they might have children, and in good time, four sons were born. The eldest of them was Rama.

Now, as it should be, these four brothers were thoroughly educated in all branches of learning. To avoid future quarrels there was in ancient India a custom for the king in his own lifetime to nominate his eldest son as his successor, the Yuvaraja, young king, as he is called.

---

[1]Oudh refers to Awadh as known in British historical texts.

Now, there was another king, called Janaka, and this king had a beautiful daughter named Sita. Sita was found in a field; she was a daughter of the earth, and was born without parents. The word 'Sita' in ancient Sanskrit means the furrow made by a plough. In the ancient mythology of India you will find persons born of one parent only, or persons born without parents, born of sacrificial fire, born in the field, and so on—dropped from the clouds as it were. All those sorts of miraculous birth were common in the mythological lore of India.

Sita, being the daughter of the earth, was pure and immaculate. She was brought up by King Janaka. When she was of a marriageable age, the king wanted to find a suitable husband for her.

There was an ancient Indian custom called Svayamvara, by which the princesses used to choose husbands. A number of princes from different parts of the country were invited, and the princess in splendid array, with a garland in her hand, and accompanied by a crier who enumerated the distinctive claims of each of the royal suitors, would pass in the midst of those assembled before her, and select the prince she liked for her husband by throwing the garland of flowers round his neck. They would then be married with much pomp and grandeur.

There were numbers of princes who aspired for the hand of Sita; the test demanded on this occasion was the breaking of a huge bow, called Haradhanu. All the princes put forth all their strength to accomplish this feat, but failed. Finally, Rama took the mighty bow in his hands and with easy grace broke it in twain. Thus, Sita selected Rama, the son of King Dasharatha for her husband, and they were wedded with great rejoicings. Then, Rama took his bride to his home, and his old father thought that the time was now come for him to retire and appoint Rama as Yuvaraja.

Everything was accordingly made ready for the ceremony and the whole country was jubilant over the affair, till the younger queen Kaikeyi was reminded by one of her maidservants of two promises made to her by the king long ago. At one time, she had pleased the king very much, and he offered to grant her two boons: 'Ask any two things in my power and I will grant them to you,' said he, but she made no request then. She had forgotten all about it, but the evil-minded maidservant in her employ began to work upon her jealousy with regard to Rama being installed on the throne, and insinuated to her how nice it would be for her if her own son had succeeded the king, until the queen was almost mad with jealousy. Then the servant suggested to her to ask from the king the two promised boons: one would be that her own son Bharata should be placed on the throne, and the other that Rama should be sent to the forest and be exiled for 14 years.

Now, Rama was the life and soul of the old king and when this wicked request was made to him, he as a king felt he could not go back on his word. So he did not know what to do. But Rama came to the rescue and willingly offered to give up the throne and go into exile, so that his father might not be guilty of falsehood. So Rama went into exile for 14 years, accompanied by his loving wife Sita and his devoted brother Lakshmana, who would on no account be parted from him.

The Aryans did not know who were the inhabitants of these wild forests. In those days, the forest tribes they called 'monkeys', and some of the so-called 'monkeys', if unusually strong and powerful, were called 'demons'.

So, into the forest, inhabited by demons and monkeys, Rama, Lakshmana and Sita went. When Sita had offered to accompany Rama, he exclaimed, 'How can you, a princess, face hardships and accompany me into a forest full of unknown dangers!' But Sita replied, 'Wherever Rama goes, there goes Sita. How can you talk of "princess" and "royal birth" to me? I go with you!' So, Sita went. And the younger brother, he also went with them. They penetrated far into the forest, until they reached the river Godavari. On the banks of the river they built little cottages, near which Rama and Lakshmana used to hunt deer and collect fruits.

After they had lived thus for some time, one day there came a demon giantess. She was the sister of the giant king of Lanka (Ceylon). Roaming through the forest at will, she came across Rama, and seeing that he was a very handsome man, she fell in love with him at once. But Rama was the purest of men and also was a married man; so, of course, he could not return her love. In revenge, she went to her brother, the giant king, and told him all about the beautiful Sita, the wife of Rama.

Rama was the most powerful of mortals; there were no giants or demons or anybody else strong enough to conquer him. So, the giant king had to resort to subterfuge. He got hold of another giant who was a magician and changed him into a beautiful golden deer; the deer went prancing round about the place where Rama lived, until Sita was fascinated by its beauty and asked Rama to go and capture the deer for her. Rama went into the forest to catch the deer, leaving his brother in charge of Sita. Then Lakshmana laid a circle of fire round the cottage, and he said to Sita, 'Today I see something may befall you; and, therefore, I tell you not to go outside of this magic circle. Some danger may befall you if you do.' In the meanwhile, Rama had pierced the magic deer with his arrow, and immediately the deer, changed into the form of a man and died.

Immediately, at the cottage was heard the voice of Rama, crying, 'Oh, Lakshmana, come to my help!' and Sita said, 'Lakshmana, go at once into the forest to help Rama!'

'That is not Rama's voice,' protested Lakshmana. But at the entreaties of Sita, Lakshmana had to go in search of Rama.

As soon as he went away, the giant king, who had taken the form of a mendicant monk, stood at the gate and asked for alms. 'Wait awhile,' said Sita, 'until my husband comes back and I will give you plentiful alms.'

'I cannot wait, good lady,' said he, 'I am very hungry, give me anything you have.' At this, Sita, who had a few fruits in the cottage, brought them out. But the mendicant monk after many persuasions prevailed upon her to bring the alms to him, assuring her that she need have no fear as he was a holy person. So Sita came out of the magic circle and immediately the seeming monk assumed his giant body, and grasping Sita in his arms he called his magic chariot, and putting her therein, he fled with the weeping Sita. Poor Sita! She was utterly helpless, nobody was there to come to her aid. As the giant was carrying her away, she took off a few of the ornaments from her arms and, at intervals, dropped them to the grounds.

She was taken by Ravana to his kingdom, Lanka, the island of Ceylon. He asked her to become his queen and tempted her in many ways to accede to his request. But Sita, who was chastity Itself, would not even speak to the giant; he, to punish her, made her live under a tree, day and night, until she should consent to be his wife.

When Rama and Lakshmana returned to the cottage and found that Sita was not there, their grief knew no bounds. They could not imagine what had become of her. The two brothers went on, seeking everywhere for Sita, but could find no trace of her. After searching for long, they came across a group of 'monkeys', and in the midst of them was Hanuman, the 'divine monkey'. Hanuman, the best of the monkeys, became the most faithful servant of Rama and helped him in rescuing Sita, as we shall see later on. His devotion towards Rama was so great that he is still worshipped by the Hindus as the ideal of a true servant of the Lord. You see, by the 'monkeys' and 'demons' are meant the aborigines of South India.

So, Rama, at last, fell in with these monkeys. They told him that they had seen flying through the sky a chariot, in which was seated a demon who was carrying away the most beautiful lady, and that she was weeping bitterly, and as the chariot passed over their heads she dropped one of her ornaments to attract their attention. Then they showed Rama the ornament. Lakshmana took up the ornament and said, 'I do not know whose ornament this is.' Rama took it from him and recognized it at once saying, 'Yes, it is Sita's.' Lakshmana could not recognize the ornament because in India the wife of the elder brother was held in such reverence that he had never looked upon the arms and the neck of Sita. So you see, as it was a necklace, he did not know whose it was. There is in this episode a touch of the old Indian custom. Then, the monkeys told Rama who this demon king was and where he lived, and then they all went to seek him.

Now, the monkey-king Vali and his younger brother Sugriva were then fighting amongst themselves for the kingdom. The younger brother was helped by Rama, and he regained the kingdom from Vali, who had driven him away; he, in return, promised to help Rama. They searched the country all round, but could not find Sita. At last Hanuman leaped by one bound from the coast of India to the island of Ceylon, and there went looking all over Lanka for Sita, but nowhere could he find her.

You see, this giant king had conquered the gods, the men, in fact the whole world; and he had collected all the beautiful women and made them his concubines. So, Hanuman thought to himself, 'Sita cannot be with them in the palace. She would rather die than be in such a place.' So Hanuman went to find her elsewhere. At last, he found Sita under a tree, pale and thin, like the new moon that lies low in the horizon. Now Hanuman took the form of a little monkey and settled on the tree, and there he witnessed how the giantesses sent by Ravana came and tried to frighten Sita into submission, but she would not even listen to the name of the giant king.

Then, Hanuman came nearer to Sita and told her how he became the messenger of Rama, who had sent him to find out where Sita was; and Hanuman showed to Sita the signet ring which Rama had given as a token for establishing his identity. He also informed her that as soon as Rama would know her whereabouts, he would come with an army and conquer the giant and free her. However, he suggested to Sita that if she wished it, he would take her on his shoulders and could with one leap clear the ocean and get back to Rama. But Sita could not bear the idea, as she was chastity itself, and could not touch the body of any man except her husband. So, Sita remained where she was. But she gave him a jewel from her hair to carry to Rama, and with that Hanuman returned.

Learning everything about Sita from Hanuman, Rama collected an army, and with it marched towards the southernmost point of India. There Rama's monkeys built a huge bridge, called Setu Bandha, connecting India with Ceylon. In very low water, even now, it is possible to cross from India to Ceylon over the sand banks there.

Now Rama was God incarnate, otherwise, how could he have done all these things? He was an incarnation of God, according to the Hindus. They in India believe him to be the seventh incarnation of God.

The monkeys removed whole hills, placed them in the sea and covered them with stones and trees, thus making a huge embankment. A little squirrel, so it is said, was there rolling himself in the sand and running back and forth on to the bridge. Thus, in his small way he was working for the bridge of Rama by putting in sand. The monkeys laughed, for they were bringing whole mountains, whole forests, huge loads of sand for the bridge—so they laughed at the little squirrel rolling in the sand and then shaking himself. But Rama saw it and remarked: 'Blessed be the little squirrel; he is doing his work to the best of his ability, and he is therefore quite as great as the greatest of you.' Then he gently stroked the squirrel on the back, and the marks of Rama's fingers, running lengthways, are seen on the squirrel's back even to this day.

Now, when the construction of the bridge was finished, the whole army of monkeys, led by Rama and his brother entered Ceylon. For several months afterwards tremendous war and bloodshed followed. At last, this demon king, Ravana, was conquered and killed; and his capital, with all the palaces and everything, which were entirely of solid gold, was taken. In faraway villages in the interior of India, when I tell them that I have been in Ceylon, the simple folk say, 'There, as our books tell, the houses are built of gold.' So, all these golden cities fell into the hands of Rama, who gave them over to Vibhishana, the younger brother of Ravana, and seated him on the throne in the place of his brother, as a return for the valuable services rendered by him to Rama during the war.

Then Rama with Sita and his followers left Lanka. But there ran a murmur among the followers. 'The test! The test!' they cried, 'Sita has not given the test that she was perfectly pure in Ravana's household.'

'Pure! She is chastity itself,' exclaimed Rama.

'Never mind! We want the test,' persisted the people. Subsequently, a huge sacrificial fire was made ready, into which

Sita had to plunge herself. Rama was in agony, thinking that Sita was lost, but in a moment, the God of fire himself appeared with a throne upon his head, and upon the throne was Sita. Then, there was universal rejoicing, and everybody was satisfied.

Early during the period of exile, Bharata, the younger brother had come and informed Rama, of the death of the old king and vehemently insisted on his occupying the throne. During Rama's exile Bharata would on no account ascend the throne and out of respect placed a pair of Rama's wooden shoes on it as a substitute for his brother. Then Rama returned to his capital, and by the common consent of his people he became the king of Ayodhya.

After Rama regained his kingdom, he took the necessary vows which in olden times the king had to take for the benefit of his people. The king was the slave of his people and had to bow to public opinion, as we shall see later on. Rama passed a few years in happiness with Sita, when the people again began to murmur that Sita had been stolen by a demon and carried across the ocean. They were not satisfied with the former test and clamoured for another test, otherwise she must be banished.

In order to satisfy the demands of the people, Sita was banished, and left to live in the forest, where was the hermitage of the sage and poet Valmiki. The sage found poor Sita weeping and forlorn, and hearing her sad story sheltered her in his ashrama. Sita was expecting soon to become a mother and she gave birth to twin boys. The poet never told the children who they were. He brought them up together in the Brahmacharin life. He then composed the poem known as Ramayana, set it to music and dramatized it.

Drama, in India, was a very holy thing. Drama and music are themselves held to be religion. Any song—whether it be a love song or otherwise—if one's whole soul is in that song, one attains salvation, one has nothing else to do. They say it leads to the same goal as meditation.

So, Valmiki dramatized 'The Life of Rama', and taught Rama's two children how to recite and sing it.

There came a time when Rama was going to perform a huge sacrifice, or *yajna*, such as the old kings used to celebrate. But no ceremony in India can be performed by a married man without his wife: he must have the wife with him, the sahadharmini, the 'co-religionist'—that is the expression for a wife. The Hindu householder has to perform hundreds of ceremonies, but not one can be duly performed according to the shastras, if he has not a wife to complement it with her part in it.

Now Rama's wife was not with him then as she had been banished. So, the people asked him to marry again. But at this request, Rama for the first time in his life stood against the people. He said, 'This cannot be. My life is Sita's.' So, as a substitute, a golden statue of Sita was made, in order that the ceremony could be accomplished. They arranged even a dramatic entertainment to enhance the religious feeling in this great festival. Valmiki, the great sage-poet, came with his pupils, Lava and Kusha, the unknown sons of Rama. A stage had been erected and everything was ready for the performance. Rama and his brothers attended with all his nobles and his people—a vast audience. Under the direction of Valmiki, the life of Rama was sung by Lava and Kusha, and fascinated the whole assembly by their charming voice and appearance. Poor Rama was nearly maddened, and when in the drama the scene of Sita's exile came about, he did not know what to do. Then the sage said to him, 'Do not be grieved, for I will show you Sita.' Then Sita was brought upon the stage and Rama was delighted to see his wife.

All of a sudden, the old murmur arose: 'The test! The test!' Poor Sita was so terribly overcome by the repeated cruel slight on her reputation that it was more than she could bear. She appealed to the gods to testify to her innocence. When the earth opened, Sita exclaimed, 'Here is the test,' and vanished into the bosom of the Earth. The people were taken aback at this tragic end. And Rama was overwhelmed with grief.

A few days after Sita's disappearance, a messenger came to Rama from the gods, who intimated to him that his mission on earth was finished and he was to return to heaven. These tidings brought to him the recognition of his own real Self. He plunged into the waters of Sarayu, the mighty river that laved his capital, and joined Sita in the other world.

This is the great, ancient epic of India. Rama and Sita are the ideals of the Indian nation. All children, especially girls, worship Sita. The height of a woman's ambition is to be like Sita, the pure, the devoted, the all-suffering! When you study these characters, you can at once find out how different is the ideal in India from that of the West. For the race, Sita stands as the ideal of suffering. The West says, 'Do! Show your power by doing.' India says, 'Show your power by suffering.' The West has solved the problem of how much a man can have: India has solved the problem of how little a man can have. The two extremes, you see. Sita is typical of India—the idealized India. The question is not whether she ever lived, whether the story is history or not, we know that the ideal is there. There is no other Pauranika story that has so permeated the whole nation, so entered into its very life, and has so tingled in every drop of blood of the race, as this ideal of Sita. Sita is the name in India for everything that is good, pure and holy—everything that in woman we call womanly. If a priest has to bless a woman he says, 'Be Sita!' If he blesses a child, he says, 'Be Sita!' They are all children of Sita, and are struggling to be Sita, the patient, the all-suffering, the ever-faithful, the ever-pure wife. Through all this suffering she experiences, there is not one harsh word against Rama. She takes it as her own duty and performs her own part in it. Think of the terrible injustice of her being exiled to the forest! But Sita knows no bitterness. That is, again, the Indian ideal. Says the ancient Buddha, 'When a man hurts you and you turn back to hurt him, that would not cure the first injury, it would only create in the world one more wickedness.' Sita was a true Indian by nature; she never returned injury.

Who knows which is the truer ideal? The apparent power and strength, as held in the West, or the fortitude in suffering, of the East?

The West says, 'We minimize evil by conquering it.' India says, 'We destroy evil by suffering, until evil is nothing to us, it becomes positive enjoyment.' Well, both are great ideals. Who knows which will survive in the long run? Who knows which attitude will really most benefit humanity? Who knows which will disarm and conquer animosity? Will it be suffering, or doing?

In the meantime, let us not try to destroy each other's ideals. We are both intent upon the same work, which is the annihilation of evil. You take up your method, let us take up our method. Let us not destroy the ideal. I do not say to the West, 'Take up our method.' Certainly not. The goal is the same, but the methods can never be the same. And so, after hearing about the ideals of India, I hope that you will say in the same breath to India, 'We know, the goal, the ideal is all right for us both. You follow your own ideal. You follow your method in your own way, and Godspeed to you!' My message in life is to ask the East and West not to quarrel over different ideals, but to show them that the goal is the same in both cases, however opposite it may appear. As we mend our way through this mazy vale of life, let us bid each other Godspeed.

12

THE MAHABHARATA

Delivered on 1 February 1900, at Shakespeare Club, Pasadena, California

The other epic about which I am going to speak to you this evening is called the Mahabharata. It contains the story of a race descended from King Bharata, who was the son of Dushyanta and Shakuntala. Maha means great, and Bharata means the descendants of Bharata, from whom India has derived its name, Bharata. Mahabharata means Great India, or the story of the great descendants of Bharata. The scene of this epic is the ancient kingdom of the Kurus and the story is based on the great war which took place between the Kurus and the Panchalas. So the region of the quarrel is not very big. This epic is the most popular one in India, and it exercises the same authority in India as Homer's poems did over the Greeks. As ages went on, more and more matter was added to it, until it has become a huge book of about a hundred thousand couplets. All sorts of tales, legends and myths, philosophical treatises, scraps of history and various discussions have been added to it from time to time, until it is a vast, gigantic mass of literature; through it all runs the old, original story. The central story of the Mahabharata is of a war between two families of cousins, one family called the Kauravas, the other the Pandavas—for the empire of India.

The Aryans came into India in small companies. Gradually,

these tribes began to extend, until at last they became the undisputed rulers of India and then arose this fight to gain the mastery, between two branches of the same family. Those of you who have studied the Gita know how the book opens with a description of the battlefield, with two armies arrayed against one other. That is the war of the Mahabharata.

There were two brothers, sons of the emperor. The elder one was called Dhritarashtra and the other was called Pandu. Dhritarashtra, the elder one, was born blind. According to Indian law, no blind, halt, maimed, consumptive, or any other constitutionally diseased person, can inherit. He can only get maintenance. So, Dhritarashtra could not ascend the throne, though he was the elder son, and Pandu became the emperor.

Dhritarashtra had a 100 sons and Pandu had only five. After the death of Pandu at an early age, Dhritarashtra became king of the Kurus and brought up the sons of Pandu along with his own children. When they grew up they were placed under the tutorship of the great priest-warrior, Drona, and were well-trained in the various material arts and sciences befitting princes. The education of the princes being finished, Dhritarashtra put Yudhishthira, the eldest of the sons of Pandu, on the throne of his father.

The sterling virtues of Yudhishthira and the valour and devotion of his other brothers aroused jealousies in the hearts of the sons of the blind king and at the instigation of Duryodhana, the eldest of them, the five Pandava brothers were prevailed upon to visit Varanavata, on the plea of a religious festival that was being held there. There they were accommodated in a palace made, under Duryodhana's instructions, of hemp, resin, lac and other inflammable materials, which were subsequently set fire to secretly. But the good Vidura, the step-brother of Dhritarashtra, having become cognizant of the evil intentions of

Duryodhana and his party, had warned the Pandavas of the plot and they managed to escape without anyone's knowledge. When the Kurus saw the house was reduced to ashes, they heaved a sigh of relief and thought all obstacles were now removed out of their path. Then the children of Dhritarashtra got hold of the kingdom. The five Pandava brothers had fled to the forest with their mother, Kunti. They lived there by begging and went about in disguise giving themselves out as Brahmana students. Many were the hardships and adventures they encountered in the wild forests, but their fortitude of mind, strength and valour made them conquer all dangers. Things went on until they came to hear of the approaching marriage of the princess of a neighbouring country.

I told you last night of the peculiar form of the ancient Indian marriage. It was called svayamvara, the choosing of the husband by the princess. A great gathering of princes and nobles assembled, amongst whom the princess would choose her husband. Preceded by her trumpeters and heralds she would approach, carrying a garland of flowers in her hand. At the throne of each candidate for her hand, the praises of that prince and all his great deeds in battle would be declared by the heralds. And when the princess decided which prince she desired to have for a husband, she would signify the fact by throwing the marriage-garland round his neck. Then the ceremony would turn into a wedding. King Drupada was a great king, king of the Panchalas, and his daughter, Draupadi, famed far and wide for her beauty and accomplishments, was going to choose a hero.

At a svayamvara, there was always a great feat of arms or something of the kind. On this occasion, a mark in the form of a fish was set up high in the sky; under that fish was a wheel with a hole in the centre, continually turning round, and beneath was a tub of water. A man looking at the reflection of the fish in the tub of water was asked to send an arrow and hit the eye of the fish through the chakra or wheel, and he who succeeded would be married to the princess. Now, there came kings and princes from different parts of India, all anxious to win the hand of the princess, and one after another they tried their skill, and every one of them failed to hit the mark.

You know, there are four castes in India: the highest caste is that of the hereditary priest, the Brahmana; next is the caste of the Kshatriya, composed of kings and fighters; next, the Vaishyas, the traders or businessmen, and then Shudras, the servants. Now, this princess was, of course, a Kshatriya, one of the second caste.

When all those princes failed in hitting the mark, then the son of King Drupada rose up in the midst of the court and said: 'The Kshatriya, the king caste has failed; now the contest is open to the other castes. Let a Brahmana, even a Shudra, take part in it; whosoever hits the mark, marries Draupadi.'

Among the Brahmanas were seated the five Pandava brothers. Arjuna, the third brother, was the hero of the bow. He arose and stepped forward. Now, Brahmanas as a caste are very quiet and rather timid people. According to the law, they must not touch a warlike weapon, they must not wield a sword, they must not go into any enterprise that is dangerous. Their life is one of contemplation, study and control of the inner nature. Judge, therefore, how quiet and peaceable a people they are. When the Brahmanas saw this man get up, they thought this man was going to bring the wrath of the Kshatriyas upon them and that they would all be killed. So they tried to dissuade him, but Arjuna did not listen to them because he was a soldier. He lifted the bow in his hand, strung it without any effort, and drawing it, sent the arrow right through the wheel and hit the eye of the fish.

Then there was great jubilation. Draupadi, the princess, approached Arjuna and threw the beautiful garland of flowers over his head. But there arose a great cry among the princes, who could not bear the idea that this beautiful princess who was a Kshatriya should be won by a poor Brahmana, from among this huge assembly of kings and princes. So, they wanted to fight Arjuna and snatch her from him by force. The brothers had a tremendous fight with the warriors, but held their own, and carried off the bride in triumph.

The five brothers now returned home to Kunti with the princess. Brahmanas have to live by begging. So they, who lived as Brahmanas, used to go out, and what they got by begging they brought home and the mother divided it among them. Thus the five brothers, with the princess, came to the cottage where the mother lived. They shouted out to her jocosely, 'Mother, we have brought home the most wonderful alms today.' The mother replied, 'Enjoy it in common, all of you, my children.' Then the mother seeing the princess, exclaimed, 'Oh! What have I said! It is a girl!' But what could be done! The mother's word was spoken once for all. It must not be disregarded. The mother's words must be fulfilled. She could not be made to utter an untruth, as she never had done so. So Draupadi became the common wife of all the five brothers.

Now, you know, in every society there are stages of development. Behind this epic there is a wonderful glimpse of the ancient historic times. The author of the poem mentions the fact of the five brothers marrying the same woman, but he tries to gloss it over to find an excuse and a cause for such an act: it was the mother's command, the mother sanctioned this strange betrothal and so on. You know, in every nation there has been a certain stage in society that allowed polyandry—all the brothers of a family would marry one wife in common. Now, this was evidently a glimpse of the past polyandrous stage.

In the meantime, the brother of the princess was perplexed in his mind and thought: 'Who are these people? Who is this man whom my sister is going to marry? They have not any chariots, horses, or anything. Why, they go on foot!' So he had followed them at a distance and at night overheard their conversation, and became fully convinced that they were really Kshatriyas. Then King Drupada came to know who they were and was greatly delighted.

Though at first much objection was raised, it was declared by Vyasa that such a marriage was allowable for these princes and it was permitted. So the King Drupada had to yield to this polyandrous marriage and the princess was married to the five sons of Pandu.

Then the Pandavas lived in peace and prosperity and became more powerful with every passing day. Though Duryodhana and his party conceived of fresh plots to destroy them, King Dhritarashtra was prevailed upon by the wise counsels of the elders to make peace with the Pandavas; and so he invited them home amidst the rejoicings of the people and gave them half of the kingdom. Then, the five brothers built for themselves a beautiful city, called Indraprastha, and extended their dominions, laying all the people under tribute to them. Then the eldest, Yudhishthira, in order to declare himself emperor over all the kings of ancient India, decided to perform a Rajasuya Yajna or imperial sacrifice in which the conquered kings would have to come with tribute and swear allegiance and help the performance of the sacrifice by personal services. Shri Krishna, who had become their friend and a relative, came to them and approved of the idea. But there was alas one obstacle to its performance. A king, Jarasandha by name, who intended to offer a sacrifice of a hundred kings, had kept 86 of them with him as captives. Shri Krishna counselled an attack on Jarasandha. So he, Bhima and Arjuna challenged the king, who accepted the challenge and was finally conquered by Bhima after 14 days of continuous wrestling. The captive kings were then set free.

Then the four younger brothers went out with armies on a conquering expedition, each in a different direction and brought all the kings under subjection to Yudhishthira. Returning, they laid all the vast wealth they secured at the feet of the eldest brother to meet the expenses of the great sacrifice.

So, to this Rajasuya sacrifice all the liberated kings came, along with those conquered by the brothers and rendered homage to Yudhishthira. King Dhritarashtra and his sons were also invited to come and take a share in the performance of the sacrifice. At the conclusion of the sacrifice, Yudhishthira was crowned emperor and declared as lord paramount. This was the sowing of the future feud. Duryodhana came back from the sacrifice filled with jealousy against Yudhishthira as their sovereignty and vast splendour and wealth were more than he could bear; and so he devised plans to effect their fall by guile as he knew that to overcome them by force was beyond his power. This king, Yudhishthira, had the love of gambling and he was challenged at an evil hour to play dice with Shakuni, the crafty gambler and the evil genius of Duryodhana.

In ancient India, if a man of the military caste was challenged to fight, he must at any price accept the challenge to uphold his honour. And if he was challenged to play dice, it was a point of honour to play, and dishonourable to decline the challenge. King Yudhishthira, says the Epic, was the incarnation of all virtues. Even he, the great sage-king, had to accept the challenge. Shakuni and his party had made false dice. So

Yudhishthira lost game after game, and stung with his losses, he went on with the fatal game, staking everything he had and losing all, until all his possessions, his kingdom and everything were lost. The last stage came when, under further challenge, he had no other resources left, but to stake his brothers and then himself, and last of all, the fair Draupadi, and lost all. Now they were completely at the mercy of the Kauravas, who cast all sorts of insults upon them and subjected Draupadi to the most inhuman treatment. At last, through the intervention of the blind king, they got their liberty, and were asked to return home and rule their kingdom. But Duryodhana saw the danger and forced his father to allow one more throw of the dice in which the party which would lose, should retire to the forests for 12 years and then live unrecognized in a city for one year; if they were found out, the same term of exile should have to be undergone once again and then only the kingdom was to be restored to the exiled. This last game too was lost by Yudhishthira and the five Pandava brothers retired to the forests with Draupadi as homeless exiles. They lived in the forests and mountains for 12 years. There they performed many deeds of virtue and valour and would go out now and then on a long round of pilgrimages, visiting many holy places. That part of the poem is very interesting and instructive, and various are the incidents, tales and legends with which this part of the book is replete. There are in it beautiful and sublime stories of ancient India, religious and philosophical. Great sages came to see the brothers in their exile and narrated to them many telling stories of ancient India, so as to make them bear lightly the burden of their exile. One only I will relate to you here.

There was a king called Ashvapati. The king had a daughter, who was so good and beautiful that she was called Savitri, which is the name of a sacred prayer of the Hindus. When Savitri grew old enough, her father asked her to choose a husband for herself. These ancient Indian princesses were very independent, you see, and chose their own princely suitors.

Savitri consented and travelled in distant regions, mounted in a golden chariot, with her guards and aged courtiers to whom her father entrusted her, stopping at different courts and seeing different princes, but not one of them could win the heart of Savitri. They came at last to a holy hermitage in one of those forests that in ancient India were reserved for animals and where no animals were allowed to be killed. The animals lost the fear of man—even the fish in the lakes came and took food out of the hand. For thousands of years no one had killed anything therein. The sages and the aged went there to live among the deer and the birds. Even criminals were safe there. When a man got tired of life, he would go to the forest; in the company of sages, talking of religion and meditating thereon, he passed the remainder of his life.

Now it happened that there was a king, Dyumatsena, who was defeated by his enemies and was deprived of his kingdom when he was struck with age and had lost his sight. This poor, old, blind king, with his queen and his son, took refuge in the forest and passed his life in rigid penance. His boy's name was Satyavan.

It came to pass that after having visited all the different royal courts, Savitri at last came to this hermitage, or holy place. Not even the greatest king could pass by the hermitages or ashramas as they were called, without going to pay homage to the sages for such honour and respect was felt for these holy men. The greatest emperor of India would be only too glad to trace his descent to some sage who lived in a forest, subsisting on roots, fruits and clad in rags. We are all children of sages. That is the respect that is paid to religion. So, even kings, when they pass by the hermitages, feel honoured to go in and pay their respects to the sages. If they approach on horseback, they descend and walk as they advance towards them. If they arrive in a chariot, chariot and armour must be left outside when they enter. No fighting man can enter unless he comes in the manner of a religious man, quiet and gentle.

So Savitri came to this hermitage and saw Satyavan there, the hermit's son and her heart was conquered. She had escaped all the princes of the palaces and the courts, but here in the forest-refuge of King Dyumatsena, his son, Satyavan, stole her heart.

When Savitri returned to her father's house, he asked her, 'Savitri, dear daughter, speak. Did you see anybody whom you would like to marry.'

Then softly with blushes, said Savitri, 'Yes, father.'

'What is the name of the prince?'

'He is no prince, but the son of King Dyumatsena who has lost his kingdom—a prince without a patrimony, who lives a monastic life, the life of a sannyasin in a forest, collecting roots and herbs, helping and feeding his old father and mother, who live in a cottage.'

On hearing this, the father consulted Sage Narada, who happened to be then present there, and he declared it was the most ill-omened choice that was ever made. The king then asked him to explain why it was so. And Narada said, 'Within 12 months from this time, the young man will die.'

Then the king started with terror and spoke, 'Savitri, this young man is going to die in 12 months and you will become a widow: think of that! Desist from your choice, my child, you shall never be married to a short-lived and fated bridegroom.'

'Never mind, father, do not ask me to marry another person and sacrifice the chastity of mind for I love and have accepted in my mind that good and brave Satyavan only as my husband. A maiden chooses only once, and she never departs from her troth.'

When the king found that Savitri was resolute in mind and heart, he complied. Then Savitri married prince Satyavan and she quietly went from the palace of her father into the forest to live with her chosen husband and help her husband's parents. Now, though Savitri knew the exact date when Satyavan was to die, she kept it hidden from him. Daily he went into the depths of the forest, collected fruits and flowers, gathered faggots, came back to the cottage and she cooked the meals and helped the old people. Thus their lives went on until the fatal day came near and three short days remained only. She took a severe vow of three nights' penance and holy fasts and kept her hard vigils. Savitri spent sorrowful and sleepless nights with fervent prayers and unseen tears, till the dreaded morning dawned. That day Savitri could not bear him out of her sight, even for a moment. She begged permission from his parents to accompany her husband, when he went to gather the usual herbs and fuel, and gaining their consent she went. Suddenly, in faltering accents, he complained to his wife of feeling faint, 'My head is dizzy and my senses reel, dear Savitri, I feel sleep stealing over me; let me rest beside thee for a while.'

In fear and trembling she replied, 'Come, lay your head upon my lap, my dearest lord.' And he laid his burning head in the lap of his wife, and ere long sighed and expired. Clasping him to her, her eyes flowing with tears, there she sat in the lonesome forest, until the emissaries of Death approached to take away the soul of Satyavan. But they could not come near to the place where Savitri sat with the dead body of her husband, his head resting in her lap. There was a zone of fire surrounding her, and not one of the emissaries of Death could come within it. They all fled back from it, returned to King Yama, the God of Death and told him why they could not obtain the soul of this man.

Then came Yama, the God of Death, the Judge of the dead. He was the first man that died—the first man that died on earth—and he had become the presiding deity over all those that die. He judges whether, after a man has died, he is to be punished or rewarded. So he came himself. Of course, he could go inside that charmed circle as he was a god. When he came to Savitri, he said, 'Daughter, give up this dead body, for know, death is the fate of mortals, and I am the first of mortals who died. Since then, everyone has had to die. Death is the fate of man.' Thus told, Savitri walked off, and Yama drew the soul out. Yama having possessed himself of the soul of the young man proceeded on his way. Before he had gone far, he heard footfalls upon the dry leaves. He turned back. 'Savitri, daughter, why are you following me? This is the fate of all mortals.'

'I am not following thee, Father,' replied Savitri, 'but this is, also, the fate of woman, she follows where her love takes her, and the Eternal Law separates not loving man and faithful wife.'

Then said the God of Death, 'Ask for any boon, except the life of your husband.'

'If thou art pleased to grant a boon, O Lord of Death, I ask that my father-in-law may be cured of his blindness and made happy.'

'Let thy pious wish be granted, duteous daughter.' And then the King of Death travelled on with the soul of Satyavan. Again the same footfall was heard from behind. He looked round. 'Savitri, my daughter, you are still following me?'

'Yes, my Father; I cannot help doing so; I am trying all the time to go back, but the mind goes after my husband and the body follows. The soul has already gone, for in that soul is also mine; and when you take the soul, the body follows, does it not?'

'Pleased am I with your words, fair Savitri. Ask yet another boon of me, but it must not be the life of your husband.'

'Let my father-in-law regain his lost wealth and kingdom, Father, if thou art pleased to grant another supplication.'

'Loving daughter,' Yama answered, 'this boon I now bestow, but return home, for living mortal cannot go with King Yama.'

And then Yama pursued his way. But Savitri, meek and faithful still followed her departed husband. Yama again turned back. 'Noble Savitri, follow not in hopeless woe.'

'I cannot choose, but follow where thou takest my beloved one.'

'Then suppose Savitri that your husband was a sinner and has to go to hell. In that case goes Savitri with the one she loves?'

'Glad am I to follow where he goes be it life or death, heaven or hell,' said the loving wife.

'Blessed are your words, my child, pleased am I with you, ask yet another boon, but the dead come not to life again.'

'Since you so permit me, then, let the imperial line of my father-in-law be not destroyed; let his kingdom descend to Satyavan's sons.'

And then the God of Death smiled. 'My daughter, thou shalt have thy desire now: here is the soul of thy husband, he shall live again. He shall live to be a father and thy children also shall reign in due course. Return home. Love has conquered Death! Woman never loved like thee, and thou art the proof that even I, the God of Death, am powerless against the power of the true love that abideth!'

This is the story of Savitri, and every girl in India must aspire to be like Savitri, whose love could not be conquered by death, and who through this tremendous love snatched back from even Yama, the soul of her husband.

The book is full of hundreds of beautiful episodes like this. I began by telling you that the Mahabharata is one of the greatest books in the world and consists of about a hundred thousand verses in 18 Parvans, or volumes.

To return to our main story. We left the Pandava brothers in exile. Even there they were not allowed to remain unmolested from the evil plots of Duryodhana, but all of them were futile.

A story of their forest life, I shall tell you here. One day, the brothers became thirsty in the forest. Yudhishthira bade his brother, Nakula, go and fetch water. He quickly proceeded towards the place where there was water and soon came to a crystal lake and was about to drink of it when he heard a voice utter these words: 'Stop, O child. First answer my questions and then drink of this water.' But Nakula, who was exceedingly thirsty, disregarded these words, drank of the water, and having drunk of it, dropped down dead. As Nakula did not return, King Yudhishthira told Sahadeva to seek his brother and bring back water with him. So Sahadeva proceeded to the lake and beheld his brother lying dead. Afflicted at the death of his brother and suffering severely from thirst, he went towards the water, when the same words were heard by him: 'O child, first answer my questions and then drink of the water.' He also disregarded these words, and having satisfied his thirst, dropped down dead. Subsequently, Arjuna and Bhima were sent, one after the other, on a similar quest, but neither returned, having drunk of the lake and dropped down dead. Then Yudhishthira rose up to go in search of his brothers. At length, he came to the beautiful lake and saw his brothers lying dead. His heart was full of grief at the sight and he began to lament. Suddenly he heard the same voice saying, 'Do not, O child, act rashly.

I am a Yaksha living as a crane on tiny fish. It is by me that thy younger brothers have been brought under the sway of the Lord of departed spirits. If thou, O Prince, answer not the questions put by me even thou shalt number the fifth corpse. Having answered my questions first, do thou, O Kunti's son, drink and carry away as much as thou requires.'

Yudhishthira replied, 'I shall answer thy questions according to my intelligence. Do thou ask met.' The Yaksha then asked him several questions, all of which Yudhishthira answered satisfactorily. One of the questions asked was: 'What is the most wonderful fact in this world?'

'We see our fellow beings every moment falling off around us, but those that are left behind think that they will never die. This is the most curious fact: in face of death, none believes that he will die!'

Another question asked was: 'What is the path of knowing the secret of religion?'

And Yudhishthira answered, 'By argument nothing can be settled; doctrines there are many; various are the scriptures, one part contradicting the other. There are not two sages who do not differ in their opinions. The secret of religion is buried deep, as it were, in dark caves. So the path to be followed is that which the great ones have trodden.'

Then the Yaksha said, 'I am pleased. I am Dharma, the God of Justice in the form of the crane. I came to test you. Now, your brothers, see, not one of them is dead. It is all my magic. Since abstention from injury is regarded by thee as higher than both profit and pleasure, therefore, let all thy brothers live, O Bull of the Bharata race.' And at these words of the Yaksha, the four Pandavas rose up.

Here is a glimpse of the nature of King Yudhishthira. We find by his answers that he was more of a philosopher, more of a yogi, than a king.

Now, as the thirteenth year of the exile was drawing nigh, the Yaksha bade them go to Virata's kingdom and live there in such disguises as they would think best.

So, after the term of the 12 years' exile had expired, they went to the kingdom of Virata in different disguises to spend the remaining one year in concealment, and entered into menial services in the king's household. Thus, Yudhishthira became a Brahmana courtier of the king, as one skilled in dice; Bhima was appointed a cook; Arjuna, dressed as a eunuch, was made a teacher of dancing and music to Uttara, the princess and remained in the inner apartments of the king; Nakula became the keeper of the king's horses; and Sahadeva got the charge of the cows; and Draupadi, disguised as a waiting-woman, was also admitted into the queen's household. Thus concealing their identity, the Pandava brothers and Draupadi safely spent a year, and the search of Duryodhana to find them out was of no avail. They were only discovered just when the year was out.

Then Yudhishthira sent an ambassador to Dhritarashtra and demanded that half of the kingdom should, as their share, be restored to them. But Duryodhana hated his cousins and would not consent to their legitimate demands. They were even willing to accept a single province, nay, even five villages. But the headstrong Duryodhana declared that he would not yield without fight even as much land as a needle's point would hold. Dhritarashtra pleaded again and again for peace, but all in vain. Krishna also went and tried to avert the impending war and death of kinsmen, so did the wise elders of the royal court, but all negotiations for a peaceful partition of the kingdom were futile. So, at last, preparations were made on both sides for war, and all the warlike nations took part in it.

The old Indian customs of the Kshatriyas were observed

in it. Duryodhana took one side, Yudhishthira the other. From Yudhishthira, messengers were at once sent to all the surrounding kings, entreating their alliance, since honourable men would grant the request that first reached them. So, warriors from all parts assembled to espouse the cause of either the Pandavas or the Kauravas according to the precedence of their requests; and thus one brother joined this side and the other that side, the father on one side and the son on the other. The most curious thing was the code of war of those days; as soon as the battle for the day ceased and evening came, the opposing parties were good friends, even going to each other's tents; however, when the morning came, again they proceeded to fight each other. That was the strange trait that the Hindus carried down to the time of the Mohammedan invasion. Then again, a man on horseback must not strike one on foot; must not poison the weapon; must not vanquish the enemy in any unequal fight, or by dishonesty; and must never take undue advantage of another and so on. If any deviated from these rules, he would be covered with dishonour and shunned.

The Kshatriyas were trained in that way. And when the foreign invasion came from Central Asia, the Hindus treated the invaders in the selfsame way. They defeated them several times and on as many occasions sent them back to their homes with presents etc. The code laid down was that they must not usurp anybody's country; and when a man was beaten, he must be sent back to his country with due regard to his position. The Mohammedan conquerors treated the Hindu kings differently, and when they got them once, they destroyed them without remorse.

Mind you, in those days—in the times of our story, the poem says—the science of arms was not the mere use of bows and arrows at all; it was magic archery in which the use of mantras, concentration, etc., played a prominent part. One man could fight millions of men and burn them at will. He could send one arrow and it would rain thousands of arrows and thunder; he could make anything burn and so on—it was all divine magic. One fact is most curious in both these poems—the Ramayana and the Mahabharata—along with these magic arrows and all these things going on, you see the cannon already in use. The cannon is an old, old thing, used by the Chinese and the Hindus. Upon the walls of the cities were hundreds of curious weapons made of hollow iron tubes, which filled with powder and ball would kill hundreds of men. The people believed that the Chinese, by magic, put the devil inside a hollow iron tube, and when they applied a little fire to a hole, the devil came out with a terrific noise and killed many people.

So in those old days, they used to fight with magic arrows. One man would be able to fight millions of others. They had their military arrangements and tactics: there were the foot soldiers, termed the pada; then the cavalry, Turaga; and two other divisions which the moderns have lost and given up—there was the elephant corps—hundreds and hundreds of elephants, with men on their backs, formed into regiments and protected with huge sheets of iron mail; these elephants would bear down upon a mass of the enemy. Then there were the chariots, of course (you have all seen pictures of those old chariots, they were used in every country). These were the four divisions of the army in those old days.

Now, both parties alike wished to secure the alliance of Krishna. He declined to take an active part and fight in this war, but offered himself as charioteer to Arjuna and as the friend and counsellor of the Pandavas while to Duryodhana he gave his army of mighty soldiers.

Then was fought on the vast plain of Kurukshetra the

great battle in which Bhisma, Drona, Karna and the brothers of Duryodhana with the kinsmen on both sides and thousands of other heroes falling to death. The war lasted 18 days. Indeed, out of the 18 Akshauhinis of soldiers very few men were left. The death of Duryodhana ended the war in favour of the Pandavas. It was followed by the lament of Gandhari, the queen and the widowed women, and the funerals of the deceased warriors.

The greatest incident of the war was the marvellous and immortal poem of the Gita, the Song Celestial. It is the popular scripture of India and the loftiest of all teachings. It consists of a dialogue held by Arjuna with Krishna, just before the commencement of the fight on the battle-field of Kurukshetra. I would advise those of you who have not read that book to read it. If you only knew how much it has influenced your own country even! If you want to know the source of Emerson's inspiration, it is this book, the Gita. He went to see Carlyle and Carlyle made him a present of the Gita; and that little book is responsible for the Concord Movement. All the broad movements in America, in one way or other, are indebted to the Concord party.

The central figure of the Gita is Krishna. As you worship Jesus of Nazareth as God come down as man, so the Hindus worship many incarnations of God. They believe in not one or two only, but in many, who have come down from time to time, according to the needs of the world, for the preservation of dharma and destruction of wickedness. Each sect has one, and Krishna is one of them. Krishna, perhaps, has a larger number of followers in India than any other incarnation of God. His followers hold that he was the most perfect of those incarnations. Why? 'Because,' they say, 'look at Buddha and other incarnations: they were only monks and they had no sympathy for married people. How could they have? But look at Krishna: he was great as a son, as a king, as a father and all through his life he practiced the marvellous teachings which he preached. He, who in the midst of the greatest activity finds the sweetest peace and in the midst of the greatest calmness is most active, has known the secret of life.'

Krishna shows the way how to do this—by being non-attached: do everything but do not get identified with anything. You are the soul, the pure, the free, all the time; you are the witness. Our misery comes, not from work, but by our getting attached to something. Take for instance, money: money is a great thing to have, earn it, says Krishna; struggle hard to get money, but don't get attached to it. So with children, with wife, husband, relatives, fame, everything; you have no need to shun them, only don't get attached. There is only one attachment and that belongs to the Lord and to none other. Work for them, love them, do good to them, sacrifice a hundred lives, if need be, for them, but never be attached. His own life was the exact exemplification of that.

Remember that the book which delineates the life of Krishna is several thousand years old, and some parts of his life are very similar to those of Jesus of Nazareth. Krishna was of royal birth; there was a tyrant king, called Kamsa, and there was a prophecy that one would be born of such and such a family, who would be king. So Kamsa ordered all the male children to be massacred. The father and mother of Krishna were cast by King Kamsa into prison, where the child was born. A light suddenly shone in the prison and the child spoke saying, 'I am the light of the world, born for the good of the world.' You find Krishna again symbolically represented with cows—'The Great Cowherd,' as he is called. Sages affirmed that God Himself was born, and they went to pay him homage. In other parts of the story, the similarity between the two does not continue.

Shri Krishna conquered this tyrant Kamsa, but he never thought of accepting or occupying the throne himself. He had nothing to do with that. He had done his duty and there it ended.

After the conclusion of the Kurukshetra War, the great warrior and venerable grandsire, Bhishma, who fought 10 days out of the 18 days' battle, still lay on his deathbed and gave instructions to Yudhishthira on various subjects, such as the duties of the king, the duties of the four castes, the four stages of life, the laws of marriage, the bestowing of gifts, etc., basing them on the teachings of the ancient sages. He explained Sankhya philosophy and Yoga philosophy and narrated numerous tales and traditions about saints and gods and kings. These teachings occupy nearly one-fourth of the entire work and form an invaluable storehouse of Hindu laws and moral codes. Yudhishthira had in the meantime been crowned king. But the awful bloodshed and extinction of superiors and relatives weighed heavily on his mind; and then, under the advice of Vyasa, he performed the Ashvamedha sacrifice.

After the war, for 15 years, Dhritarashtra dwelt in peace and honour, obeyed by Yudhishthira and his brothers. Then the aged monarch leaving Yudhishthira on the throne, retired to the forest with his devoted wife and Kunti, the mother of the Pandava brothers, to pass his last days in asceticism.

Thirty-six years had now passed since Yudhishthira regained his empire. Then came to him the news that Krishna had left his mortal body. Krishna, the sage, his friend, his prophet, his counsellor, had departed. Arjuna hastened to Dwaraka and came back only to confirm the sad news that Krishna and the Yadavas were all dead. Then the king and the other brothers, overcome with sorrow, declared that the time for them to go, too, had arrived. So they cast off the burden of royalty, placed

Parikshit, the grandson of Arjuna, on the throne, and retired to the Himalayas, on the Great Journey, the *mahaprasthana*. This was a peculiar form of sannyasa. It was a custom for old kings to become sannyasins. In ancient India, when men became very old, they would give up everything. So did the kings. When a man did not want to live any more, then he went towards the Himalayas, without eating or drinking and walked on and on till the body failed. All the time thinking of God, he just marched on till the body gave way.

Then came the gods, the sages and they told King Yudhishthira that he should go and reach heaven. To go to heaven one has to cross the highest peaks of the Himalayas. Beyond the Himalayas is Mount Meru. On the top of Mount Meru is heaven. None ever went there in this body. There the gods reside. And Yudhishthira was called upon by the gods to go there.

So the five brothers and their wife clad themselves in robes of bark and set out on their journey. On the way, they were followed by a dog. On and on they went, and they turned their weary feet northward to where the Himalayas lifts his lofty peaks, and they saw the mighty Mount Meru in front of them. Silently they walked on in the snow, until suddenly the queen fell, to rise no more.

To Yudhishthira who was leading the way, Bhima, one of the brothers, said, 'Behold, O King, the queen has fallen.' The king shed tears, but he did not look back.

'We are going to meet Krishna,' he says. 'No time to look back. March on.'

After a while, again Bhima said, 'Behold, our brother, Sahadeva has fallen.' The king shed tears, but paused not.

'March on," he cried.

One after the other, in the cold and snow, all the four

brothers dropped down, but unshaken, though alone, the king advanced onward. Looking behind, he saw the faithful dog was still following him. And so the king and the dog went on, through snow and ice, over hill and dale, climbing higher and higher, till they reached Mount Meru; and there they began to hear the chimes of heaven, and celestial flowers were showered upon the virtuous king by the gods. Then descended the chariot of the gods and Indra prayed to him, 'Ascend in this chariot, greatest of mortals: thou that alone art given to enter heaven without changing the mortal body.' But no, that Yudhishthira would not do without his devoted brothers and his queen; then Indra explained to him that the brothers had already gone thither before him.

And Yudhishthira looked around and said to his dog, 'Get into the chariot, child.'

The god stood aghast. 'What! The dog?' he cried. 'Do thou cast off this dog! The dog goeth not to heaven! Great King, what dost thou mean? Art thou mad? Thou, the most virtuous of the human race, thou only canst go to heaven in thy body.'

'But he has been my devoted companion through snow and ice. When all my brothers were dead, my queen dead, he alone never left me. How can I leave him now?'

'There is no place in heaven for men with dogs. He has to be left behind. There is nothing unrighteous in this.'

'I do not go to heaven,' replied the king, 'without the dog. I shall never give up such a one who has taken refuge with me, until my own life is at an end. I shall never swerve from righteousness, nay, not even for the joys of heaven or the urging of a god.'

'Then,' said Indra, 'on one condition the dog goes to heaven. You have been the most virtuous of mortals and he has been a dog, killing and eating animals; he is sinful, hunting and taking other lives. You can exchange heaven with him.'

'Agreed,' says the king. 'Let the dog go to heaven.'

At once, the scene changed. Hearing these noble words of Yudhishthira, the dog revealed himself as Dharma; the dog was no other than Yama, the Lord of Death and Justice. And Dharma exclaimed, 'Behold, O King, no man was ever so unselfish as thou, willing to exchange heaven with a little dog and for his sake disclaiming all his virtues and ready to go to hell even for him. Thou art well born, O King of kings. Thou hast compassion for all creatures, O Bharata, of which this is a bright example. Hence, regions of undying felicity are thine! Thou hast won them, O King, and shine is a celestial and high goal.'

Then Yudhishthira, with Indra, Dharma and other gods, proceeds to heaven in a celestial car. He undergoes some trials, bathes in the celestial Ganga and assumes a celestial body. He meets his brothers who are now immortals, and all at last is bliss.

Thus ends the story of the Mahabharata, setting forth in a sublime poem the triumph of virtue and defeat of vice.

In speaking of the Mahabharata to you, it is simply impossible for me to present the unending array of the grand and majestic characters of the mighty heroes depicted by the genius and master-mind of Vyasa. The internal conflicts between righteousness and filial affection in the mind of the god-fearing, yet feeble, old, blind King Dhritarashtra; the majestic character of the grandsire Bhishma; the noble and virtuous nature of the royal Yudhishthira, and of the other four brothers, as mighty in valour as in devotion and loyalty; the peerless character of Krishna, unsurpassed in human wisdom; and not less brilliant, the characters of the women—the stately queen Gandhari, the loving mother Kunti, the ever-devoted and all-suffering

Draupadi—these and hundreds of other characters of this epic and those of the Ramayana have been the cherished heritage of the whole Hindu world for the last several thousands of years and form the basis of their thoughts and of their moral and ethical ideas. In fact, the Ramayana and the Mahabharata are the two encyclopedias of the ancient Aryan life and wisdom, portraying an ideal civilization which humanity has yet to aspire after.

13

THE GITA I

Delivered on 26 May 1900, in San Francisco

To understand the Gita requires its historical background. The Gita is a commentary on the Upanishads. The Upanishads are the Bible of India. They occupy the same place as the New Testament does. There are [more than] a hundred books comprising the Upanishads, some very small and some big, each a separate treatise. The Upanishads do not reveal the life of any teacher, but simply teach principles. They are [as it were] shorthand notes taken down of discussion in [learned assemblies], generally in the courts of kings. The word Upanishad may mean 'sittings' [or 'sitting near a teacher'].

Those of you who may have studied some of the Upanishads can understand how they are condensed shorthand sketches. After long discussions had been held, they were taken down, possibly from memory. The difficulty is that you get very little of the background. Only the luminous points are mentioned there. The origin of ancient Sanskrit is 5000 BC; the Upanishads [are at least] 2,000 years before that. Nobody knows [exactly] how old they are. The Gita takes the ideas of the Upanishads and in [some] cases the very words. They are strung together with the idea of bringing out, in a compact, condensed and systematic form the whole subject the Upanishads deal with.

The [original] scriptures of the Hindus are called the vedas. They were so vast—the mass of writings—that if the texts alone were brought here, this room would not contain them. Many of them are lost. They were divided into branches, each branch put into the head of certain priests and kept alive by memory. Such men still exist. They will repeat book after book of the vedas without missing a single intonation. The larger portion of the vedas has disappeared. The small portion left makes a whole library by itself. The oldest of these contains the hymns of the Rig Veda. It is the aim of the modern scholar to restore [the sequence of the Vedic compositions]. The old, orthodox idea is quite different, as your orthodox idea of the Bible is quite different from the modern scholar's. The vedas are divided into two portions: one the Upanishads, the philosophical portion, the other the work portion.

We will try to give a little idea of the work portion. It consists of rituals and hymns, various hymns addressed to various gods. The ritual portion is composed of ceremonies, some of them very elaborate. A great many priests are required. The priestly function became a science by itself, owing to the elaboration of the ceremonials. Gradually the popular idea of veneration grew round these hymns and rituals. The gods disappeared and in their place were left the rituals. That was the curious development in India. The orthodox Hindu [the Mimamsaka] does not believe in gods, the unorthodox believe in them. If you ask the orthodox Hindu what the meaning is of these gods in the Vedas, [he will not be able to give any satisfactory answer]. The priests sing these hymns and pour libations and offering into the fire. When you ask the orthodox Hindu the meaning of this, he says that words have the power to produce certain effects. That is all. There is all the natural and supernatural power that ever existed. The vedas are simply words that have the mystical power to produce effects if the sound intonation is right. If one sound is wrong it will not do. Each one must be perfect. [Thus] what in other religions is called prayer disappeared and the vedas became the gods. So you see the tremendous importance that was attached to the words of the vedas. These are the eternal words out of which the whole universe has been produced. There cannot be any thought without the word. Thus, whatever there is in this world is the manifestation of thought and thought can only manifest itself through words. This mass of words by which the unmanifested thought becomes manifest, that is what is meant by the vedas. It follows that the external existence of everything [depends on the vedas, for thought] does not exist without the word. If the word 'horse' did not exist, none could think of a horse. [So] there must be [an intimate relation between] thought, word and the external object. What are these words [in reality]? The vedas. They do not call it Sanskrit language at all. It is Vedic language, a divine language. Sanskrit is a degenerate form. So are all other languages. There is no language older than Vedic. You may ask, 'Who wrote the vedas?' They were not written. The words are the vedas. A word is veda, if I can pronounce it rightly. Then it will immediately produce the [desired] effect.

This mass of vedas eternally exists and all the world is the manifestation of this mass of words. Then when the cycle ends, all this manifestation of energy becomes finer and finer, becomes only words, then thought. In the next cycle, first the thought changes into words and then out of those words [the whole universe] is produced. If there is something here that is not in the vedas, that is your delusion. It does not exist.

[Numerous] books upon that subject alone defend the vedas. If you tell [their authors] that the vedas must have been pronounced by men first, [they will simply laugh]. You never heard of any [man uttering them for the first time]. Take Buddha's words. There is a tradition that he lived and spoke these words [many times before]. If the Christian stands up and says, 'My religion is a historical religion and therefore yours is wrong and ours is true,' [the Mimamsaka replies], 'Yours being historical, you confess that a man invented it 1,900 years ago. That which is true must be infinite and eternal. That is the one test of truth. It never decays, it is always the same. You confess your religion was created by such-and-such a man. The vedas were not. By no prophets or anything... Only infinite words, infinite by their very nature, from which the whole universe comes and goes.' In the abstract, it is perfectly correct... The sound must be the beginning of creation. There must be germ sounds like germ plasm. There cannot be any ideas without the words... Wherever there are sensations, ideas, emotions, there must be words. The difficulty is when they say that these four books are the vedas and nothing else. [Then] the Buddhist will stand up and say, 'Ours are vedas. They were revealed to us later on.' That cannot be. Nature does not go on in that way. Nature does not manifest her laws bit by bit, an inch of gravitation today and [another inch] tomorrow. No, every law is complete. There is no evolution in law at all. It is [given] once and for ever. It is all nonsense, this 'new religion and better inspiration,' and all that. It means nothing.

There may be a hundred thousand laws and man may know only a few today. We discover them—that is all. Those old priests with their tremendous [claims about eternal words], having dethroned the gods, took the place of the gods. [They said], 'You do not understand the power of words. We know how to use them. We are the living gods of the world. Pay us; we will manipulate the words and you will get what you want. Can you pronounce the words yourself? You cannot, for, mind you, one mistake will produce the opposite effect. You want to be rich, handsome, have a long life, a fine husband?' Only pay the priest and keep quiet!

Yet there is another side. The ideal of the first part of the vedas is entirely different from the ideal of the other part, the Upanishads. The ideal of the first part coincides with [that of] all other religions of the world except the Vedanta. The ideal is enjoyment here and hereafter—man and wife, husband and children. Pay your dollar, the priest will give you a certificate and you will have a happy time afterwards in heaven. You will find all your people there and have this merry-go-round without end. No tears, no weeping—only laughing. No stomach ache, but yet eating. No headache, but yet [parties]. That, considered the priests, was the highest goal of man.

There is another idea in this philosophy which is according to your modern ideas. Man is a slave of nature and slave eternally he has got to remain. We call it karma. Karma means law and it applies everywhere. Everything is bound by karma. 'Is there no way out?' 'No! Remain slaves all through the years—fine slaves. We will manipulate the words so that you will only have the good and not the bad side of all—if you will pay [us] enough.' That was the ideal of [the Mimamsakas]. These are the ideals which are popular throughout the ages. The vast mass of mankind are never thinkers. Even if they try to think, the [effect of the] vast mass of superstitions on them is terrible. The moment they weaken, one blow comes and the backbone breaks into 20 pieces. They can only be moved by lures and threats. They can never move of their own accord. They must be frightened, horrified, or terrorized and they are your slaves forever. They have nothing else to do but to pay and obey. Everything else is done by the priest... How much easier religion becomes! You see, you have nothing to do. Go home and sit quietly. Somebody is doing the whole thing for you. Poor, poor animals!

Side by side, there was the other system. The Upanishads are diametrically opposite in all their conclusions. First of all, the Upanishads believe in God, the creator of the universe, its ruler. You find later on [the idea of a benign providence]. It is an entirely opposite [conception]. Now, although we hear the priest, the ideal is much more subtle. Instead of many gods, they made one God.

The second idea, that you are all bound by the law of karma, the Upanishads admit, but they declare the way out. The goal of man is to go beyond law. And enjoyment can never be the goal because enjoyment can only be in nature.

In the third place, the Upanishads condemn all the sacrifices and say that is mummery. That may give you all you want, but it is not desirable, for the more you get, the more you [want] and you run round and round in a circle eternally, never getting to the end—enjoying and weeping. Such a thing as eternal happiness is impossible anywhere. It is only a child's dream. The same energy becomes joy and sorrow.

I have changed my psychology a bit today. I have found the most curious fact. You have a certain idea and you do not want to have it, you think of something else and the idea you want to suppress is entirely suppressed. What is that idea? I saw it come out in 15 minutes. It came out and staggered me. It was strong and it came in such a violent and terrible fashion [that] I thought here was a madman. And when it was over, all that had happened [was a suppression of the previous emotion]. What came out? It was my own bad impression which had to be worked out. 'Nature will have her way. What can suppression do?' That is a terrible [statement] in the Gita. It seems it may be a vain struggle after all. You may have a hundred thousand [urges competing] at the same time. You may repress [them], but the moment the spring rebounds, the whole thing is there again.

[But there is hope]. If you are powerful enough, you can divide your consciousness into 20 parts all at the same time. I am changing my psychology. Mind grows. That is what the yogis say. There is one passion and it rouses another, and the first one dies. If you are angry and then happy, the next moment the anger passes away. Out of that anger you manufactured the next state. These states are always interchangeable. Eternal happiness and misery are a child's dream. The Upanishads point out that the goal of man is neither misery nor happiness, but we have to be master of that out of which these are manufactured. We must be masters of the situation at its very root, as it were.

The other point of divergence is: the Upanishads condemn all rituals, especially those that involve the killing of animals. They declare those all nonsense. One school of old philosophers says that you must kill such an animal at a certain time if the effect is to be produced. [You may reply], 'But [there is] also the sin of taking the life of the animal; you will have to suffer for that.' They say that is all nonsense. How do you know what is right and what is wrong? Your mind says so? Who cares what your mind says? What nonsense are you talking? You are setting your mind against the scriptures. If your mind says something and the vedas say something else, stop your mind and believe in the vedas. If they say, killing a man is right, that is right. If you say, 'No, my conscience says [otherwise,' it won't do]. The moment you believe in any book as the eternal word, as sacred, no more can you question. I do not see how you people here believe in the Bible whenever you say about [it], 'How wonderful those words are, how right and how good!' Because, if you believe in the Bible as the word of God, you have no right to judge at all. The moment you judge, you think you are higher than the Bible. [Then] what is the use of the Bible to you? The priests say, 'We refuse to make the comparison with your Bible or anybody's. It is no use comparing because what is the authority? There it ends. If you think something is not right, go and get it right according to the vedas.'

The Upanishads believe in that, [but they have a higher standard too]. On the one hand, they do not want to overthrow the vedas and on the other they see these animal sacrifices and the priests stealing everybody's money. But in the psychology they are all alike. All the differences have been in the philosophy, [regarding] the nature of the soul. Has it a body and a mind? And is the mind only a bundle of nerves, the motor nerves and the sensory nerves? Psychology, they all take for granted, is a perfect science. There cannot be any difference there. All the fight has been regarding philosophy—the nature of the soul, God and all that.

Then another great difference between the priests and the Upanishads come. The Upanishads say, renounce. That is the test of everything. Renounce everything. It is the creative faculty that brings us into all this entanglement. The mind is in its own nature when it is calm. The moment you can calm it, that [very] moment you will know the truth. What is it that is whirling the mind? Imagination, creative activity. Stop creation and you know the truth. All power of creation must stop, and then you know the truth at once.

On the other hand, the priests are all for [creation]. Imagine a species of life [in which there is no creative activity. It is unthinkable]. The people had to have a plan [of evolving a stable society. A system of rigid selection was adopted. For instance,] no people who are blind and halt can be married. [As a result] you will find so much less deformity [in India] than in any other country in the world. Epileptics and insane [people] are very rare [there]. That is owing to direct selection. The priests say, 'Let them become sannyasins.' On the other hand, the Upanishads say, 'Oh no, [the] earth's best and finest [and] freshest flowers should be laid upon the altar. The strong, the young, with sound intellect and sound body—they must struggle for the truth.'

So with all these divergences of opinion, I have told you that the priests already differentiated themselves into a separate caste. The second is the caste of the kings… All the Upanishadic philosophy is from the brains of kings, not priests. There [runs] an economic struggle through every religious struggle. This animal called man has some religious influence, but he is guided by economy. Individuals are guided by something else, but the mass of mankind never made a move unless economy was [involved]. You may [preach a religion that may not be perfect in every detail], but if there is an economic background [to it], and you have the most [ardent champions] to preach it, you can convince a whole country…

Whenever any religion succeeds, it must have economic value. Thousands of similar sects will be struggling for power, but only those who meet the real economic problem will have it. Man is guided by the stomach. He walks and the stomach goes first and the head afterwards. Have you not seen that? It will take ages for the head to go first. By the time a man is 60 years of age, he is called out of [the world]. The whole of life is one delusion and just when you begin to see things the way they are, you are snatched off. So long as the stomach went first you were all right. When children's dreams begin to vanish and you begin to look at things the way they are, the head goes. Just when the head goes first, [you go out].

[For] the religion of the Upanishads to be popularized was a hard task. Very little economy is there, but tremendous altruism…

The Upanishads had very little kingdom, although they were

discovered by kings that held all the royal power in their hands. So the struggle...began to be fiercer. Its culminating point came 2,000 years after, in Buddhism. The seed of Buddhism is here, [in] the ordinary struggle between the king and the priest; and [in the struggle] all religion declined. One wanted to sacrifice religion, the other wanted to cling to the sacrifices, to Vedic gods, etc. Buddhism...broke the chains of the masses. All castes and creeds alike became equal in a minute. So the great religious ideas in India exist, but have yet to be preached, otherwise they do no good...

In every country it is the priest who is conservative, for two reasons—because it is his bread and because he can only move with the people. All priests are not strong. If the people say, 'Preach two thousand gods,' the priests will do it. They are the servants of the congregation who pay them. God does not pay them. So blame yourselves before blaming the priests. You can only get the government, the religion, the priesthood you deserve and no better.

So the great struggle began in India and it comes to one of its culminating points in the Gita. When it was causing fear that all India was going to be broken up between [the] two... [groups], there rose this man Krishna, and in the Gita he tries to reconcile the ceremony and the philosophy of the priests and the people. Krishna is loved and worshipped in the same way as Christ. The difference is only in the age. The Hindus keep the birthday of Krishna as you do for Christ. Krishna lived 5,000 years ago and his life is full of miracles, some of them very similar to those in the life of Christ. The child was born in prison. The father took him away and put him with the shepherds. All children born in that year were ordered to be killed...He was killed; that was his fate.

Krishna was a married man. There are thousands of books

about him. They do not interest me much. The Hindus are great in telling stories, you see. [If] the Christian missionaries tell one story from their Bible, the Hindus will produce 20 stories. You say the whale swallowed Jonah; the Hindus say someone swallowed an elephant... Since I was a child, I have heard about Krishna's life. I take it for granted there must have been a man called Krishna, and his Gita shows he has [left] a wonderful book. I told you, you can understand the character of a man by analysing the fables about him. The fables have the nature [of decorations]. You must find they are all polished and manipulated to fit into the character. For instance, take Buddha. The central idea [is] sacrifice. There are thousands of folklore, but in every case the sacrifice must have been kept up. There are thousands of stories about Lincoln, about some characteristic of that great man. You take all the fables and find the general idea and [know] that that was the central character of the man. You find in Krishna that non-attachment is the central idea. He does not need anything. He does not want anything. He works for work's sake. 'Work for work's sake. Worship for worship's sake. Do good because it is good to do good. Ask no more.' That must have been the character of the man. Otherwise these fables could not be brought down to the one idea of non-attachment. The Gita is not his only sermon...

He is the most rounded man I know of, wonderfully developed equally in brain and heart and hand. Every moment [of his] is alive with activity, either as a gentleman, warrior, minister, or something else. Great as a gentleman, as a scholar, as a poet. This all-rounded and wonderful activity and combination of brain and heart you see in the Gita and other books. Most wonderful heart, exquisite language, and nothing can approach it anywhere. This tremendous activity of the man—the impression is still there. Five thousand years have passed and he has influenced millions and millions. Just think what an influence this man has over the whole world, whether you know it or not. My regard for him is for his perfect sanity. No cobwebs in that brain, no superstition. He knows the use of everything, and when it is necessary to [assign a place to each], he is there. Those that talk, go everywhere, question about the mystery of the vedas, etc., they do not know the truth. They are no better than frauds. There is a place in the vedas [even] for superstition, for ignorance. The whole secret is to find out the proper place for everything.

Then that heart! He is the first man, way before Buddha, to open the door of religion to every caste. That wonderful mind! That tremendously active life! Buddha's activity was on one plane, the plane of teaching. He could not keep his wife and child and become a teacher at the same time. Krishna preached in the midst of the battlefield. 'He who in the midst of intense activity finds himself in the greatest calmness and in the greatest peace finds intense activity, that is the greatest [yogi as well as the wisest man].' It means nothing to this man—the flying of missiles about him. Calm and sedate he goes on discussing the problems of life and death. Each one of the prophets is the best commentary on his own teaching. If you want to know what is meant by the doctrine of the New Testament, you go to Mr So-and-so. [But] read again and again [the four Gospels and try to understand their importance in the light of the wonderful life of the master as depicted there]. The great men think, and you and I [also] think. But there is a difference. We think and our bodies do not follow. Our actions do not harmonize with our thoughts. Our words have not the power of the words that become Vedas... Whatever they think must be accomplished. If they say, 'I do this,' the body does it. Perfect obedience. This is the end. You can think yourself God in one minute, but you cannot be [God]. That is the difficulty. They become what they think. We will become [only] by [degrees].

You see, that was about Krishna and his time. In the next lecture we will know more of his book.

14

THE GITA II

Delivered on 28 May 1900, in San Francisco

The Gita requires a little preliminary introduction. The scene is laid on the battlefield of Kurukshetra. There were two branches of the same race fighting for the empire of India about 5,000 years ago. The Pandavas had the right, but the Kauravas had the might. The Pandavas were five brothers and they were living in a forest. Krishna was the friend of the Pandavas. The Kauravas would not grant them as much land as would cover the point of a needle.

The opening scene is the battlefield and both sides see their relatives and friends—one brother on one side and another on the other side; a grandfather on one side, grandson on the other side… When Arjuna sees his own friends and relatives on the other side and knows that he may have to kill them, his heart gives way and he says that he will not fight. Thus begins the Gita.

For all of us in this world, life is a continuous fight… Many a time comes when we want to interpret our weakness and cowardice as forgiveness and renunciation. There is no merit in the renunciation of a beggar. If a person who can [give a blow] forbears, there is merit in that. If a person who has, gives up, there is merit in that. We know how often in our lives through laziness and cowardice we give up the battle and try to hypnotize our minds into the belief that we are brave.

The Gita opens with this very significant verse: 'Arise, O Prince! Give up this faint-heartedness, this weakness! Stand up and fight!' Then Arjuna, trying to argue the matter [with Krishna], brings higher moral ideas, how non-resistance is better than resistance and so on. He is trying to justify himself, but he cannot fool Krishna. Krishna is the higher Self, or God. He sees through the argument at once. In this case [the motive] is weakness. Arjuna sees his own relatives and he cannot strike them…

There is a conflict in Arjuna's heart between his emotionalism and his duty. The nearer we are to [beasts and] birds, the more we are in the hells of emotion. We call it love. It is self-hypnotization. We are under the control of our [emotions] like animals. A cow can sacrifice its life for its young. Every animal can. What of that? It is not the blind, birdlike emotion that leads to perfection… [To reach] the eternal consciousness, that is the goal of man! There emotion has no place, nor sentimentalism, nor anything that belongs to the senses—only the light of pure reason. [There] man stands as spirit.

Now, Arjuna is under the control of this emotionalism. He is not what he should be—a great self-controlled, enlightened sage working through the eternal light of reason. He has become like an animal, like a baby, just letting his heart carry away his brain, making a fool of himself and trying to cover his weakness under the flowery names of 'love' and so on. Krishna sees through that. Arjuna talks like a man of little learning and brings out many reasons, but at the same time he talks the language of a fool.

'The sage is not sorry for those that are living, nor for those that die.' [Krishna says :] 'You cannot die nor can I. There was never a time when we did not exist. There will never be a time when we shall not exist. As in this life a man begins with childhood, and [passes through youth and old age, so at death he merely passes into another kind of body]. Why should a wise man be sorry?' And where is the beginning of this emotionalism that has got hold of you? It is in the senses. 'It is the touch of the senses that brings all this quality of existence: heat and cold, pleasure and pain. They come and go.' Man is miserable this moment, happy the next. As such he cannot experience the nature of the soul...

'Existence can never be non-existence, neither can non-existence ever become existence... Know, therefore, that that which pervades all this universe is without beginning or end. It is unchangeable. There is nothing in the universe that can change [the changeless]. Though this body has its beginning and end, the dweller in the body is infinite and without end.'

Knowing this, stand up and fight! Not one step back, that is the idea... Fight it out, whatever comes. Let the stars move from the sphere! Let the whole world stand against us! Death means only a change of garment. What of it? Thus fight! You gain nothing by becoming cowards... Taking a step backward, you do not avoid any misfortune. You have cried to all the gods in the world. Has misery ceased? The masses in India cry to 60 million gods and still die like dogs. Where are these gods? ... The gods come to help you when you have succeeded. So what is the use? Die game...This bending the knee to superstitions, this selling yourself to your own mind does not befit you, my soul. You are infinite, deathless, birthless. Because you are infinite spirit, it does not befit you to be a slave... Arise! Awake! Stand up and fight! Die if you must. There is none to help you. You are all the world. Who can help you?

'Beings are unknown to our human senses before birth and after death. It is only in the interim that they are manifest. What is there to grieve about? Some look at it [the Self] with wonder. Some talk of it as wonderful. Others hear of it as wonderful. Others, hearing of it, do not understand.'

But if you say that killing all these people is sinful, then consider this from the standpoint of your own caste duty... 'Making pleasure and misery the same, making success and defeat the same, do thou stand up and fight.'

This is the beginning of another peculiar doctrine of the Gita—the doctrine of non-attachment. That is to say, we have to bear the result of our own actions because we attach ourselves to them... 'Only what is done as duty for duty's sake...can scatter the bondage of karma.' There is no danger that you can overdo it... 'If you do even a little of it, [this yoga will save you from the terrible round of birth and death].'

'Know, Arjuna, the mind that succeeds is the mind that is concentrated. The minds that are taken up with 2,000 subjects (have) their energies dispersed. Some can talk flowery language and think there is nothing beyond the vedas. They want to go to heaven. They want good things through the power of the vedas, and so they make sacrifices.' Such will never attain any success [in spiritual life] unless they give up all these materialistic ideas.

That is another great lesson. Spirituality can never be attained unless all material ideas are given up... What is in the senses? The senses are all delusion. People wish to retain them [in heaven] even after they are dead—a pair of eyes, a nose. Some imagine they will have more organs than they have now. They want to see God sitting on a throne through all eternity—the material body of God... Such men's desires are for the body, for food and drink and enjoyment. It is the materialistic life prolonged. Man cannot think of anything beyond this life. This life is all for the body. 'Such a man never comes to that concentration which leads to freedom.'

'The vedas only teach things belonging to the three *gunas*, to *sattva* [calmness], *rajas* [passion] and *tamas* [ignorance].' The vedas only teach about things in nature. People cannot think anything they do not see on earth. If they talk about heaven, they think of a king sitting on a throne, of people burning incense. It is all nature, nothing beyond nature. The vedas, therefore, teach nothing but nature. 'Go beyond nature, beyond the dualities of existence, beyond your own consciousness, caring for nothing, neither for good nor for evil.'

We have identified ourselves with our bodies. We are only body, or rather, possessed of a body. If I am pinched, I cry. All this is nonsense, since I am the soul. All this chain of misery, imagination, animals, gods and demons, everything, the whole world all this comes from the identification of ourselves with the body. I am spirit. Why do I jump if you pinch me?... Look at the slavery of it. Are you not ashamed? We are religious! We are philosophers! We are sages! Lord bless us! What are we? Living hells, that is what we are. Lunatics, that is what we are!

We cannot give up the idea [of body]. We are earthbound... Our ideas are burial grounds. When we leave the body we are bound by thousands of elements to those [ideas].

Who can work without any attachment? That is the real question. Such a man is the same whether his work succeeds or fails. His heart does not give one false beat even if his whole life-work is burnt to ashes in a moment. 'This is the sage who always works for work's sake without caring for the results. Thus, he goes beyond the pain of birth and death. Thus he becomes free.' Then he sees that this attachment is all delusion. The Self can never be attached... Then he goes beyond all the scriptures and philosophies. If the mind is deluded and pulled into a whirlpool by books and scriptures, what is the good of all these scriptures? One says this, another says that. What book shall you take? Stand alone! See the glory of your own soul and see that you will have to work. Then you will become a man of firm will.

Arjuna asks: 'Who is a person of established will?'

[Krishna answers:] 'The man who has given up all desires, who desires nothing, not even this life, nor freedom, nor gods, nor work, nor anything. When he has become perfectly satisfied, he has no more cravings.' He has seen the glory of the Self and has found that the world, the gods and heaven are…within his own Self. Then the gods become no gods, death becomes no death, life becomes no life. Everything has changed. 'A man is said to be [illumined] if his will has become firm, if his mind is not disturbed by misery, if he does not desire any happiness, if he is free of all [attachment], of all fear, of all anger…

'As the tortoise can draw in his legs, and if you strike him, not one foot comes out, even so the sage can draw all his sense-organs inside,' and nothing can force them out. Nothing can shake him, no temptation or anything. Let the universe tumble about him, it does not make one single ripple in his mind.

Then comes a very important question. Sometimes people fast for days… When the worst man has fasted for 20 days, he becomes quite gentle. Fasting and torturing themselves have been practiced by people all over the world. Krishna's idea is that this is all nonsense. He says that the senses will for the moment recede from the man who tortures himself, but will emerge again with 20 times more [power]…What should you do? The idea is to be natural—no asceticism. Go on, work, only mind that you are not attached. The will can never be fixed strongly in the man who has not learnt and practiced the secret of non-attachment.

I go out and open my eyes. If something is there, I must see it. I cannot help it. The mind runs after the senses. Now the senses must give up any reaction to nature.

'Where it is dark night for the [sense-bound] world, the self controlled [man] is awake. It is daylight for him… And where the world is awake, the sage sleeps.' Where is the world awake? In the senses. People want to eat and drink and have children, and then they die a dog's death… They are always awake for the senses. Even their religion is just for that. They invent a God to help them, to give them more women, more money, more children—never a God to help them become more godlike! 'Where the whole world is awake, the sage sleeps. But where the ignorant are asleep, there the sage stays awake'—in the world of light where man looks upon himself not as a bird, not as an animal, not as a body, but as infinite spirit, deathless, immortal. There, where the ignorant are asleep, and do not have time, nor intellect, nor the power to understand, there the sage is awake. That is daylight for him.

'As all the rivers of the world constantly pour their waters into the ocean, but the ocean's grand, majestic nature remains undisturbed and unchanged, so even though all the senses bring in sensations from nature, the ocean-like heart of the sage knows no disturbance, knows no fear.' Let miseries come in millions of rivers and happiness in hundreds! I am no slave to misery! I am no slave to happiness!

15

THE GITA III

Delivered on 29 May 1900, in San Francisco

Arjuna asks: 'You just advised action and yet you uphold knowledge of Brahman as the highest form of life. Krishna, if you think that knowledge is better than action, why do you tell me to act?'

[Shri Krishna]: 'From ancient times, these two systems have come down to us. The Sankhya philosophers advance the theory of knowledge. The yogis advance the theory of work. But none can attain peace by renouncing actions. None in this life can stop activity even for a moment. Nature's qualities [gunas] will make him act. He who stops his activities and at the same time is still thinking about them attains to nothing; he only becomes a hypocrite. But he who by the power of his mind gradually brings his sense-organs under control, employing them in work, that man is better. Therefore do thy work.' …

'Even if you have known the secret that you have no duty, that you are free, still you have to work for the good of others. Because whatever a great man does, ordinary people will do also. If a great man who has attained peace of mind and freedom ceases to work, then all the rest without that knowledge and peace will try to imitate him, and thus confusion would arise.'

'Behold, Arjuna, there is nothing that I do not possess and nothing that I want to acquire. And yet I continue to work. If I stopped work for a moment, the whole universe would [be destroyed]. That which the ignorant do with desire for results and gain, let the wise do without any attachment and without any desire for results and gain.'

Even if you have knowledge, do not disturb the childlike faith of the ignorant. On the other hand, go down to their level and gradually bring them up. That is a very powerful idea and it has become the ideal in India. That is why you can see a great philosopher going into a temple and worshipping images. It is not hypocrisy.

Later on we read what Krishna says, 'Even those who worship other deities are really worshipping me.' It is God incarnate whom man is worshipping. Would God be angry if you called Him by the wrong name? He would be no God at all! Can't you understand that whatever a man has in his own heart is God—even if he worships a stone? What of that!

We will understand more clearly if we once get rid of the idea that religion consists in doctrines. One idea of religion has been that the whole world was born because Adam ate the apple and there is no way of escape. Believe in Jesus Christ—in a certain man's death! But in India, there is quite a different idea. [There] religion means realization, nothing else. It does not matter whether one approaches the destination in a carriage with four horses, in an electric car, or rolling on the ground. The goal is the same. For the [Christians], the problem is how to escape the wrath of the terrible God. For the Indians, it is how to become what they really are, to regain their lost Selfhood…

Have you realized that you are spirit? When you say, 'I do,' what is meant by that—this lump of flesh called the body or the spirit, the infinite, ever blessed, effulgent, immortal? You may be the greatest philosopher, but as long as you have the idea that you are the body, you are no better than the little worm crawling under your foot! No excuse for you! So much the worse for you that you know all the philosophies and at the same time think you are the body! Body-gods, that is what you are! Is that religion?

Religion is the realization of spirit as spirit. What are we doing now? Just the opposite, realizing spirit as matter. Out of the immortal God we manufacture death and matter, and out of dead dull matter we manufacture spirit...

If you [can realize Brahman] by standing on your head, or on one foot, or by worshipping five thousand gods with three heads each—welcome to it!... Do it any way you can! Nobody has any right to say anything. Therefore, Krishna says, if your method is better and higher, you have no business to say that another man's method is bad, however wicked you may think it.

Again, we must consider, religion is a [matter of] growth, not a mass of foolish words. Two thousand years ago a man saw God. Moses saw God in a burning bush. Does what Moses did when he saw God save you? No man's seeing God can help you the least bit except that it may excite you and urge you to do the same thing. That is the whole value of the ancients' examples. Nothing more. [Just] signposts on the way. No man's eating can satisfy another man. No man's seeing God can save another man. You have to see God yourself. All these people fighting about what God's nature is on whether He has three heads in one body or five heads in six bodies. Have you seen God? No... And they do not believe they can ever see Him. What fools we mortals be! Sure, lunatics!

[In India], it has come down as a tradition that if there is a God, He must be your God and my God. To whom does the sun belong! You say Uncle Sam is everybody's uncle. If there is a God, you ought to be able to see Him. If not, let Him go.

Each one thinks his method is the best. Very good! But remember, it may be good for you. One food which is very indigestible to one is very digestible to another. Because it is good for you, do not jump to the conclusion that your method is everybody's method, that Jack's coat fits John and Mary. All the uneducated, uncultured, unthinking men and women have been put into that sort of strait jacket! Think for yourselves. Become atheists! Become materialists! That would be better. Exercises the mind!... What right have you to say that this man's method is wrong? It may be wrong for you. That is to say, if you undertake the method, you will be degraded, but that does not mean that he will be degraded. Therefore, says Krishna, if you have knowledge and see a man weak, do not condemn him. Go to his level and help him if you can. He must grow. I can put five bucketfuls of knowledge into his head in five hours. But what good will it do? He will be a little worse than before.

Whence comes all this bondage of action? Because we chain the soul with action. According to our Indian system, there are two existences: nature on the one side and the Self, the atman on the other. By the word nature is meant not only all this external world, but also our bodies, the mind, the will, even down to what says 'I'. Beyond all that is the infinite life and light of the soul—the Self, the atman... According to this philosophy, the Self is entirely separate from nature, always was and always will be... There never was a time, when the spirit could be identified even with the mind...

It is self-evident that the food you eat is manufacturing the mind all the time. It is matter. The Self is above any connection with food. Whether you eat or not does not matter. Whether you think or not...does not matter. It is infinite light. Its light is the same always. If you put a blue or a green glass [before a light], what has that to do with the light? Its colour is unchangeable. It is the mind which changes and gives the different colours. The moment the spirit leaves the body, the whole thing goes to pieces.

The reality in nature is spirit. Reality itself—the light of the spirit—moves and speaks and does everything [through our bodies, minds, etc.]. It is the energy and soul and life of the spirit that is being worked upon in different ways by matter... The spirit is the cause of all our thoughts and body action and everything, but it is untouched by good or evil, pleasure or pain, heat or cold, and all the dualism of nature, although it lends its light to everything.

'Therefore, Arjuna, all these actions are in nature. Nature... is working out her own laws in our bodies and minds. We identify ourselves with nature and say, "I am doing this." This way delusion seizes us.'

We always act under some compulsion. When hunger compels me, I eat. And suffering is still worse—slavery. That real 'I' is eternally free. What can compel it to do anything? The sufferer is in nature. It is only when we identify ourselves with the body that we say, 'I am suffering; I am Mr So-and-so'—all such nonsense. But he who has known the truth, holds himself aloof. Whatever his body does, whatever his mind does, he does not care. But mind you, the vast majority of mankind are under this delusion; and whenever they do any good, they feel that they are [the doers]. They are not yet able to understand higher philosophy. Do not disturb their faith! They are shunning evil and doing good. Great idea! Let them have it!... They are workers for good. By degrees they will think that there is greater glory than that of doing good. They will only witness and things are done... Gradually they will understand. When they have shunned all evil and done all good, then they will begin to realize that they are beyond all nature. They are not the doers. They stand [apart]. They are the…witness. They simply stand and look. Nature is begetting all the universe…They turn their backs. 'In the beginning, O beloved, there only existed that existence. Nothing else existed. And that [brooding], everything else was created.'

'Even those who know the path act impelled by their own nature. Everyone acts according to his nature. He cannot transcend it.' The atom cannot disobey the law. Whether it is the mental or the physical atom, it must obey the law. 'What is the use of [external restraint]?'

What makes the value of anything in life? Not enjoyment, not possessions. Analyse everything. You will find there is no value except in experience, to teach us something. And in many cases it is our hardships that give us better experience than enjoyment. Many times blows give us better experience than the caresses of nature…Even famine has its place and value…

According to Krishna, we are not new beings just come into existence. Our minds are not new minds… In modern times, we all know that every child brings [with him] all the past, not only of humanity, but of the plant life. There are all the past chapters, this present chapter and there are a whole lot of future chapters before him. Everyone has his path mapped and sketched and planned out for him. And in spite of all this darkness, there cannot be anything uncaused—no event, no circumstance… It is simply our ignorance. The whole infinite chain of causation…is bound one link to another back to nature. The whole universe is bound by that sort of chain. It is the universal [chain of] cause and effect, you receiving one link, one part, I another…And that [part] is our own nature.

Now Shri Krishna says: 'Better die in your own path than attempt the path of another.' This is my path, and I am down here. And you are way up there, and I am always tempted to give up my path thinking I will go there and be with you.

And if I go up, I am neither there nor here. We must not lose sight of this doctrine. It is all [a matter of] growth. Wait and grow, and you attain everything; otherwise there will be [great spiritual danger]. Here is the fundamental secret of teaching religion.

What do you mean by 'saving people' and all believing in the same doctrine? It cannot be. There are the general ideas that can be taught to mankind. The true teacher will be able to find out for you what your own nature is. Maybe you do not know it. It is possible that what you think is your own nature is all wrong. It has not developed to consciousness. The teacher is the person who ought to know… He ought to know by a glance at your face and put you on [your path]. We grope about and struggle here and there and do all sorts of things and make no progress until the time comes when we fall into that life-current and are carried away. The sign is that the moment we are in that stream we will float. Then there is no more struggle. This is to be found out. Then die in that [path] rather than giving it up and taking hold of another.

Instead, we start a religion and make a set of dogmas and betray the goal of mankind and treat everyone [as having] the same nature. No two persons have the same mind or the same body… No two persons have the same religion…

If you want to be religious, enter not the gate of any organized religions. They do a 100 times more evil than good because they stop the growth of each one's individual development. Study everything, but keep your own seat firm. If you take my advice, do not put your neck into the trap. The moment they try to put their noose on you, get your neck out and go somewhere else. [As] the bee culling honey from many flowers remains free, not bound by any flower, be not bound… Enter not the door of any organized religion.

[Religion] is only between you and your God, and no third person must come between you. Think what these organized religions have done! What Napoleon was more terrible than those religious persecutions? . . . If you and I organize, we begin to hate every person. It is better not to love, if loving only means hating others. That is no love. That is hell! If loving your own people means hating everybody else, it is the quintessence of selfishness and brutality, and the effect is that it will make you brutes. Therefore, better die working out your own natural religion than following another's natural religion, however great it may appear to you.

'Beware, Arjuna, lust and anger are the great enemies. These are to be controlled. These cover the knowledge even of those [who are wise]. This fire of lust is unquenchable. Its location is in the sense organs and in the mind. The Self desires nothing.'

'This yoga I taught in ancient times [to Vivaswan; Vivaswan taught it to Manu]… Thus it was that the knowledge descended from one thing to another. But in time this great yoga was destroyed. That is why I am telling it to you again today.'

Then Arjuna asks, 'Why do you speak thus? You are a man born only the other day, and [Vivaswan was born long before you]. What do you mean that you taught him?'

Then Krishna says, 'O Arjuna, you and I have run the cycle of births and deaths many times, but you are not conscious of them all. I am without beginning, birthless, the absolute Lord of all creation. I through my own nature take form. Whenever virtue subsides and wickedness prevails, I come to help mankind. For the salvation of the good, for the destruction of wickedness, for the establishment of spirituality I come from time to time. Whosoever wants to reach me through whatsoever ways, I reach him through that. But know, Arjuna, none can ever swerve from my path.' None ever did. How can we? None swerves from His path.

...All societies are based upon bad generalization. The law can only be formed upon perfect generalization. What is the old saying: Every law has its exception?... If it is a law, it cannot be broken. None can break it. Does the apple break the law of gravitation? The moment a law is broken, no more universe exists. There will come a time when you will break the law, and that moment your consciousness, mind and body will melt away.

There is a man stealing there. Why does he steal? You punish him. Why can you not make room for him and put his energy to work?... You say, 'You are a sinner,' and many will say he has broken the law. All this herd of mankind is forced [into uniformity] and hence all the trouble, sin and weakness... The world is not as bad as you think. It is we fools who have made it evil. We manufacture our own ghosts and demons and then...we cannot get rid of them. We put our hands before our eyes and cry: 'Somebody give us light.' Fools! Take your hands from your eyes! That is all there is to it...We call upon the gods to save us and nobody blames himself. That is the pity of it. Why is there so much evil in society? What is it they say? Flesh and the devil and the woman. Why make these things [up]? Nobody asks you to make them [up]. 'None, O Arjuna, can swerve from my path.' We are fools and our paths are foolish. We have to go through all this Maya. God made the heaven, and man made the hell for himself.

'No action can touch me. I have no desire for the results of action. Whosoever knows me thus knows the secret and is not bound by action. The ancient sages, knowing this secret [could safely engage in action]. Do thou work in the same fashion.'

He who sees in the midst of intense activity, intense calm and in the midst of most intense peace is intensely active [is wise indeed]... This is the question: with every sense and every organ active, have you that tremendous peace [so that] nothing can disturb you? Standing on Market Street, waiting for the car with all the rush...going on around you, are you in meditation—calm and peaceful? In the cave, are you intensely active there with all quiet about you? If you are, you are a yogi, otherwise not.

'[The seers call him wise] whose every attempt is free, without any desire for gain, without any selfishness.' Truth can never come to us as long as we are selfish. We colour everything with our own selves. Things come to us as they are. Not that they are hidden, not at all! *We* hide them. We have the brush. A thing comes, we do not like it and we brush a little and then look at it... We do not want to know. We paint everything with ourselves. In all action, the motive power is selfishness. Everything is hidden by ourselves. We are like the caterpillar which takes the thread out of his own body and of that makes the cocoon, and behold, he is caught. By his own work he imprisons himself. That is what we are doing. The moment I say 'me', the thread makes a turn. 'I and mine', another turn. So it goes...

We cannot remain without action for a moment. Act! But just as when your neighbour asks you, 'Come and help me!', have you exactly the same idea when you are helping yourself. No more. Your body is of no more value than that of John. Don't do anything more for your body than you do for John. That is religion.

'He whose efforts are bereft of all desire and selfishness has burnt all this bondage of action with the fire of knowledge, he is wise.' Reading books cannot do that. The ass can be burdened with the whole library; that does not make him learned at all. What is the use of reading many books? 'Giving up all attachment to work, always satisfied, not hoping for gain, the wise man acts and is beyond action.'

Naked I came out of my mother's womb and naked I return. Helpless I came and helpless I go. Helpless I am now. And we do not know [the goal]. It is terrible for us to think about it. We get such odd ideas! We go to a medium and see if the ghost can help us. Think of the weakness! Ghosts, devils, gods, anybody—come on! And all the priests, all the charlatans! That is just the time they get hold of us, the moment we are weak. Then they bring in all the gods.

I see in my country a man becomes strong, educated, becomes a philosopher and says, 'All this praying and bathing is nonsense...' The man's father dies and his mother dies. That is the most terrible shock a Hindu can have. You will find him bathing in every dirty pool, going into the temple, licking the dust... Help anyone! But we are helpless. There is no help from anyone. That is the truth. There have been more gods than human beings; and yet no help. We die like dogs—no help. Everywhere beastliness, famine, disease, misery, evil! And all are crying for help. But no help. And yet, hoping against hope, we are still screaming for help. Oh, the miserable condition! Oh, the terror of it! Look into your own heart! One half of [the trouble] is not our fault, but the fault of our parents. Born with this weakness, more and more of it was put into our heads. Step by step we go beyond it.

It is a tremendous error to feel helpless. Do not seek help from anyone. We are our own help. If we cannot help ourselves, there is none to help us... 'Thou thyself art thy only friend, thou thyself thy only enemy. There is no other enemy but this self of mine, no other friend but myself.' This is the last and greatest lesson, and Oh, what a time it takes to learn it! We seem to get hold of it and the next moment the old wave comes. The backbone breaks. We weaken and again grasp for that superstition and help. Just think of that huge mass of misery and all caused by this false idea of going to seek help!

Possibly the priest says his routine words and expects something. Sixty thousand people look to the skies and pray and pay the priest. Month after month they still look, still pay and pray... Think of that! Is it not lunacy? What else is it? Who is responsible? You may preach religion, but to excite the minds of undeveloped children...! You will have to suffer for that. In your heart of hearts, what are you? For every weakening thought you have put into anybody's head, you will have to pay with compound interest. The law of karma must have its pound of flesh...

There is only one sin. That is weakness. When I was a boy I read Milton's *Paradise Lost*. The only good man I had any respect for was Satan. The only saint is that soul that never weakens, faces everything and determines to die game.

Stand up and die game!... Do not add one lunacy to another. Do not add your weakness to the evil that is going to come. That is all I have to say to the world. Be strong!... You talk of ghosts and devils. We are the living devils. The sign of life is strength and growth. The sign of death is weakness. Whatever is weak, avoid! It is death. If it is strength, go down into hell and get hold of it! There is salvation only for the brave. None but the brave deserves the fair.' None but the bravest deserves salvation. Whose hell? Whose torture? Whose sin? Whose weakness? Whose death? Whose disease?

You believe in God. If you do, believe in the real God. 'Thou art the man, thou the woman, thou the young man walking in the strength of youth...thou the old man tottering with his stick.' Thou art weakness. Thou art fear. Thou art heaven and thou art hell. Thou art the serpent that would sting. Come thou as fear! Come thou as death! Come thou as misery!...

All weakness, all bondage is imagination. Speak one word to it, it must vanish. Do not weaken! There is no other way out... Stand up and be strong! No fear. No superstition. Face the truth as it is! If death comes—that is the worst of our miseries—let it come! We are determined to die game. That is all the religion I know. I have not attained to it, but I am struggling to do it. I may not, but you may. Go on!

Where one sees another, one hears another so long as there are two, there must be fear, and fear is the mother of all [misery]. Where none sees another, where it is all One, there is none to be miserable, none to be unhappy. [There is only] the One without a second. Therefore be not afraid. Awake, arise and stop not till the goal is reached!

16

CHRIST, THE MESSENGER

Delivered in 1900 at Los Angeles, California

The wave rises on the ocean and there is a hollow. Again another wave rises, perhaps bigger than the former, to fall down again, similarly, again to rise—driving onward. In the march of events, we notice the rise and fall, and we generally look towards the rise, forgetting the fall. But both are necessary and both are great. This is the nature of the universe. Whether in the world of our thoughts, the world of our relations in society, or in our spiritual affairs, the same movement of succession, of rises and falls is going on. Hence great predominances in the march of events, the liberal ideals, are marshaled ahead, to sink down, to digest, as it were, to ruminate over the past—to adjust, to conserve, to gather strength once more for a rise and a bigger rise.

The history of nations also has ever been like that. The great soul, the messenger we are to study this afternoon, came at a period of the history of his race which we may well designate as a great fall. We catch only little glimpses here and there of the stray records that have been kept of his sayings and doings; for verily it has been well said that the doings and sayings of that great soul would fill the world if they had all been written down. And the three years of his ministry were like one compressed, concentrated age, which it has taken 1,900 years to unfold, and who knows how much longer it will yet take! Little men like you and me are simply the recipients of just a little energy. A few minutes, a few hours, a few years at best, are enough to spend it all, to stretch it out, as it were, to its fullest strength and then we are gone forever. But mark this giant that came; centuries and ages pass, yet the energy that he left upon the world is not yet stretched, nor yet expended to its full. It goes on adding new vigour as the ages roll on.

Now what you see in the life of Christ is the life of all the past. The life of every man is, in a manner, the life of the past. It comes to him through heredity, through surroundings, through education, through his own reincarnation—the past of the race. In a manner, the past of the earth, the past of the whole world is there, upon every soul. What are we, in the present, but a result, an effect, in the hands of that infinite past? What are we but floating waveless in the eternal current of events, irresistibly moved forward and onward and incapable of rest? But you and I are only little things, bubbles. There are always some giant waves in the ocean of affairs and in you and me the life of the past race has been embodied only a little. But there are giants who embody, as it were, almost the whole of the past and who stretch out their hands for the future. These are the sign-posts here and there which point to the march of humanity; these are verily gigantic, their shadows covering the earth—they stand undying, eternal! As it has been said by the same messenger, 'No man hath seen God at any time, but through the Son.' And that is true. And where shall we see God, but in the Son? It is true that you and I, and the poorest of us, the meanest even, embody that God, even reflect that God. The vibration of light is everywhere, omnipresent, but we have to strike the light of the lamp before we can see the light. The omnipresent God of the universe cannot be seen until He is reflected by these giant lamps of the earth—the prophets, the man-Gods, the incarnations, the embodiments of God.

We all know that God exists, yet we do not see Him, we do not understand Him. Take one of these great messengers of light, compare his character with the highest ideal of God that you ever formed and you will find that your God falls short of the ideal and that the character of the prophet exceeds your conceptions. You cannot even form a higher ideal of God than what the actually embodied have practically realized and set before us as an example. Is it wrong, therefore, to worship these as God? Is it a sin to fall at the feet of these man-Gods and worship them as the only divine beings in the world? If they are really, actually, higher than all our conceptions of God, what harm is there in worshipping them? Not only is there no harm, but it is the only possible and positive way of worship. However much you may try by struggle, by abstraction, by whatsoever method you like, still so long as you are a man in the world of men, your world is human, your religion is human and your God is human. And that must be so. Who is not practical enough to take up an actually existing thing and give up an idea which is only an abstraction, which he cannot grasp, and is difficult of approach except through a concrete medium? Therefore, these incarnations of God have been worshipped in all ages and in all countries.

We are now going to study a little of the life of Christ, the incarnation of the Jews. When Christ was born, the Jews were in that state which I call a state of fall between two waves; a state of conservatism; a state where the human mind is, as it were, tired for the time being of moving forward and is taking care only of what it has already; a state when the attention is more bent upon particulars, upon details, than upon the great, general and bigger problems of life; a state of stagnation, rather than a towing ahead; a state of suffering more than of doing.

Mark you, I do not blame this state of things. We have no right to criticize it—because had it not been for this fall, the next rise, which was embodied in Jesus of Nazareth would have been impossible. The Pharisees and Sadducees might have been insincere, they might have been doing things which they ought not to have done; they might have been even hypocrites, but whatever they were, these factors were the very cause of which the messenger was the effect. The Pharisees and Sadducees at one end were the very impetus which came out at the other end as the gigantic brain of Jesus of Nazareth.

The attention to forms, to formulas, to the everyday details of religion, to rituals may sometimes be laughed at, but nevertheless, within them is strength. Many times in the rushing forward we lose much strength. As a fact, the fanatic is stronger than the liberal man. Even the fanatic, therefore, has one great virtue: he conserves energy, a tremendous amount of it. As with the individual, so with the race, energy is gathered to be conserved. Hemmed in all around by external enemies, driven to focus in a centre by the Romans, by the Hellenic tendencies in the world of intellect, by waves from Persia, India and Alexandria—hemmed in physically, mentally and morally—there stood the race with an inherent, conservative, tremendous strength, which their descendants have not lost even today. And the race was forced to concentrate and focus all its energies upon Jerusalem and Judaism. But all power when once gathered cannot remain collected; it must expend and expand itself. There is no power on earth which can be kept long confined within a narrow limit. It cannot be kept compressed too long to allow of expansion at a subsequent period.

This concentrated energy amongst the Jewish race found its expression at the next period in the rise of Christianity. The gathered streams collected into a body. Gradually, all the little streams joined together, and became a surging wave on the top of which we find standing out the character of Jesus of Nazareth. Thus, every prophet is a creation of his own times, the creation of the past of his race; he himself is the creator of the future. The cause of today is the effect of the past and the cause for the future. In this position stands the messenger. In him is embodied all that is the best and greatest in his own race, the meaning, the life, for which that race has struggled for ages; he himself is the impetus for the future, not only to his own race, but to unnumbered other races of the world.

We must bear another fact in mind: that my view of the great Prophet of Nazareth would be from the standpoint of the Orient. Many times you forget, also, that the Nazarene himself was an Oriental of Orientals. With all your attempts to paint him with blue eyes and yellow hair, the Nazarene was still an Oriental. All the similes, the imageries, in which the Bible is written—the scenes, the locations, the attitudes, the groups, the poetry and symbol—speak to you of the Orient, of the bright sky, of the heat, of the sun, of the desert, of the thirsty men and animals; of men and women coming with pitchers on their heads to fill them at the wells; of the flocks, of the ploughmen, of the cultivation that is going on around; of the water-mill and wheel, of the mill-pond, of the millstones. All these are to be seen today in Asia.

The voice of Asia has been the voice of religion. The voice of Europe is the voice of politics. Each is great in its own sphere. The voice of Europe is the voice of ancient Greece. To the Greek mind, his immediate society was all in all, beyond that it is Barbarian. None but the Greek has the right to live. Whatever the Greeks do is right and correct; whatever else there exists in the world is neither right nor correct, nor should be allowed to live. It is intensely human in its sympathies, intensely natural, intensely artistic, therefore. The Greek lives entirely in this world. He does not care to dream. Even his poetry is practical. His gods and goddesses are not only human beings, but intensely human, with all human passions and feelings almost the same as with any of us. He loves what is beautiful, but, mind you, it is always external nature: the beauty of the hills, of the snows, of the flowers, the beauty of forms and of figures, the beauty in the human face, and, more often, in the human form—that is what the Greeks liked. And the Greeks being the teachers of all subsequent Europeanism, the voice of Europe is Greek.

There is another type in Asia. Think of that vast, huge continent, whose mountain-tops go beyond the clouds, almost touching the canopy of heaven's blue; a rolling desert of miles upon miles where a drop of water cannot be found, neither will a blade of grass grow; interminable forests and gigantic rivers rushing down into the sea. In the midst of all these surroundings, the oriental love of the beautiful and of the sublime developed itself in another direction. It looked inside and not outside. There is also the thirst for nature, and there is also the same thirst for power; there is also the same thirst for excellence, the same idea of the Greek and Barbarian, but it has extended over a larger circle.

In Asia, even today, birth or colour or language never makes a race. That which makes a race is its religion. We are all Christians, we are all Mohammedans, we are all Hindus, or all Buddhists. No matter if a Buddhist is a Chinaman, or is a man from Persia, they think that they are brothers, because of their professing the same religion. Religion is the tie, unity of humanity. And then again, the Oriental, for the same reason, is a visionary, is a born dreamer. The ripples of the waterfalls, the songs of the birds, the beauties of the sun and moon and the stars and the whole earth are pleasant enough, but they are not sufficient for the oriental mind. He wants to dream a dream beyond. He wants to go beyond the present. The present, as it were, is nothing to him. The Orient has been the cradle of the human race for ages and all the vicissitudes of fortune are there—kingdoms succeeding kingdoms, empires succeeding empires, human power, glory and wealth rolling down there: a Golgotha of power and learning. That is the Orient: a Golgotha of power, of kingdoms, of learning. No wonder, the oriental mind looks with contempt upon the things of this world and naturally wants to see something that changeth not, something which dieth not, something which in the midst of this world of misery and death is eternal, blissful, undying. An oriental prophet never tires of insisting upon these ideals; and, as for prophets, you may also remember that without one exception, all the messengers were Orientals.

We see, therefore, in the life of this area, messenger of life, the first watchword: 'Not this life, but something higher'; and, like the true son of the Orient, he is practical in that. You people of the West are practical in your own department, in military affairs, in managing political circles and other things. Perhaps, the Oriental is not practical in those ways, but he is practical in his own field; he is practical in religion. If one preaches a philosophy, tomorrow there are hundreds who will struggle their best to make it practical in their lives. If a man preaches that standing on one foot would lead one to salvation, he will immediately get 500 to stand on one foot. You may call it ludicrous, but, mark you, beneath that is their philosophy—that intense practicality. In the West, plans of salvation mean intellectual gymnastics—plans which are never worked out, never brought into practical life. In the West, the preacher who talks the best is the greatest preacher.

So, we find Jesus of Nazareth, in the first place, the true son of the Orient, intensely practical. He has no faith in this evanescent world and all its belongings. No need of text-torturing, as is the fashion in the West in modern times, no need of stretching out texts until they will not stretch any more. Texts are not India rubber, and even that has its limits. Now, no making of religion to pander to the sense vanity of the present day! Mark you, let us all be honest. If we cannot follow the ideal, let us confess our weakness, but not degrade it; let not any try to pull it down. One gets sick at heart at the different accounts of the life of the Christ that Western people give. I do not know what he was or what he was not! One would make him a great politician; another, perhaps, would make of him a great military general; another, a great patriotic Jew; and so on. Is there any warrant in the books for all such assumptions? The best commentary on the life of a great teacher is his own life. 'The foxes have holes, the birds of the air have nests, but the Son of man hath not where to lay his head.' That is what Christ says as the only way to salvation; he lays down no other way. Let us confess in sackcloth and ashes that we cannot do that. We still have fondness for 'me and mine'. We want property, money, wealth. Woe unto us! Let us confess and not put to shame that great teacher of humanity! He had no family ties. But do you think that, that man had any physical ideas in him? Do you think that, this mass of light, this God and not-man, came down to earth, to be the brother of animals? And yet, people make him preach all sorts of things. He had no sex ideas! He was a soul! Nothing but a soul—just working for the good of humanity; and that was all his relation to the body. In the soul, there is no sex. The disembodied soul has no relationship to the animal, no relationship to the body. The ideal may be far away beyond us. But never mind, keep to the ideal. Let us confess that it is our ideal, but we cannot approach it yet.

He had no other occupation in life, no other thought except that one, that he was a spirit. He was a disembodied, unfettered, unbound spirit. And not only so, but he, with his marvellous vision, had found that every man and woman, whether Jew or Gentile, whether rich or poor, whether saint or sinner, was the embodiment of the same undying spirit as himself. Therefore, the one work his whole life showed was to call upon them to realize their own spiritual nature. Give up, he says, these superstitious dreams that you are low and that you are poor. Think not that you are trampled upon and tyrannized over as if you were slaves, for within you is something that can never be tyrannized over, never be trampled upon, never be troubled, never be killed. You are all Sons of God, immortal spirit. 'Know', he declared, 'the Kingdom of Heaven is within you.' 'I and my Father are one.' Dare you stand up and say, not only that 'I am the Son of God', but I shall also find in my heart of hearts that 'I and my Father are one'? That was what Jesus of Nazareth said. He never talks of this world and of this life. He has nothing to do with it, except that he wants to get hold of the world as it is, give it a push and drive it forward and onward until the whole world has reached to the effulgent light of God, until everyone has realized his spiritual nature, until death is vanished and misery banished.

We have read the different stories that have been written about him; we know the scholars and their writings and the higher criticism; and we know all that has been done by study. We are not here to discuss how much of the New Testament is true, we are not here to discuss how much of that life is historical. It does not matter at all whether the New Testament was written within 500 years of his birth, nor does it matter even how much of that life is true. But there is something behind it, something we want to imitate. To tell a lie, you have to imitate a truth, and that truth is a fact. You cannot imitate that which never existed. You cannot imitate that which you never perceived. But there must have been a nucleus, a tremendous power that came down, a marvellous manifestation of spiritual power—and of that we are speaking. It stands there. Therefore, we are not afraid of all the criticisms of the scholars. If I, as an Oriental, have to worship Jesus of Nazareth, there is only one way left to me, that is, to worship him as God and nothing else. Have we no right to worship him in that way, do you mean to say? If we bring him down to our own level and simply pay him a little respect as a great man, why should we worship at all? Our scriptures say, 'These great children of light, who manifest the light themselves, who are light themselves, they being worshipped become, as it were, one with us and we become one with them.'

For, you see, in three ways man perceives God. At first, the undeveloped intellect of the uneducated man sees God as far away, up in the heavens somewhere, sitting on a throne as a great judge. He looks upon Him as a fire, as a terror. Now, that is good, for there is nothing bad in it. You must remember that humanity travels not from error to truth, but from truth to truth; it may be, if you like it better, from lower truth to higher truth, but never from error to truth. Suppose you start from here and travel towards the sun in a straight line. From here the sun looks only small in size. Suppose you go forward a million miles, the sun will be much bigger. At every stage the sun will become bigger and bigger. Suppose 20,000 photographs had been taken of the same sun, from different standpoints; these 20,000 photographs will all certainly differ from one another. But can you deny that each is a photograph of the same sun? So all forms of religion, high or low, are just different stages toward that eternal state of light, which is God Himself. Some embody a lower view, some a higher, and that is all the difference. Therefore, the religions of the unthinking masses all over the world must be, and have always been, of a God who is outside of the universe, who lives in heaven, who governs from that place, who is a punisher of the bad and a rewarder of the good and so on. As man advanced spiritually, he began to feel that God was omnipresent, that He must be in him, that He must be everywhere, that He was not a distant God, but dearly the soul of all souls. As my soul moves my body, even so is God the mover of my soul. Soul within soul. And a few individuals who had developed enough and were pure enough, went still further, and at last found God. As the New Testament says, 'Blessed are the pure in heart, for they shall see God.' And they found at last that they and the Father were one.

You find that all these three stages are taught by the great teacher in the New Testament. Note the common prayer he taught: 'Our Father which art in Heaven, hallowed be Thy name,' and so on—a simple prayer, a child's prayer. Mark you, it is the 'common prayer' because it is intended for the uneducated masses. To a higher circle, to those who had advanced a little more, he gave a more elevated teaching: 'I am in my Father, and ye in me, and I in you.' Do you remember that? And then, when the Jews asked him who he was, he declared that he and his Father were one, and the Jews thought that that was blasphemy. What did he mean by that? This has been also told by your old prophets, 'Ye are gods and all of you are children of the Most High.' Mark the same three stages. You will find that it is easier for you to begin with the first and end with the last.

The messenger came to show the path that the spirit is not in forms, that it is not through all sorts of vexations and knotty problems of philosophy that you know the spirit. Better that you had no learning, better that you never read a book in your life. These are not at all necessary for salvation—neither wealth, nor position nor power, not even learning, but what is necessary is that one thing, purity. 'Blessed are the pure in heart,' for the spirit in its own nature is pure. How can it be otherwise? It is of God, it has come from God. In the language of the Bible, 'It is the breath of God.' In the language of the Koran, 'It is the soul of God.' Do you mean to say that the spirit of God can ever be impure? But, alas, it has been, as it were, covered over with the dust and dirt of ages, through our own actions, good and evil. Various works which were not correct, which were not true, have covered the same spirit with the dust and dirt of the ignorance of ages. It is only necessary to clear away the dust and dirt, and then the spirit shines immediately. 'Blessed are the pure in heart, for they shall see God.' 'The kingdom of Heaven is within you.' Where goest thou to seek for the kingdom of God, asks Jesus of Nazareth, when it is there, within you? Cleanse the spirit and it is there. It is already yours. How can you get what is not yours? It is yours by right. You are the heirs of immortality, sons of the Eternal Father.

This is the great lesson of the messenger, and another which is the basis of all religions, is renunciation. How can you make the spirit pure? By renunciation. A rich young man asked Jesus, 'Good master, what shall I do that I may inherit eternal life?' And Jesus said unto him, 'One thing thou lackest; go thy way, sell whatsoever thou hast and give to the poor, and thou shalt have treasures in heaven: and come, take up thy cross and follow Me.' And he was sad at that saying and went away grieved, for he had great possessions. We are all more or less like that. The voice is ringing in our ears day and night. In the midst of our pleasures and joys, in the midst of worldly things, we think that we have forgotten everything else. Then comes a moment's pause and the voice rings in our ears, 'Give up all that thou hast and follow Me.' 'Whosoever will save his life shall lose it; and whosoever shall lose his life for My sake shall find it.' For whoever gives up this life for His sake, finds the life immortal. In the midst of all our weakness there is a moment of pause and the voice rings: 'Give up all that thou hast; give it to the poor and follow me.' This is the one ideal he preaches, and this has been the ideal preached by all the great prophets of the world: renunciation. What is meant by renunciation? That there is only one ideal in morality: unselfishness. Be selfless. The ideal is perfect unselfishness. When a man is struck on the right cheek, he turns the left also. When a man's coat is carried off, he gives away his cloak also.

We should work in the best way we can, without dragging the ideal down. Here is the ideal. When a man has no more self in him, no possession, nothing to call 'me' or 'mine', has given himself up entirely, destroyed himself as it were—in that man is God Himself; for in him self-will is gone, crushed out, annihilated. That is the ideal man. We cannot reach that state yet; yet, let us worship the ideal, and slowly struggle to reach the ideal, though maybe with faltering steps. It may be tomorrow, or it may be a thousand years hence, but that ideal has to be reached. For it is not only the end, but also the means. To be unselfish, perfectly selfless, is salvation itself, for the man within dies and God alone remains.

One more point. All the teachers of humanity are unselfish. Suppose Jesus of Nazareth was teaching and a man came and told him, 'What you teach is beautiful. I believe that it is the way to perfection, and I am ready to follow it, but I do not care to worship you as the only begotten Son of God.' What would be the answer of Jesus of Nazareth? 'Very well, brother, follow the ideal and advance in your own way. I do not care whether you give me the credit for the teaching or not. I am not a shopkeeper. I do not trade in religion. I only teach truth and truth is nobody's property. Nobody can patent truth. Truth is God Himself. Go forward.' But what the disciples say nowadays is: 'No matter whether you practise the teachings or not, do you give credit to the Man? If you credit the master, you will be saved; if not, there is no salvation for you.' And thus the whole teaching of the master is degenerated, and all the struggle and fight is for the personality of the man. They do not know that in imposing that difference, they are, in a manner, bringing shame to the very man they want to honour—the very man that would have shrunk with shame from such an idea. What did he care if there was one man in the world that remembered him or not? He had to deliver his message and he gave it. And if he had 20,000 lives, he would give them all up for the poorest man in the world. If he had to be tortured millions of times for a million despised Samaritans, and if for each one of them the sacrifice of his own life would be the only condition of salvation, he would have given his life. And all this without wishing to have his name known even to a single person. Quiet, unknown, silent, would he work, just as the Lord works. Now, what would the disciple say? He will tell you that you may be a perfect man, perfectly unselfish, but unless you give the credit to our teacher, to our saint, it is of no avail. Why? What is the origin of this superstition, this ignorance? The disciple thinks that the Lord can manifest Himself only once. There lies the whole mistake. God manifests Himself to you in man. But throughout nature, what happens once must have happened before and must happen in future. There is nothing in nature which is not bound by law. That means that whatever happens once must go on and must have been going on.

In India they have the same idea of the incarnations of God. One of their great incarnations, Krishna, whose grand sermon, the Bhagavad Gita, some of you might have read, says, 'Though I am unborn, of changeless nature, and Lord of beings, yet subjugating My *prakriti*, I come into being by My own Maya. Whenever virtue subsides and immorality prevails, then I body Myself forth. For the protection of the good, for the destruction of the wicked and for the establishment of dharma, I come into being, in every age.' Whenever the world goes down, the Lord comes to help it forward; and so He does from time to time and place to place. In another passage, He speaks to this effect: Wherever thou findest a great soul of immense power and purity struggling to raise humanity, know that he is born of My splendour, that I am there working through him.

Let us, therefore, find God not only in Jesus of Nazareth, but in all the great ones that have preceded him, in all that came after him and all that are yet to come. Our worship is unbounded and free. They are all manifestations of the same infinite god. They are all pure and unselfish; they struggled and gave up their lives for us, poor human beings. They each and all suffer vicarious atonement for every one of us, and also for all that are to come hereafter.

In a sense you are all prophets; every one of you is a prophet, bearing the burden of the world on your own shoulders. Have you ever seen a man, have you ever seen a woman, who is not quietly, patiently, bearing his or her little burden of life? The great prophets were giants—they bore a gigantic world on their shoulders. Compared with them we are pigmies, no doubt, yet we are doing the same task; in our little circles, in our little homes, we are bearing our little crosses. There is no one so evil, no one so worthless, but he has to bear his own cross. But with all our mistakes, with all our evil thoughts and evil deeds, there is a bright spot somewhere, there is still somewhere the golden thread through which we are always in touch with the divine. For, know for certain, that the moment the touch of the divine is lost there would be annihilation. And because none can be annihilated, there is always somewhere in our heart of hearts, however low and degraded we may be, a little circle of light which is in constant touch with the divine.

Our salutations go to all the past prophets whose teachings and lives we have inherited, whatever might have been their race, clime, or creed! Our salutations go to all those Godlike men and women who are working to help humanity, whatever be their birth, colour, or race! Our salutations to those who are coming in the future—living Gods—to work unselfishly for our descendants.

17

KRISHNA

Delivered on 1 April 1900, in California

Almost the same circumstances which gave birth to Buddhism in India surrounded the rise of Krishna. Not only this, the events of that day we find happening in our own times.

There is a certain ideal. At the same time, there must always be a large majority of the human race who cannot come up to the ideal, not even intellectually... The strong ones carry it out and many times have no sympathy for the weak. The weak to the strong are only beggars. The strong ones march ahead... Of course, we see at once that the highest position to take is to be sympathetic and helpful to those who are weak. But then, in many cases the philosopher bars the way to our being sympathetic. If we go by the theory that the whole of this infinite life has to be determined by the few years' existence here and now...then it is very hopeless for us...and we have no time to look back upon those who are weak. But if these are not the conditions—if the world is only one of the many schools through which we have to pass, if the eternal life is to be moulded and fashioned and guided by the eternal law, and eternal law, eternal chances await everyone—then we need not be in a hurry. We have time to sympathize, to look around, stretch out a helping hand to the weak and bring them up.

With Buddhism we have two words in Sanskrit: one is

translated religion, the other, a sect. It is the most curious fact that the disciples and descendants of Krishna have no name for their religion [although] foreigners call it Hinduism or Brahmanism. There is one religion and there are many sects. The moment you give it a name, individualize it and separate it from the rest, it is a sect, no more a religion. A sect [proclaims] its own truth and declares that there is no truth anywhere else. Religion believes that there has been, and still is, one religion in the world. There never were two religions. It is the same religion [presenting] different aspects in different places. The task is to conceive the proper understanding of the goal and scope of humanity.

This was the great work of Krishna: to clear our eyes and make us look with broader vision upon humanity in its march upward and onward. His was the first heart that was large enough to see truth in all, his the first lips that uttered beautiful words for each and all.

This Krishna preceded Buddha by some thousand years... A great many people do not believe that he ever existed. Some believe that [the worship of Krishna grew out of] the old sun worship. There seem to be several Krishnas: one was mentioned in the Upanishads, another was king, another a general. All have been lumped into one Krishna. It does not matter much. The fact is [that] some individual comes, who is unique in spirituality. Then all sorts of legends are invented around him. But, all the Bibles and stories which come to be cast upon this one person have to be recast in [the mould of] his character. All the stories of the New Testament have to be modelled upon the accepted life [and] character of Christ. In all of the Indian stories about Buddha, the one central note of that whole life is kept up—sacrifice for others...

In Krishna we find...two ideas [standing] supreme in his

message: The first is the harmony of different ideas; the second is non-attachment. A man can attain perfection, the highest goal, sitting on a throne, commanding armies, working out big plans for nations. In fact, Krishna's great sermon was preached on the battlefield.

Krishna saw plainly through the vanity of all the mummeries, mockeries and ceremonials of the old priests; and yet he saw some good in them.

If you are a strong man, very good! But do not curse others who are not strong enough for you… Everyone says, 'Woe unto you people!!' Who says, 'Woe unto me that I cannot help you?' The people are doing all right to the best of their ability and means and knowledge. Woe unto me that I cannot lift them to where I am!

So the ceremonials, worship of gods, myths are all right, Krishna says…Why? Because they all lead to the same goal. Ceremonies, books, and forms—all these are links in the chain. Get hold! That is the one thing. If you are sincere and have really got hold of one link, do not let go; the rest is bound to come. [But people] do not get hold. They spend the time quarrelling and determining what they should get hold of, and do not get hold of anything,,. We are always after truth, but never want to get it. We simply want the pleasure to go about and ask. We have a lot of energy and spend it that way. That is why Krishna says: get hold of any one of these chains that are stretched out from the common centre. No one step is greater than another… Blame no view of religion so far as it is sincere. Hold on to one of these links and it will pull you to the centre. Your heart itself will teach all the rest. The teacher within will teach all the creeds, all the philosophies…

Krishna talks of himself as God, as Christ does. He sees the Deity in himself. And he says, 'None can go a day out of my path. All have to come to me. Whosoever wants to worship in whatsoever form, I give him faith in that form, and through that I meet him…' His heart is all for the masses.

Independent, Krishna stands out. The very boldness of it frightens us. We depend upon everything…upon a few good words, upon circumstances. When the soul wants to depend upon nothing, not even upon life, that is the height of philosophy, the height of manhood. Worship leads to the same goal. Krishna lays great stress upon worship. Worship God!

Various sorts of worship we see in this world. The sick man is very worshipful to God… There is the man who loses his fortune; he also prays very much, to get money. The highest worship is that of the man who loves God for God's sake. [The question may be asked:] 'Why should there be so much sorrow if there is a God?' The worshipper replies, '…There is misery in the world, [but] because of that I do not cease to love God. I do not worship Him to take away my [misery]. I love Him because He is love itself.' The other [types of worship] are lower-grade, but Krishna has no condemnation for anything. It is better to do something than to stand still. The man who begins to worship God will grow by degrees and begin to love God for love's sake…

How to attain purity living this life? Shall we all go to the forest caves? What good would it do? If the mind is not under control, it is no use living in a cave because the same mind will bring all disturbances there. We will find 20 devils in the cave because all the devils are in the mind. If the mind is under control, we can have the cave anywhere, wherever we are.

It is our own mental attitude which makes the world what it is for us. Our thoughts make things beautiful, our thoughts make things ugly. The whole world is in our own minds. Learn to see things in the proper light. First, believe in this world—that there is meaning behind everything. Everything in the world is good, is holy and beautiful. If you see something evil, think that you are not understanding it in the right light. Throw the burden on yourselves!... Whenever we are tempted to say that the world is going to the dogs, we ought to analyse ourselves, and we shall find that we have lost the faculty of seeing things as they are.

Work day and night! 'Behold, I am the Lord of the universe. I have no duty. Every duty is bondage. But I work for work's sake. If I ceased to work for a minute, [there would be chaos].' So do thou work, without any idea of duty...

This world is a play. You are His playmates. Go on and work, without any sorrow, without any misery. See His play in the slums, in the saloons! Work to lift people! Not that they are vile or degraded; Krishna does not say that.

Do you know why so little good work is done? My lady goes to the slum... She gives a few ducats and says, 'My poor men, take that and be happy!'... Or my fine woman, walking through the street, sees a poor fellow and throws him five cents. Think of the blasphemy of it! Blessed are we that the Lord has given us his teaching in your own Testament. Jesus says, 'Inasmuch as ye have done it unto the least of these my brethren, ye have done it unto me.' It is blasphemy to think that you can help anyone. First root out this idea of helping and then go to worship. God's children are your master's children. [And children are but different forms of the father.] You are His servant... Serve the living God! God comes to you in the blind, in the halt, in the poor, in the weak, in the diabolical. What a glorious chance for you to worship! The moment you think you are 'helping', you undo the whole thing and degrade yourself. Knowing this, work. 'What follows?' you say. You do not get that heartbreak, that awful misery... Then work is no more slavery. It becomes a play, and joy itself... Work! Be unattached! That is the whole secret. If you get attached, you become miserable...

With everything we do in life, we identify ourselves. Here is a man who says harsh words to me. I feel anger coming on me. In a few seconds, anger and I are one, and then comes misery. Attach yourselves to the Lord and to nothing else, because everything else is unreal. Attachment to the unreal will bring misery. There is only one existence that is real, only one life in which there is neither object nor [subject]...

But unattached love will not hurt you. Do anything— marry, have children... Do anything you like—nothing will hurt you. Do nothing with the idea of 'mine'. Duty for duty's sake; work for work's sake. What is that to you? You stand aside.

When we come to that non-attachment, then we can understand the marvellous mystery of the universe; how it is intense activity and vibration, and at the same time most intense peace and calm; how it is work every moment and rest every moment. That is the mystery of the universe—the impersonal and personal in one, the infinite and finite in one. Then we shall find the secret. 'He who finds in the midst of intense activity the greatest rest and in the midst of the greatest rest intense activity, he has become a yogi.' He alone is a real worker, none else. We do a little work and break ourselves. Why? We become attached to that work. If we do not become attached, side by side with it we have infinite rest...

How hard it is to arrive at this sort of non-attachment! Therefore Krishna shows us the lower ways and methods. The easiest way for everyone is to do [his or her] work and not take the results. It is our desire that binds us. If we take the results of actions, whether good or evil, we will have to bear them. But if we work not for ourselves, but all for the glory of the

Lord, the results will take care of themselves. 'To work you have the right, but not to the fruits thereof.' The soldier works for no results. He does his duty. If defeat comes, it belongs to the general, not to the soldier. We do our duty for love's sake—love for the general, love for the Lord...

If you are strong, take up the Vedanta philosophy and be independent. If you cannot do that, worship God; if not, worship some image. If you lack strength even to do that, do some good works without the idea of gain. Offer everything you have unto the service of the Lord. Fight on! 'Leaves and water and one flower—whosoever lays anything on my altar, I receive it with equal delights.' If you cannot do anything, not a single good work, then take refuge [in the Lord]. 'The Lord resides within the heart of the being, making them turn upon His wheel. Do thou with all thy soul and heart take refuge in Him...

These are some of the general ideas that Krishna preached on this idea of love [in the Gita]. There are [in] other great books, sermons on love—as with Buddha, as with Jesus...

A few words about the life of Krishna. There is a great deal of similarity between the lives of Jesus and Krishna. A discussion is going on as to which borrowed of the other. There was the tyrannical king in both places. Both were born in a manger. The parents were bound in both cases. Both were saved by angels. In both cases all the boys born in that year were killed. The childhood is the same... Again, in the end, both were killed. Krishna was killed by accident; he took the man who killed him to heaven. Christ was killed, and blessed the robber and took him to heaven.

There are a great many similarities between the New Testament and the Gita. The human thought goes the same way...I will find you the answer in the words of Krishna himself: 'Whenever virtue subsides and irreligion prevails, I come down. Again and again I come. Therefore, whenever thou seest a great soul struggling to uplift mankind, know that I am come and worship…'

At the same time, if he comes as Jesus or as Buddha, why is there so much schism? The preachings must be followed! A Hindu devotee would say: It is God himself who became Christ and Krishna and Buddha and all these [great teachers]. A Hindu philosopher would say: these are the great souls; they are already free. And though free, they refuse to accept their liberation while the whole world is suffering. They come again and again, take a human embodiment and help mankind. They know from their childhood what they are and what they come for… They do not come through bondage like we do… They come out of their own free will, and cannot help having tremendous spiritual power. We cannot resist it. The vast mass of mankind is dragged into the whirlpool of spirituality and the vibration goes on and on because one of these [great souls] gives a push. So it continues until all mankind is liberated and the play of this planet is finished.

Glory unto the great souls whose lives we have been studying! They are the living gods of the world. They are the persons whom we ought to worship. If He comes to me, I can only recognize Him if He takes a human form. He is everywhere, but do we see Him? We can only see Him if He takes the limitation of man… If men and…animals are manifestations of God, these teachers of mankind are leaders, are gurus. Therefore, salutations unto you, whose footstool is worshipped by angels! Salutations unto you leaders of the human race! Salutations unto you great teachers! You leaders have our salutations forever and ever!

18

MOHAMMED

Delivered on 25 March 1900, in San Francisco Bay Area

The ancient message of Krishna is one harmonizing three—Buddha's, Christ's and Mohammed's. Each of the three started an idea and carried it to its extreme. Krishna antedates all the other prophets. [Yet, we might say,] Krishna takes the old ideas and synthesizes them, [although] his is the most ancient message. His message was for the time being submerged by the advance wave of Buddhism. Today it is the message peculiar to India. If you will have it so, this afternoon I will take Mohammed and bring out the particular work of the great Arabian prophet...

Mohammed [as] a young man...did not [seem to] care much for religion. He was inclined to make money. He was considered a nice young man and very handsome. There was a rich widow. She fell in love with this young man and they married. When Mohammed had become emperor over the larger part of the world, the Roman and Persian empires were all under his feet and he had a number of wives. When one day he was asked which wife he liked best, he pointed to his first wife: 'Because she believed [in] me first.' Women have faith... Gain independence, gain everything, but do not lose that characteristic of women!...

Mohammed's heart was sick at the sin, idolatry and mock worship, superstitions and human sacrifices and so on. The

Jews were degraded by the Christians. On the other hand, the Christians were worse degraded than his own countrymen.

We are always in a hurry. [But] if any great work is to be done, there must be great preparation... After much praying, day and night, Mohammed began to have dreams and visions. Gabriel appeared to him in a dream and told him that he was the messenger of truth. He told him that the message of Jesus, of Moses, and all the prophets would be lost and asked him to go and preach. Seeing the Christians preaching politics in the name of Jesus, seeing the Persians preaching dualism, Mohammed said: 'Our God is one God. He is the Lord of all that exists. There is no comparison between Him and any other.'

God is God. There is no philosophy, no complicated code of ethics. 'Our God is one without a second, and Mohammed is the prophet.' ...Mohammed began to preach it in the streets of Mecca... They began to persecute him, and he fled into the city of [Medina]. He began to fight and the whole race became united. [Mohammedanism] deluged the world in the name of the Lord. The tremendous conquering power! ...

You...people have very hard ideas and are so superstitious and prejudiced! These messengers must have come from God, else how could they have been so great? You look at every defect. Each one of us has his defects. Who hasn't? I can point out many defects in the Jews. The wicked are always looking for defects... Flies come and seek for the [ulcer], and bees come only for the honey in the flower. Do not follow the way of the fly, but that of the bee...

Mohammed married quite a number of wives afterwards. Great men may marry two hundred wives each. 'Giants' like you, I would not allow to marry one wife. The characters of the great souls are mysterious, their methods past our finding out. We must not judge them. Christ may judge Mohammed.

Who are you and I? Little babies. What do we understand of these great souls?...

[Mohammedanism] came as a message for the masses... The first message was equality... There is one religion—love. No more question of race, colour, [or] anything else. Join it! That practical quality carried the day... The great message was perfectly simple. Believe in one God, the creator of heaven and earth. All was created out of nothing by Him. Ask no questions...

Their temples are like Protestant churches...no music, no paintings, no pictures. A pulpit in the corner, on that lies the Koran. The people all stand in line. No priest, no person, no bishop...The man who prays must stand at the side of the audience. Some parts are beautiful...

These old people were all messengers of God. I fall down and worship them; I take the dust of their feet. But they are dead!... And we are alive. We must go ahead!... Religion is not an imitation of Jesus or Mohammed. Even if an imitation is good, it is never genuine. Be not an imitation of Jesus, but be Jesus, you are quite as great as Jesus, Buddha, or anybody else. If we are not...we must struggle and be. I would not be exactly like Jesus. It is unnecessary that I should be born a Jew...

The greatest religion is to be true to your own nature. Have faith in yourselves! If you do not exist, how can God exist, or anybody else? Wherever you are, it is this mind that perceives even the infinite. I see God, therefore He exists. If I cannot think of God, He does not exist [for me]. This is the grand march of our human progress.

These [great souls] are signposts on the way. That is all they are. They say, 'Onward, brothers!' We cling to them; we never want to move. We do not want to think; we want others to think for us. The messengers fulfil their mission. They ask to be up and doing. A 100 years later we cling to the message and go to sleep.

Talking about faith and belief and doctrine is easy, but it is so difficult to build character and to stem the tide of the senses. We succumb. We become hypocrites...

[Religion] is not a doctrine, [not] a rule. It is a process. That is all. [Doctrines and rules] are all for exercise. By that exercise we get strong and at last break the bonds and become free. Doctrine is of no use except for gymnastics... Through exercise the soul becomes perfect. That exercise is stopped when you say, 'I believe...'

'Whenever virtue subsides and immorality abounds, I take human form. In every age I come for the salvation of the good, for the destruction of the wicked, for the establishment of spirituality.'

[Such] are the great messengers of light. They are our great teachers, our elder brothers. But we must go our own way!

19

ON LORD BUDDHA

Delivered in Detroit

In every religion, we find one type of self-devotion particularly developed. The type of working without a motive is most highly developed in Buddhism. Do not mistake Buddhism and Brahminism. In this country, you are very apt to do so. Buddhism is one of our sects. It was founded by a great man called Gautama, who became disgusted at the eternal metaphysical discussions of his day, the cumbrous rituals and more especially with the caste system. Some people say that we are born to a certain state and therefore we are superior to others who are not thus born. He was also against the tremendous priestcraft. He preached a religion in which there was no motive power, and was perfectly agnostic about metaphysics or theories about God. He was often asked if there was a God, and he answered, he did not know. When asked about right conduct, he would reply, 'Do good and be good.'

There came five Brahmins, who asked him to settle their discussion. One said, 'Sir, my book says that God is such and such, and that this is the way to come to God.'

Another said, 'That is wrong, for my book says such and such, and this is the way to come to God' and so did the others.

He listened calmly to all of them and then asked them one by one, 'Does any one of your books say that God becomes angry, that He ever injures anyone, that He is impure?'

'No, Sir, they all teach that God is pure and good.'

'Then, my friends, why do you not become pure and good first so that you may know what God is?'

Of course I do not endorse all his philosophy. I want a good deal of metaphysics, for myself. I entirely differ in many respects, but because I differ, is that any reason why I should not see the beauty of the man? He was the only man who was bereft of all motive power. There were other great men who all said they were the incarnations of God Himself, and that those who would believe in them would go to heaven. But what did Buddha say with his dying breath? 'None can help you; help yourself; work out your own salvation.' He said about himself, 'Buddha is the name of infinite knowledge, infinite as the sky; I, Gautama, have reached that state; you will all reach that too if you struggle for it.' Bereft of all motive power, he did not want to go to heaven, did not want money; he gave up his throne and everything else and went about begging his bread through the streets of India, preaching for the good of men and animals with a heart as wide as the ocean.

He was the only man who was ever ready to give up his life for animals to stop a sacrifice. He once said to a king, 'If the sacrifice of a lamb helps you to go to heaven, sacrificing a man will help you better; so sacrifice me.' The king was astonished. And yet this man was without any motive power. He stands as the perfection of the active type, and the very height to which he attained shows that through the power of work we can also attain to the highest spirituality.

To many the path becomes easier if they believe in God. But the life of Buddha shows that even a man who does not believe in God, has no metaphysics, belongs to no sect and does not go to any church, or temple and is a confessed materialist, even he can attain to the highest. We have no right to judge him.

I wish I had one infinitesimal part of Buddha's heart. Buddha may or may not have believed in God; that does not matter to me. He reached the same state of perfection to which others come by bhakti—love of God—yoga, or jnana. Perfection does not come from belief or faith. Talk does not count for anything. Parrots can do that. Perfection comes through the disinterested performance of action.

20

BUDDHA'S MESSAGE TO THE WORLD

Delivered on 18 March 1900, in San Francisco

Buddhism is historically the most important religion—historically, not philosophically—because it was the most tremendous religious movement that the world ever saw, the most gigantic spiritual wave ever to burst upon human society. There is no civilization on which its effect has not been felt in some way or the other.

The followers of Buddha were most enthusiastic and very missionary in spirit. They were the first among the adherents of various religions not to remain content with the limited sphere of their Mother Church. They spread far and wide. They travelled east and west, north and south. They reached into darkest Tibet; they went into Persia, Asia Minor; they went into Russia, Poland and many other countries of the Western world. They went into China, Korea, Japan; they went into Burma, Siam, the East Indies and beyond. When Alexander the Great, through his military conquests, brought the Mediterranean world in contact with India, the wisdom of India at once found a channel through which to spread over vast portions of Asia and Europe. Buddhist priests went out teaching among the different nations; and as they taught, superstition and priestcraft began to vanish like mist before the sun.

To understand this movement properly you should know

what conditions prevailed in India at the time Buddha came, just as to understand Christianity you have to grasp the state of Jewish society at the time of Christ. It is necessary that you have an idea of Indian society 600 years before the birth of Christ, by which time Indian civilization had already completed its growth.

When you study the civilization of India, you find that it has died and revived several times; this is its peculiarity. Most races rise once and then decline forever. There are two kinds of people; those who grow continually and those whose growth comes to an end. The peaceful nations, India and China, fall down, yet rise again, but the others, once they go down, do not come up—they die. Blessed are the peacemakers, for they shall enjoy the earth.

At the time Buddha was born, India was in need of a great spiritual leader, a prophet. There was already a most powerful body of priests. You will understand the situation better if you remember the history of the Jews—how they had two types of religious leaders, priests and prophets, the priests keeping the people in ignorance and grinding superstitions into their minds. The methods of worship the priests prescribed were only a means by which they could dominate the people. All through the Old Testament, you find the prophets challenging the superstitions of the priests. The outcome of this fight was the triumph of the prophets and the defeat of the priests.

Priests believe that there is a God, but that this God can be approached and known only through them. People can enter the Holy of Holies only with the permission of the priests. You must pay them, worship them, place everything in their hands. Throughout the history of the world, this priestly tendency has cropped up again and again—this tremendous thirst for power, this tiger-like thirst, seems a part of human nature. The priests dominate you, lay down a thousand rules for you. They describe simple truths in roundabout ways. They tell you stories to support their own superior position. If you want to thrive in this life or go to heaven after death, you have to pass through their hands. You have to perform all kinds of ceremonies and rituals. All this has made life so complicated and has so confused the brain that if I give you plain words, you will go home unsatisfied. You have become thoroughly befuddled. The less you understand, the better you feel! The prophets have been giving warnings against the priests and their superstitions and machinations, but the vast mass of people have not yet learnt to heed to these warnings—education is yet to come to them.

Men must have education. They speak of democracy, of the equality of all men, these days. But how will a man know he is equal with all? He must have a strong brain, a clear mind free of nonsensical ideas; he must pierce through the mass of superstitions encrusting his mind to the pure truth that is in his inmost Self. Then he will know that all perfections, all powers are already within himself, that these have not been given to him by others. When he realizes this, he becomes free that moment, he achieves equality. He also realizes that everyone else is equally as perfect as he, and he does not have to exercise any power, physical, mental or moral, over his brother men. He abandons the idea that there was ever any man who was lower than himself. Then he can talk of equality; not until then.

Now, as I was telling you, among the Jews there was a continuous struggle between the priests and the prophets; and the priests sought to monopolize power and knowledge, till they themselves began to lose them and the chains they had put on the feet of the people were on their own feet. The masters always become slaves before long. The culmination of the struggle was the victory of Jesus of Nazareth. This triumph is the history of

Christianity. Christ at last succeeded in overthrowing the mass of witchcraft. This great prophet killed the dragon of priestly selfishness, rescued from its clutches the jewel of truth and gave it to all the world, so that whosoever desired to possess it would have absolute freedom to do so, and would not have to wait on the pleasure of any priest or priests.

The Jews were never a very philosophical race—they had not the subtlety of the Indian brain, nor did they have the Indian's psychic power. The priests in India, the Brahmins possessed great intellectual and psychic powers. It was they who began the spiritual development of India and they accomplished wonderful things. But the time came when the free spirit of development that had at first actuated the Brahmins disappeared. They began to arrogate powers and privileges to themselves. If a Brahmin killed a man, he would not be punished. The Brahmin, by his very birth, is the lord of the universe! Even the most wicked Brahmin must be worshipped!

But while the priests were flourishing, there existed also the poet-prophets called sannyasins. All Hindus, whatever their castes may be, must, for the sake of attaining spirituality, give up their work and prepare for death. No more is the world to be of any interest to them. They must go out and become sannyasins. The sannyasins have nothing to do with the 2,000 ceremonies that the priests have invented: Pronounce certain words—10 syllables, 20 syllables and so on—all these things are nonsense.

So these poet-prophets of ancient India repudiated the ways of the priest and declared the pure truth. They tried to break the power of the priests, and they succeeded a little. But in two generations, their disciples went back to the superstitious, roundabout ways of the priests—became priests themselves: 'You can get truth only through us!' Truth became crystallized again, and again prophets came to break the encrustations and free the truth, and so it went on. Yes, there must be all the time the man, the prophet, or else humanity will die.

You wonder why there have to be all these roundabout methods of the priests. Why can you not come directly to the truth? Are you ashamed of God's truth that you have to hide it behind all kinds of intricate ceremonies and formulas? Are you ashamed of God that you cannot confess His truth before the world? Do you call that being religious and spiritual? The priests are the only people fit for the truth! The masses are not fit for it! It must be diluted! Water it down a little!

Take the Sermon on the Mount and the Git—they are simplicity itself. Even the streetwalker can understand them. How grand! In them you find the truth clearly and simply revealed. But no, the priests would not accept that truth can be found so directly. They speak of 2,000 heavens and 2,000 hells. If people follow their prescriptions, they will go to heaven! If they do not obey the rules, they will go to hell!

But the people shall learn the truth. Some are afraid that if the full truth is given to all, it will hurt them. They should not be given the unqualified truth—so they say. But the world is not much better off by compromising truth. What worse can it be than it is already? Bring truth out! If it is real, it will do good. When people protest and propose other methods, they only make apologies for witchcraft.

India was full of it in Buddha's day. There were the masses of people and they were debarred from all knowledge. If just a word of the vedas entered the ears of a man, terrible punishment was visited upon him. The priests had made a secret of the vedas—the vedas that contained the spiritual truths discovered by the ancient Hindus!

At last one man could bear it no more. He had the brain,

the power, and the heart—a heart as infinite as the broad sky. He felt how the masses were being led by the priests and how the priests were glorying in their power, and he wanted to do something about it. He did not want any power over any one and he wanted to break the mental and spiritual bonds of men. His heart was large. The heart, many around us may have, and we also want to help others. But we do not have the brain; we do not know the ways and means by which help can be given. But this man had the brain to discover the means of breaking the bondages of souls. He learnt why men suffer and he found the way out of the suffering. He was a man of accomplishment, he worked everything out; he taught one and all without distinction and made them realize the peace of enlightenment. This was the man Buddha.

You know from Arnold's poem, *The Light of Asia*, how Buddha was born a prince and how the misery of the world struck him deeply; how, although brought up and living in the lap of luxury, he could not find comfort in his personal happiness and security; how he renounced the world, leaving his princess and new-born son behind; how he wandered searching for truth from teacher to teacher; and how he at last attained to enlightenment. You know about his long mission, his disciples, his organizations. You all know these things.

Buddha was the triumph in the struggle that had been going on between the priests and the prophets in India. One thing can be said for these Indian priests—they were not and never are intolerant of religion; they never have persecuted religion. Any man was allowed to preach against them. Theirs is such a religion; they never molested any one for his religious views. But they suffered from the peculiar weaknesses of all the priests: they also sought power, they also promulgated rules and regulations and made religion unnecessarily complicated, and thereby undermined the strength of those who followed their religion.

Buddha cut through all these excrescences. He preached the most tremendous truths. He taught the very gist of the philosophy of the vedas to one and all without distinction, he taught it to the world at large, because one of his great messages was the equality of man. Men are all equal. No concession there to anybody! Buddha was the great preacher of equality. Every man and woman has the same right to attain spirituality—that was his teaching. The difference between the priests and the other castes he abolished. Even the lowest were entitled to the highest attainments; he opened the door of Nirvana to one and all. His teaching was bold even for India. No amount of preaching can ever shock the Indian soul, but it was hard for India to swallow Buddha's doctrine. How much harder it must be for you!

His doctrine was this: why is there misery in our life? Because we are selfish. We desire things for ourselves—that is why there is misery. What is the way out? The giving up of the self. The self does not exist; the phenomenal world, all this that we perceive, is all that exists. There is nothing called soul underlying the cycle of life and death. There is the stream of thought, one thought following another in succession, each thought coming into existence and becoming non-existent at the same moment, that is all; there is no thinker of the thought, no soul. The body is changing all the time; so is mind, consciousness. The self therefore is a delusion. All selfishness comes of holding on to the self, to this illusory self. If we know the truth that there is no self, then we will be happy and make others happy.

This was what Buddha taught. And he did not merely talk; he was ready to give up his own life for the world. He said, 'If sacrificing an animal is good, sacrificing a man is better', and he offered himself as a sacrifice. He said, 'This animal sacrifice is another superstition. God and soul are the two big superstitions. God is only a superstition invented by the priests. If there is a God, as these Brahmins preach, why is there so much misery in the world? He is just like me, a slave to the law of causation. If he is not bound by the law of causation, then why does he create? Such a God is not at all satisfactory. There is the ruler in heaven that rules the universe according to his sweet will and leaves us all here to die in misery—he never has the goodness to look at us for a moment. Our whole life is continuous suffering, but this is not sufficient punishment—after death we must go to places where we have other punishments. Yet we continually perform all kinds of rites and ceremonies to please this creator of the world!'

Buddha said, 'These ceremonials are all wrong. There is but one ideal in the world. Destroy all delusions; what is true will remain. As soon as the clouds are gone, the sun will shine.' How to kill the self? Become perfectly unselfish, ready to give up your life even for an ant. Work not for any superstition, not to please any God, not to get any reward, but because you are seeking your own release by killing your self. Worship and prayer and all that, these are all nonsense. You all say, 'I thank God'—but where does He live? You do not know and yet you are all going crazy about God.

Hindus can give up everything except their God. To deny God is to cut off the very ground from under the feet of devotion. Devotion and God the Hindus must cling to. They can never relinquish these. And here, in the teaching of Buddha, are no God and no soul—simply work. What for? Not for the self, for the self is a delusion. We shall be ourselves when this delusion has vanished. Very few are there in the world that can rise to that height and work for work's sake.

Yet the religion of Buddha spread fast. It was because of the marvellous love which, for the first time in the history of humanity, overflowed a large heart and devoted itself to the service not only of all men but of all living things—a love which did not care for anything except to find a way of release from suffering for all beings.

Man was loving God and had forgotten all about his brother man. The man who in the name of God can give up his very life, can also turn around and kill his brother man in the name of God. That was the state of the world. They would sacrifice the son for the glory of God, would rob nations for the glory of God, would kill thousands of beings for the glory of God, would drench the earth with blood for the glory of God. This was the first time they turned to the other God—man. It is man that is to be loved. It was the first wave of intense love for all men—the first wave of true unadulterated wisdom—that, starting from India, gradually inundated country after country, north, south, east, west.

This teacher wanted to make truth shine as truth. No softening, no compromise, no pandering to the priests, the powerful, the kings. No bowing before superstitious traditions, however hoary; no respect for forms and books just because they came down from the distant past. He rejected all scriptures, all forms of religious practice. Even the very language, Sanskrit, in which religion had been traditionally taught in India, he rejected, so that his followers would not have any chance to imbibe the superstitions which were associated with it.

There is another way of looking at the truth we have been discussing: the Hindu way. We claim that Buddha's great doctrine of selflessness can be better understood if it is looked at in our way. In the Upanishads, there is already the great doctrine of the atman and the Brahman. The atman, Self, is the same as Brahman, the Lord. This Self is all that is; it is the only reality. Maya, delusion, makes us see it as different. There is one Self, not many. That one Self shines in various forms. Man is man's brother because all men are one. A man is not only my brother, say the vedas, he is myself. Hurting any part of the universe, I only hurt myself. I am the universe. It is a delusion that I think I am Mr So-and-so—that is the delusion.

The more you approach your real Self, the more this delusion vanishes. The more all differences and divisions disappear, the more you realize all as the one Divinity. God exists, but He is not the man sitting upon a cloud. He is pure Spirit. Where does He reside? Nearer to you than your very self. He is the Soul. How can you perceive God as separate and different from yourself? When you think of Him as some one separate from yourself, you do not know Him. He is you yourself. That was the doctrine of the prophets of India.

It is selfishness that you think that you see Mr So-and-so and that all the world is different from you. You believe you are different from me. You do not take any thought of me. You go home and have your dinner and sleep. If I die, you still eat, drink and are merry. But you cannot really be happy when the rest of the world is suffering. We are all one. It is the delusion of separateness that is the root of misery. Nothing exists but the Self, there is nothing else.

Buddha's idea is that there is no God, only man himself. He repudiated the mentality which underlies the prevalent ideas of God. He found it made men weak and superstitious. If you pray to God to give you everything, who is it then that goes out and works? God comes to those who work hard. God helps them that help themselves. An opposite idea of God weakens our nerves, softens our muscles, makes us dependent. Everything independent is happy; everything dependent is miserable. Man has infinite power within himself, and he can realize it—he can realize himself as the one infinite Self. It can be done, but you do not believe it. You pray to God and keep your powder dry all the time.

Buddha taught the opposite. Do not let men weep. Let them have none of this praying and all that. God is not keeping shop. With every breath you are praying in God. I am talking; that is a prayer. You are listening, that is a prayer. Is there ever any movement of yours, mental or physical, in which you do not participate in the infinite divine energy? It is all a constant prayer. If you call only a set of words prayer, you make prayer superficial. Such prayers are not much good; they can scarcely bear any real fruit.

Is prayer a magic formula, by repeating which, even if you do not work hard, you gain miraculous results? No. All have to work hard; all have to reach the depths of that infinite energy. Behind the poor, behind the rich, there is the same infinite energy. It is not that one man works hard and another by repeating a few words achieves results. This universe is a constant prayer. If you take prayer in this sense, I am with you. Words are not necessary. Better is silent prayer.

The vast majority of people do not understand the meaning of this doctrine. In India any compromise regarding the Self means that we have given power into the hands of the priests and have forgotten the great teachings of the prophets. Buddha knew this; so he brushed aside all the priestly doctrines and practices and made man stand on his own feet. It was necessary for him to go against the accustomed ways of the people; he had to bring about revolutionary changes. As a result this sacrificial religion passed away from India forever and was never revived.

Buddhism apparently has passed away from India, but really

it has not. There was an element of danger in the teaching of Buddha—it was a reforming religion. In order to bring about the tremendous spiritual change he did, he had to give many negative teachings. But if a religion emphasizes the negative side too much, it is in danger of eventual destruction. Never can a reforming sect survive if it is only reforming; the formative elements alone—the real impulse, that is, the principles—live on and on. After a reform has been brought about, it is the positive side that should be emphasized; after the building is finished, the scaffolding must be taken away.

It so happened in India that as time went on, the followers of Buddha emphasized the negative aspect of his teachings too much and thereby caused the eventual downfall of their religion. The positive aspects of truth were suffocated by the forces of negation; and thus India repudiated the destructive tendencies that flourished in the name of Buddhism. That was the decree of the Indian national thought.

The negative elements of Buddhism—there is no God and no soul—died out. I can say that God is the only being that exists; it is a very positive statement. He is the one reality. When Buddha says there is no soul, I say, 'Man, thou art one with the universe; thou art all things.' How positive! The reformative element died out, but the formative element has lived through all time. Buddha taught kindness towards lower beings; and since then there has not been a sect in India that has not taught charity to all beings, even to animals. This kindness, this mercy, this charity—greater than any doctrine—are what Buddhism left to us.

The life of Buddha has an especial appeal. All my life I have been very fond of Buddha, but not of his doctrine. I have more veneration for that character than for any other—that boldness, that fearlessness and that tremendous love! He was born for the good of men. Others may seek God, others may seek truth for themselves; he did not even care to know truth for himself. He sought truth because people were in misery. How to help them, that was his only concern. Throughout his life, he never had a thought for himself. How can we ignorant, selfish, narrow-minded human beings ever understand the greatness of this man?

And consider his marvellous brain! No emotionalism. That giant brain never was superstitious. Believe not because an old manuscript has been produced, because it has been handed down to you from your forefathers, because your friends want you to—but think for yourself; search truth for yourself; realize it yourself. Then if you find it beneficial to one and many, give it to people. Soft-brained men, weak-minded, chicken-hearted, cannot find the truth. One has to be free and as broad as the sky. One has to have a mind that is crystal clear, only then can truth shine in it. We are so full of superstitions! Even in your country where you think you are highly educated, how full of narrownesses and superstitions you are! Just think, with all your claims to civilization in this country, on one occasion I was refused a chair to sit on because I was a Hindu.

Six hundred years before the birth of Christ, at the time when Buddha lived, the people of India must have had wonderful education. Extremely free-minded they must have been. Great masses followed him. Kings gave up their thrones, queens gave up their thrones. People were able to appreciate and embrace his teaching, so revolutionary, so different from what they had been taught by the priests through the ages! But their minds have been unusually free and broad.

And consider his death. If he was great in life, he was also great in death. He ate food offered to him by a member of a race similar to your American Indians. Hindus do not touch them because they eat everything indiscriminately. He told his disciples, 'Do not eat this food, but I cannot refuse it. Go to the man and tell him he has done me one of the greatest services of my life—he has released me from the body.' An old man came and sat near him—he had walked miles and miles to see the master—and Buddha taught him. When he found a disciple weeping, he reproved him, saying, 'What is this? Is this the result of all my teaching? Let there be no false bondage, no dependence on me, no false glorification of this passing personality. The Buddha is not a person; he is a realization. Work out your own salvation.'

Even when dying, he would not claim any distinction for himself. I worship him for that. What you call Buddhas and Christs are only the names of certain states of realization. Of all the teachers of the world, he was the one who taught us most to be self-reliant, who freed us not only from the bondages of our false selves, but from dependence on the invisible being or beings called God or gods. He invited everyone to enter into that state of freedom which he called Nirvana. All must attain to it one day; and that attainment is the complete fulfilment of man.

21

WOMEN OF INDIA

Delivered on 18 January 1900, at Shakespeare Club House, in Pasadena, California

Swami Vivekananda: 'Some persons desire to ask questions about Hindu Philosophy before the lecture and to question in general about India after the lecture, but the chief difficulty is I do not know what I am to lecture on. I would be very glad to lecture on any subject, either on Hindu Philosophy or on anything concerning the race, its history, or its literature. If you, ladies and gentlemen, will suggest anything, I would be very glad.'

Questioner: 'I would like to ask, Swami, what special principle in Hindu Philosophy you would have us Americans, who are a very practical people, adopt and what that would do for us beyond what Christianity can do.'

Swami Vivekananda: 'That is very difficult for me to decide; it rests upon you. If you find anything which you think you ought to adopt, and which will be helpful, you should take that. You see I am not a missionary, and I am not going about converting people to my idea. My principle is that all such ideas are good and great, so that some of your ideas may suit some people in India, and some of our ideas may suit some people here; so ideas must be cast abroad, all over the world.'

Questioner: 'We would like to know the result of your philosophy; has your philosophy and religion lifted your women above our women?'

Swami Vivekananda: 'You see, that is a very invidious question: I like our women and your women too.'

Questioner: 'Well, will you tell us about your women, their customs, education and the position they hold in the family?'

Swami Vivekananda: 'Oh, yes, those things I would be very glad to tell you. So you want to know about Indian women tonight, and not philosophy and other things?'

THE LECTURE

I must begin by saying that you may have to bear with me a good deal because I belong to an order of people who never marry; so my knowledge of women in all their relations, as mother, as wife, as daughter and sister, must necessarily not be so complete as it may be with other men. And then, India, I must remember, is a vast continent, not merely a country, and is inhabited by many different races. The nations of Europe are nearer to each other, more similar to each other, than the races in India. You may get just a rough idea of it if I tell you that there are eight different languages in all India. Different languages—not dialects—each having a literature of its own. The Hindi language, alone, is spoken by 100,000,000 people; the Bengali by about 60,000,000 and so on. Then, again, the four northern Indian languages differ more from the southern Indian languages than any two European languages from each other. They are entirely different, as much different as your language differs from the Japanese, so that you will be astonished to know when I go to southern India, unless I meet some people who can talk Sanskrit, I have to speak to them in English. Furthermore, these various races differ from each other in manners, customs, food, dress and in their methods of thought.

Then, again, there is caste. Each caste has become, as it were, a separate racial element. If a man lives long enough in India, he will be able to tell from the features what caste a man belongs to. Then, between castes, the manners and customs are different. And all these castes are exclusive; that is to say, they would meet socially, but they would not eat or drink together, nor inter-marry. In those things, they remain separate. They would meet and be friends to each other, but there it would end.

Although I have more opportunity than many other men to know women in general, from my position and my occupation as a preacher, continuously travelling from one place to another and coming in contact with all grades of society—(and women, even in northern India, where they do not appear before men, in many places would break this law for religion and would come to hear us preach and talk to us)—still it would be hazardous on my part to assert that I know everything about the women of India.

So, I will try to place before you the ideal. In each nation, man or woman represents an ideal consciously or unconsciously being worked out. The individual is the external expression of an ideal to be embodied. The collection of such individuals is the nation, which also represents a great ideal; towards that it is moving. And, therefore, it is rightly assumed that to understand a nation you must first understand its ideal, for each nation refuses to be judged by any other standard than its own.

All growth, progress, well-being, or degradation is but relative. It refers to a certain standard, and each man to be understood has to be referred to that standard of his perfection. You see this more markedly in nations: what one nation thinks good might not be so regarded by another nation. Cousin-marriage is quite permissible in this country. Now, in India, it is illegal; not only so, it would be classed with the most horrible incest. Widow-marriage is perfectly legitimate in this country. Among the higher castes in India it would be the greatest degradation for a woman to marry twice. So, you see, we work through such different ideas that to judge one people by the other's standard would be neither just nor practicable. Therefore we must know what the ideal is that a nation has raised before itself. When speaking of different nations, we start with a general idea that there is one code of ethics and the same kind of ideals for all races; practically, however, when we come to judge of others, we think what is good for us must be good for everybody; what we do is the right thing, what we do not do, of course in others would be outrageous. I do not mean to say this as a criticism, but just to bring the truth home. When I hear Western women denounce the confining of the feet of Chinese ladies, they never seem to think of the corsets which are doing far more injury to the race. This is just one example; for you must know that cramping the feet does not do one-millionth part of the injury to the human form that the corset has done and is doing—when every organ is displaced and the spine is curved like a serpent. When measurements are taken, you can note the curvatures. I do not mean that as a criticism, but just to point out to you the situation, that as you stand aghast at women of other races, thinking that you are supreme, the very reason that they do not adopt your manners and customs shows that they also stand aghast at you.

Therefore, there is some misunderstanding on both sides. There is a common platform, a common ground of understanding, a common humanity, which must be the basis of our work. We ought to find out that complete and perfect human nature which is working only in parts, here and there. It has not been given to one man to have everything in perfection.

You have a part to play; I, in my humble way, another; here is one who plays a little part; there, another. The perfection is the combination of all these parts. Just as with individuals, so with races. Each race has a part to play; each race has one side of human nature to develop. And we have to take all these together, and possibly in the distant future some race will arise in which all these marvellous individual race perfections, attained by the different races, will come together and form a new race, the like of which the world has not yet dreamed. Beyond saying that, I have no criticism to offer about anybody. I have travelled not a little in my life; I have kept my eyes open; and the more I go about the more my mouth is closed. I have no criticism to offer.

Now, the ideal woman in India is the mother, the mother first, and the mother last. The word 'woman' calls up to the mind of the Hindu, motherhood; and God is called Mother. As children, every day, when we are boys, we have to go early in the morning with a little cup of water and place it before the mother, and mother dips her toe into it and we drink it.

In the West, the woman is wife. The idea of womanhood is concentrated there—as the wife. To the ordinary man in India, the whole force of womanhood is concentrated in motherhood. In the Western home, the wife rules. In an Indian home, the mother rules. If a mother comes into a Western home, she has to be subordinate to the wife; to the wife belongs the home. A mother always lives in our homes, the wife must be subordinate to her. See all the difference of ideas.

Now, I only suggest comparisons; I would state facts so that we may compare the two sides. Make this comparison. If you ask, 'What is an Indian woman as wife?', the Indian asks, 'Where is the American woman as mother? What is she, the all-glorious, who gave me this body? What is she who kept me in her body for nine months? Where is she who would give me 20 times her life, if I had need? Where is she whose love never dies, however wicked, however vile I am? Where is she, in comparison with her, who goes to the divorce court the moment I treat her a little badly? O American woman! Where is she?' I will not find her in your country. I have not found the son who thinks mother is first. When we die, even then, we do not want our wives and our children to take her place. Our mother!—we want to die with our head on her lap once more, if we die before her. Where is she? Is woman a name to be coupled with the physical body only? Ay! The Hindu mind fears all those ideals which say that the flesh must cling unto the flesh. No, no! Woman! Thou shalt not be coupled with anything connected with the flesh. The name has been called holy once and forever, for what name is there which no lust can ever approach, no carnality ever come near, than the one word mother? That is the ideal in India.

I belong to an order very much like what you have in the Mendicant Friars of the Catholic Church; that is to say, we have to go about without very much in the way of dress and beg from door to door, live thereby, preach to people when they want it, sleep where we can get a place—that way we have to follow. And the rule is that the members of this order have to call every woman 'mother'; to every woman and little girl we have to say 'mother', that is the custom. Coming to the West, that old habit remained and I would say to ladies, 'Yes, mother, and they are horrified. I could not understand why they should be horrified. Later on, I discovered the reason: because that would mean that they are old. The ideal of womanhood in India is motherhood—that marvellous, unselfish, all-suffering, ever-forgiving mother. The wife walks behind the shadow. She must imitate the life of the mother; that is her duty. But the mother is the ideal of love; she rules the family, she possesses the family. It is the father in India who thrashes the child and spanks when there is something done by the child, and always the mother puts herself between the father and the child. You see it is just the opposite here. It has become the mother's business to spank the children in this country and poor father comes in between. You see, ideals are different. I do not mean this as any criticism. It is all good—this what you do, but our way is what we have been taught for ages. You never hear of a mother cursing the child; she is forgiving, always forgiving. Instead of 'Our Father in Heaven', we say 'mother' all the time; that idea and that word are ever associated in the Hindu mind with infinite love, the mother's love being the nearest approach to God's love in this mortal world of ours. 'Mother, O Mother, be merciful; I am wicked! Many children have been wicked, but there never was a wicked mother'—so says the great saint Ramprasad.

There she is—the Hindu mother. The son's wife comes in as her daughter; just as the mother's own daughter married and went out, so her son married and brought in another daughter, and she has to fall in line under the government of the queen of queens, of his mother. Even I, who never married, belonging to an order that never marries, would be disgusted if my wife, supposing I had married, dared to displease my mother. I would be disgusted. Why? Do I not worship my mother? Why should not her daughter-in-law? Whom I worship, why not she? Who is she, then, that would try to ride over my head and govern my mother? She has to wait till her womanhood is fulfilled; and the one thing that fulfils womanhood, that is womanliness in woman, is motherhood. Wait till she becomes a mother, then she will have the same right. That, according to the Hindu mind, is the great mission of woman—to become a mother. But oh, how different! Oh, how different! My father and mother fasted and prayed, for years and years, so that I would be born. They pray for every child before it is born. Says our great law-giver, Manu, giving the definition of an Aryan, 'He is the Aryan, who is born through prayer.' Every child not born through prayer is illegitimate, according to the great law-giver. The child must be prayed for. Those children that come with curses, that slip into the world, just in a moment of inadvertence because that could not be prevented, what can we expect of such progeny? Mothers of America, think of that! Think in the heart of your hearts, are you ready to be women? Not any question of race or country, or that false sentiment of national pride. Who dares to be proud in this mortal life of ours, in this world of woes and miseries? What are we before this infinite force of God? But I ask you the question tonight: do you all pray for the children to come? Are you thankful to be mothers, or not? Do you think that you are sanctified by motherhood, or not? Ask that of your minds. If you do not, your marriage is a lie, your womanhood is false, your education is superstition, and your children, if they come without prayer, will prove a curse to humanity.

See the different ideals now coming before us. From motherhood comes tremendous responsibility. There is the basis, start from that. Well, why is mother to be worshipped so much? Because our books teach that it is the pre-natal influence that gives the impetus to the child for good or evil. Go to a hundred thousand colleges, read a million books, associate with all the learned men of the world—better off you are when born with the right stamp. You are born for good or evil. The child is a born god or a born demon; that is what the books say. Education and all these things come afterwards—are a mere bagatelle. You are what you are born. Born unhealthful, how many drug stores, swallowed wholesale, will keep you well all through your life? How many people of good, healthy lives were born of weak parents, were born of sickly, blood-poisoned parents? How many? None—none. We come with a tremendous impetus for good or evil: born demons or born gods. Education or other things are a bagatelle.

Thus say our books: direct the pre-natal influence. Why should mother be worshipped? Because she made herself pure. She underwent harsh penances sometimes to keep herself as pure as purity can be. For, mind you, no woman in India thinks of giving up her body to any man; it is her own. The English, as a reform, have introduced at present what they call 'restitution of conjugal rights', but no Indian would take advantage of it. When a man comes in physical contact with his wife, the circumstances she controls through what prayers and through what vows! For that which brings forth the child is the holiest symbol of God himself. It is the greatest prayer between man and wife, the prayer that is going to bring into the world another soul fraught with a tremendous power for good or for evil. Is it a joke? Is it a simple nervous satisfaction? Is it a brute enjoyment of the body? Says the Hindu: no, a thousand times, no!

But then, following that, there comes in another idea. The idea we started with was that the ideal is the love for the mother—herself all-suffering, all-forbearing. The worship that is accorded to the mother has its fountainhead there. She was a saint to bring me into the world; she kept her body pure, her mind pure, her food pure, her clothes pure, her imagination pure, for years, because I would be born. Because she did that, she deserves worship. And what follows? Linked with motherhood is wifehood.

You Western people are individualistic. I want to do this thing because I like it; I will elbow every one. Why? Because

I like to. I want my own satisfaction, so I marry this woman. Why? Because I like her. This woman marries me. Why? Because she likes me. There it ends. She and I are the only two persons in the whole, infinite world; and I marry her and she marries me—nobody else is injured, nobody else responsible. Your Johns and your Janes may go into the forest and there they may live their lives, but when they have to live in society, their marriage means a tremendous amount of good or evil to us. Their children may be veritable demons—burning, murdering, robbing, stealing, drinking, hideous, vile.

So what is the basis of the Indian's social order? It is the caste law. I am born for the caste, I live for the caste. I do not mean myself, because, having joined an order, we are outside. I mean those that live in civil society. Born in the caste, the whole life must be lived according to caste regulation. In other words, in the present-day language of your country, the Western man is born individualistic, while the Hindu is socialistic—entirely socialistic. Now, then, the books say: if I allow you freedom to go about and marry any woman you like, and the woman to marry any man she likes, what happens? You fall in love; the father of the woman was, perchance, a lunatic or a consumptive. The girl falls in love with the face of a man whose father was a roaring drunkard. What says the law then? The law lays down that all these marriages would be illegal. The children of drunkards, consumptives, lunatics, etc., shall not be married. The deformed, humpbacked, crazy, idiotic—no marriage for them, absolutely none, says the law.

But the Mohammedan comes from Arabia, and he has his own Arabian law; so the Arabian Desert law has been forced upon us. The Englishman comes with his law; he forces it upon us, so far as he can. We are conquered. He says, 'Tomorrow I will marry your sister.' What can we do? Our law says, those that are born of the same family, though a hundred degrees distant, must not marry, that is illegitimate, for it would deteriorate or make the race sterile. That must not be and there it stops. So I have no voice in my marriage, nor my sister. It is the caste that determines all that. We are married sometimes when children. Why? Because the caste says: if they have to be married anyway without their consent, it is better that they are married very early, before they have developed this love: if they are allowed to grow up apart, the boy may like some other girl and the girl some other boy, and then something evil will happen; and so, says the caste, stop it there. I do not care whether my sister is deformed, or good-looking, or bad-looking: she is my sister and that is enough; he is my brother and that is all I need to know. So they will love each other. You may say, 'Oh! They lose a great deal of enjoyment—those exquisite emotions of a man falling in love with a woman and a woman falling in love with a man. This is a sort of tame thing, loving each other like brothers and sisters, as though they have to.' So be it, but the Hindu says, 'We are *socialistic*. For the sake of one man's or woman's exquisite pleasure we do not want to load misery on hundreds of others.'

There they are—married. The wife comes home with her husband; that is called the second marriage. Marriage at an early age is considered the first marriage, and they grow up separately with women and with their parents. When they are grown, there is a second ceremony performed called a second marriage. And then they live together, but under the same roof with his mother and father. When she becomes a mother, she takes her place in turn as queen of the family group.

Now comes another peculiar Indian institution. I have just told you that in the first two or three castes the widows are not allowed to marry. They cannot, even if they would. Of course, it is a hardship on many. There is no denying that not all the widows like it very much because non-marrying entails upon them the life of a student. That is to say, a student must not eat meat or fish, nor drink wine, nor dress except in white clothes and so on; there are many regulations. We are a nation of monks—always making penance, and we like it. Now, you see, a woman never drinks wine or eats meat. It was a hardship on us when we were students, but not on the girls. Our women would feel degraded at the idea of eating meat. Men eat meat sometimes in some castes; women never. Still, not being allowed to marry must be a hardship to many; I am sure of that.

But we must go back to the idea; they are intensely *socialistic*. In the higher castes of every country you will find the statistics show that the number of women is always much larger than the number of men. Why? Because in the higher castes, for generation after generation, the women lead an easy life. They 'neither toil nor spin, yet Solomon in all his glory was not arrayed like one of them'. And the poor boys, they die like flies. The girl has a cat's nine lives, they say in India. You will read in the statistics that they outnumber the boys in a very short time, except now when they are taking to work quite as hard as the boys. The number of girls in the higher castes is much larger than in the lower. Conditions are quite opposite in the lower castes. There they all work hard; women a little harder sometimes because they have to do the domestic work. But, mind you, I never would have thought of that, but one of your American travellers, Mark Twain, writes this about India: 'In spite of all that Western critics have said of Hindu customs, I never saw a woman harnessed to a plough with a cow or to a cart with a dog, as is done in some European countries. I saw no woman or girl at work in the fields in India. On both sides and ahead (of the railway train) brown-bodied naked men and boys are ploughing in the fields, but not a woman. In these two hours, I have not seen a woman or a girl working in the fields. In India, even the lowest caste never does any hard work. They generally have an easy lot compared to the same class in other nations; and as to ploughing, they never do it.'

Now, there you are. Among the lower classes the number of men is larger than the number of women; what would you naturally expect? A woman gets more chances of marriage, the number of men being larger.

Relative to such questions as to widows not marrying: among the first two castes, the number of women is disproportionately large and here is a dilemma. Either you have a non-marriageable widow problem and misery, or the non-husband-getting young lady problem. To face the widow problem, or the old maid problem? There you are; either of the two. Now, go back again to the idea that the Indian mind is socialistic. It says, 'Now look here! We take the widow problem as the lesser one.' Why? 'Because they have had their chance; they have been married. If they have lost their chance, at any rate they have had one. Sit down, be quiet and consider these poor girls; they have not had one chance of marriage.' Lord bless you! I remember once in Oxford Street, it was after ten o' clock, and all those ladies coming there, hundreds and thousands of them shopping; some man, an American, looks around, and he says, 'My Lord! How many of them will ever get husbands, I wonder!' So the Indian mind said to the widows, 'Well, you have had your chance, and now we are very, very sorry that such mishaps have come to you, but we cannot help it; others are waiting.'

Then religion comes into the question; the Hindu religion comes in as a comfort. For, mind you, our religion teaches that marriage is something bad, it is only for the weak. The very spiritual man or woman would not marry at all. So the religious woman says, 'Well, the Lord has given me a better chance. What is the use of marrying? Thank God, worship God, what is the use of my loving man?' Of course, all of them cannot put their mind on God. Some find it simply impossible. They have to suffer, but the other poor people, they should not suffer for them. Now I leave this to your judgment, but that is their idea in India.

Next we come to woman as daughter. The great difficulty in the Indian household is the daughter. The daughter and caste combined ruin the poor Hindu because, you see, she must marry in the same caste, and even inside the caste exactly in the same order; so the poor man sometimes has to make himself a beggar to get his daughter married. The father of the boy demands a very high price for his son and this poor man sometimes has to sell everything just to get a husband for his daughter. The great difficulty of the Hindu's life is the daughter. And, curiously enough, the word daughter in Sanskrit is *duhita*. The real derivation is that, in ancient times, the daughter of the family was accustomed to milk the cows, and so the word 'duhita' comes from 'duh', to milk; and the word 'daughter' really means a milkmaid. Later on, they found a new meaning to that word 'duhita', the milkmaid—she who milks away all the milk of the family. That is the second meaning.

These are the different relations held by our Indian women. As I have told you, the mother is the greatest in position, the wife is next and the daughter comes after them. It is a most intricate and complicated series of gradation. No foreigner can understand it, even if he lives there for years. For instance, we have three forms of the personal pronoun; they are a sort of verbs in our language. One is very respectful, one is middling and the lowest is just like thou and thee. To children and servants the last is addressed. The middling one is used with equals. You see, these are to be applied in all the intricate relations of life. For example, to my elder sister I always throughout my life use the pronoun *apani*, but she never does in speaking to me; she says *tumi* to me. She should not, even by mistake, say *apani* to me because that would mean a curse. Love, the love toward those that are superior, should always be expressed in that form of language. That is the custom. Similarly, I would never dare address my elder sister or elder brother, much less my mother or father, as *tu* or *tum* or *tumi*. As to calling our mother and father by name, why, we would never do that. Before I knew the customs of this country, I received such a shock when the son, in a very refined family, got up and called the mother by name! However, I got used to that. That is the custom of the country. But with us, we never pronounce the name of our parents when they are present. It is always in the third person plural, even before them.

Thus we see the most complicated meshwork in the social life of our men and our women and in our degree of relationship. We do not speak to our wives before our elders; it is only when we are alone or when inferiors are present. If I were married, I would speak to my wife before my younger sister, my nephews or nieces, but not before my elder sister or parents. I cannot talk to my sisters about their husbands at all. The idea is, we are a monastic race. The whole social organization has that one idea before it. Marriage is thought of as something impure, something lower. Therefore the subject of love would never be talked of. I cannot read a novel before my sister, or my brothers, or my mother, or even before others. I close the book.

Then again, eating and drinking is all in the same category. We do not eat before superiors. Our women never eat before men, except they be the children or inferiors. The wife would die rather than, as she says, 'munch' before her husband. Sometimes, for instance, brothers and sisters may eat together; and if I and my sister are eating, and the husband comes to the door, my sister stops, and the poor husband flies out.

These are the customs peculiar to the country. A few of these I note in different countries also. As I never married myself, I am not perfect in all my knowledge about the wife. Mother, sisters—I know what they are; and other people's wives I saw; from that I gather what I have told you.

As to education and culture, it all depends upon the man. That is to say, where the men are highly cultured, there the women are; where the men are not, women are not. Now, from the oldest times, you know, the primary education, according to the old Hindu customs, belongs to the village system. All the land from time immemorial was nationalized, as you say— belonged to the government. There never is any private right in land. The revenue in India comes from the land because every man holds so much land from the government. This land is held in common by a community, it may be five, ten, twenty, or a hundred families. They govern the whole of the land, pay a certain amount of revenue to the government, maintain a physician, a village schoolmaster and so on.

Those of you who have read Herbert Spencer remember what he calls the 'monastery system' of education that was tried in Europe and which in some parts proved a success; that is, there is one schoolmaster, whom the village keeps. These primary schools are very rudimentary because our methods are so simple. Each boy brings a little mat; and his paper, to begin with, is palm leaves. Palm leaves first, paper is too costly. Each boy spreads his little mat and sits upon it, brings out his inkstand and his books and begins to write. A little arithmetic, some Sanskrit grammar, a little of language and accounts—these are taught in the primary school.

A little book on ethics, taught by an old man, we learnt by heart, and I remember one of the lessons:

'For the good of a village, a man ought to give up his family;

For the good of a country, he ought to give up his village;

For the good of humanity, he may give up his country;

For the good of the world, everything.'

Such verses are there in the books. We get them by heart, and they are explained by teacher and pupil. These things we learn, both boys and girls together. Later on, the education differs. The old Sanskrit universities are mainly composed of boys. The girls very rarely go up to those universities, but there are a few exceptions.

In these modern days, there is a greater impetus towards higher education on the European lines, and the trend of opinion is strong towards women getting this higher education. Of course, there are some people in India who do not want it, but those who do want it carried the day. It is a strange fact that Oxford and Cambridge are closed to women today, so are Harvard and Yale, but Calcutta University opened its doors to women more than 20 years ago. I remember that the year I graduated, several girls came out and graduated—the same standard, the same course, the same in everything as the boys; and they did very well indeed. And our religion does not prevent a woman from being educated at all. In this way, the girl should be educated; even thus she should be trained; and in the old books we find that the universities were equally resorted to by both girls and boys, but later the education of the whole nation was neglected. What can you expect under foreign rule? The foreign conqueror is not there to do good to us; he wants his money. I studied hard for 12 years and became a graduate of Calcutta University; now I can scarcely make $5 a month in my country. Would you believe it? It is actually a fact. So these educational institutions of foreigners are simply to get a lot of useful, practical slaves for a little money—to turn out a host of clerks, postmasters, telegraph operators and so on. There it is.

As a result, education for both boys and girls is neglected, entirely neglected. There are a great many things that should be done in that land, but you must always remember, if you will kindly excuse me and permit me to use one of your own proverbs, 'What is sauce for the goose is sauce for the gander.' Your foreign born ladies are always crying over the hardships of the Hindu woman, and never care for the hardships of the Hindu man. They are all weeping salt tears. But who are the little girls married to? Someone, when told that they are all married to old men, asked, 'And what do the young men do? What! Are all the girls married to old men, only to old men?' We are born old—perhaps all the men there.

The ideal of the Indian race is freedom of the soul. This world is nothing. It is a vision, a dream. This life is one of many millions like it. The whole of this nature is Maya, is phantasm, a pest house of phantasms. That is the philosophy. Babies smile at life and think it so beautiful and good, but in a few years they will have to revert to where they began. They began life crying and they will leave it crying. Nations in the vigour of their youth think that they can do anything and everything: 'We are the gods of the earth. We are the chosen people.' They think that God Almighty has given them a charter to rule over all the world, to advance His plans, to do anything they like, to turn the world upside down. They have a charter to rob, murder, kill; God has given them this, and they do that because they are only babes. So empire after empire has arisen—glorious, resplendent—but now vanished away, gone, nobody knows where; it may have been stupendous in its ruin.

As a drop of water upon a lotus leaf tumbles about and falls in a moment, even so is this mortal life. Everywhere we turn are ruins. Where the forest stands today was once the mighty empire with huge cities. That is the dominant idea, the tone, the colour of the Indian mind. We know, you Western people have the youthful blood coursing through your veins. We know that nations, like men, have their day. Where is Greece? Where is Rome? Where that mighty Spaniard of the other day? Who knows through it all what becomes of India? Thus they are born, and thus they die; they rise and fall. The Hindu as a child knows of the Mogul invader whose cohorts no power on earth could stop, who has left in your language the terrible word 'Tartar'. The Hindu has learnt his lesson. He does not want to prattle, like the babes of today. Western people, say what you have to say. This is your day. Onward, go on, babes; have your prattle out. This is the day of the babies, to prattle. We have learnt our lesson and are quiet. You have a little wealth today and you look down upon us. Well, this is your day. Prattle, babes, prattle—this is the Hindu's attitude.

The Lord of Lords is not to be attained by much frothy speech. The Lord of Lords is not to be attained even by the powers of the intellect. He is not gained by much power of conquest. That man who knows the secret source of things and that everything else is evanescent, unto him He, the Lord, comes; unto none else. India has learnt her lesson through ages and ages of experience. She has turned her face towards Him. She has made many mistakes; loads and loads of rubbish are heaped upon the race. Never mind; what of that? What is the clearing of rubbish, the cleaning of cities and all that? Does that give life? Those that have fine institutions, they die. And what of institutions, those tinplate Western institutions, made in five days and broken on the sixth? One of these little handful nations cannot keep alive for two centuries together. And our institutions have stood the test of ages. Says the Hindu, 'Yes, we have buried all the old nations of the earth and stand here to bury all the new races also because our ideal is not this world, but the other. Just as your ideal is, so shall you be. If your ideal is mortal, if your ideal is of this earth, so shalt thou be. If your ideal is matter, matter shalt thou be. Behold! Our ideal is the Spirit. That alone exists, nothing else exists; and like Him, we live forever.'

22

THE POWERS OF THE MIND

Delivered on 8 January 1900, at Los Angeles, California

All over the world, there has been the belief in the supernatural throughout the ages. All of us have heard of extraordinary happenings, and many of us have had some personal experience of them. I would rather introduce the subject by telling you certain facts which have come within my own experience.

I once heard of a man who, if any one went to him with questions in his mind, would answer them immediately; and I was also informed that he foretold events. I was curious and went to see him with a few friends. We each had something in our minds to ask, and, to avoid mistakes, we wrote down our questions and put them in our pockets. As soon as the man saw one of us, he repeated our questions and gave the answers to them. Then he wrote something on paper, which he folded up, asked me to sign on the back, and said, 'Don't look at it; put it in your pocket and keep it there till I ask for it again.' And so on to each one of us. He next told us about some events that would happen to us in the future. Then he said, 'Now, think of a word or a sentence, from any language you like.' I thought of a long sentence from Sanskrit, a language of which he was entirely ignorant. 'Now, take out the paper from your pocket,' he said. The Sanskrit sentence was written there! He had written it an hour before with the remark, 'In confirmation of what I have written, this man will think of this sentence.' It was correct. Another of us who had been given a similar paper which he had signed and placed in his pocket, was also asked to think of a sentence. He thought of a sentence in Arabic, which it was still less possible for the man to know; it was some passage from the Koran. And my friend found this written down on the paper.

Another of us was a physician. He thought of a sentence from a German medical book. It was written on his paper.

Several days later, I went to this man again, thinking possibly I had been deluded somehow before. I took other friends and on this occasion too he came out wonderfully triumphant.

Another time I was in the city of Hyderabad in India, and I was told of a Brahmin there who could produce numbers of things from where, nobody knew. This man was in business there; he was a respectable gentleman. And I asked him to show me his tricks. It so happened that this man had a fever, and in India there is a general belief that if a holy man puts his hand on a sick man he would be well. This Brahmin came to me and said, 'Sir, put your hand on my head, so that my fever may be cured.'

I said, 'Very good, but you show me your tricks.' He promised. I put my hand on his head as desired, and later he came to fulfil his promise. He had only a strip of cloth about his loins, we took off everything else from him. I had a blanket which I gave him to wrap round himself because it was cold, and made him sit in a corner. Twenty-five pairs of eyes were looking at him. And he said, 'Now, look, write down anything you want.' We all wrote down names of fruits that never grew in that country, bunches of grapes, oranges and so on. And we gave him those bits of paper. And there came from under his blanket, bushels of grapes, oranges, and so forth, so much that if all that fruit was weighed, it would have been twice as heavy as the man. He asked us to eat the fruit. Some of us objected, thinking it was hypnotism, but the man began eating himself—so we all ate. It was all right.

He ended by producing a mass of roses. Each flower was perfect, with dew drops on the petals, not one crushed, not one injured. And masses of them! When I asked the man for an explanation, he said, 'It is all sleight of the hand.'

Whatever it was, it seemed to be impossible that it could be sleight of the hand merely. From whence could he have got such large quantities of things?

Well, I saw many things like that. Going about India you find hundreds of similar things in different places. These are in every country. Even in this country, you will find some such wonderful things. Of course, there is a great deal of fraud, no doubt, but then, whenever you see fraud, you have also to say that fraud is an imitation. There must be some truth somewhere that is being imitated; you cannot imitate nothing. Imitation must be of something substantially true.

In very remote times in India, thousands of years ago, these facts used to happen even more than they do today. It seems to me that when a country becomes very thickly populated, psychical power deteriorates. Given a vast country thinly inhabited, there will perhaps be more of psychical power there. These facts, the Hindus, being analytically minded, took up and investigated. And they came to certain remarkable conclusions; that is, they made a science of it. They found out that all these, though extraordinary, are also natural; there is nothing supernatural. They are under laws just the same as any other physical phenomenon. It is not a freak of nature that a man is born with such powers. They can be systematically studied, practiced and acquired. This science they call the science of Raja Yoga. There are thousands of people who cultivate the study of this science, and for the whole nation it has become a part of daily worship.

The conclusion they have reached is that all these extraordinary powers are in the mind of man. This mind is a part of the universal mind. Each mind is connected with every other mind. And each mind, wherever it is located, is in actual communication with the whole world.

Have you ever noticed the phenomenon that is called thought transference? A man here is thinking something and that thought is manifested in somebody else in some other place. With preparations—not by chanc—a man wants to send a thought to another mind at a distance, and this other mind knows that a thought is coming, and he receives it exactly as it is sent out. Distance makes no difference. The thought goes and reaches the other man, and he understands it. If your mind were an isolated something here and my mind were an isolated something there, and there were no connection between the two, how would it be possible for my thought to reach you? In the ordinary cases, it is not my thought that is reaching you direct, but my thought has got to be dissolved into ethereal vibrations and those ethereal vibrations go into your brain, and they have to be resolved again into your own thoughts. Here is a dissolution of thought and there is a resolution of thought. It is a roundabout process. But in telepathy, there is no such thing; it is direct.

This shows that there is a continuity of mind, as the yogis call it. The mind is universal. Your mind, my mind, all these little minds are fragments of that universal mind, little waves in the ocean; on account of this continuity, we can convey our thoughts directly to one another.

You see what is happening all around us. The world is one of influence. Part of our energy is used up in the preservation of our own bodies. Beyond that, every particle of our energy is day and night being used in influencing others. Our bodies, our virtues, our intellect and our spirituality, all these are continuously influencing others; so, conversely, we are being influenced by them. This is going on all around us. Now, to take a concrete example: a man comes; you know he is very learned, his language is beautiful, and he speaks to you by the hour, but he does not make any impression. Another man comes and he speaks a few words, not well arranged, ungrammatical perhaps; all the same, he makes an immense impression. Many of you have seen that. So it is evident that words alone cannot always produce an impression. Words, even thoughts, contribute only one-third of the influence in making an impression, the man, two-thirds. What you call the personal magnetism of the man— that is what goes out and impresses you.

In our families there are the heads; some of them are successful, others are not. Why? We complain of others in our failures. The moment I am unsuccessful, I say, so-and-so is the cause of the failure. In failure, one does not like to confess one's own faults and weaknesses. Each person tries to hold himself faultless and lay the blame upon somebody or something else, or even on bad luck. When heads of families fail, they should ask themselves, why it is that some persons manage a family so well and others do not. Then you will find that the difference is owing to the man—his presence, his personality.

Coming to great leaders of mankind, we always find that it was the personality of the man that counted. Now, take all the great authors of the past, the great thinkers. Really speaking, how many thoughts have they thought? Take all the writings that have been left to us by the past leaders of mankind; take each one of their books and appraise them. The real thoughts, new and genuine, that have been thought in this world up to this time, amount to only a handful. Read in their books the thoughts they have left to us. The authors do not appear to be giants to us and yet we know that they were great giants in their days. What made them so? Not simply the thoughts they thought, neither the books they wrote, nor the speeches they made, it was something else that is now gone, that is their personality. As I have already remarked, the personality of the man is two-thirds, and his intellect, his words, are but one-third. It is the real man, the personality of the man that runs through us. Our actions are but effects. Actions must come when the man is there; the effect is bound to follow the cause.

The ideal of all education, all training, should be this man-making. But, instead of that, we are always trying to polish up the outside. What use in polishing up the outside when there is no inside? The end and aim of all training is to make the man grow. The man who influences, who throws his magic, as it were, upon his fellow-beings, is a dynamo of power, and when that man is ready, he can do anything and everything he likes; that personality put upon anything will make it work.

Now, we see that though this is a fact, no physical laws that we know of will explain this. How can we explain it by chemical and physical knowledge? How much of oxygen, hydrogen, carbon, how many molecules in different positions, how many cells, etc., can explain this mysterious personality? And we still see, it is a fact, and not only that, it is the real man; and it is that man that lives and moves and works, it is that man that influences, moves his fellow-beings and passes out, and his intellect and books and works are but traces left behind. Think of this. Compare the great teachers of religion with the great philosophers. The philosophers scarcely influenced anybody's inner man and yet they wrote most marvellous books. The religious teachers, on the other hand, moved countries in their lifetime. The difference was made by personality. In the philosopher, it is a faint personality that influences; in the great prophets it is tremendous. In the former we touch the intellect, in the latter we touch life. In the one case, it is simply a chemical process, putting certain chemical ingredients together which may gradually combine and under proper circumstances bring out a flash of light or may fail. In the other, it is like a torch that goes round quickly, lighting others.

The science of yoga claims that it has discovered the laws which develop this personality, and by proper attention to those laws and methods, each one can grow and strengthen his personality. This is one of the great practical things, and this is the secret of all education. This has a universal application. In the life of the householder, in the life of the poor, the rich, the man of business, the spiritual man, in everyone's life, it is a great thing, the strengthening of this personality. There are laws, very fine, which are behind the physical laws, as we know. That is to say, there are no such realities as a physical world, a mental world, a spiritual world. Whatever is, is one. Let us say, it is a sort of tapering existence; the thickest part is here, it tapers and becomes finer and finer. The finest is what we call spirit; the grossest, the body. And just as it is here in microcosm, it is exactly the same in the macrocosm. The universe of ours is exactly like that; it is the gross external thickness and it tapers into something finer and finer until it becomes God.

We also know that the greatest power is lodged in the fine, not in the coarse. We see a man take up a huge weight, we see his muscles swell and all over his body we see signs of exertion, and we think the muscles are powerful things. But it is the thin thread-like things, the nerves, which bring power to

The Powers of the Mind ◆ 249

the muscles; the moment one of these threads is cut off from reaching the muscles, they are not able to work at all. These tiny nerves bring the power from something still finer, and that again in its turn brings it from something finer still—thought, and so on. So, it is the fine that is really the seat of power. Of course, we can see the movements in the gross, but when fine movements take place, we cannot see them. When a gross thing moves, we catch it, and thus we naturally identify movement with things which are gross. But all the power is really in the fine. We do not see any movement in the fine, perhaps because the movement is so intense that we cannot perceive it. But if by any science, any investigation, we are helped to get hold of these finer forces which are the cause of the expression, the expression itself will be under control. There is a little bubble coming from the bottom of a lake; we do not see it coming all the time, we see it only when it bursts on the surface; so, we can perceive thoughts only after they develop a great deal, or after they become actions.

We constantly complain that we have no control over our actions, over our thoughts. But how can we have it? If we can get control over the fine movements, if we can get hold of thought at the root, before it has become thought, before it has become action, then it would be possible for us to control the whole. Now, if there is a method by which we can analyse, investigate, understand, and finally grapple with those finer powers, the finer causes, then alone is it possible to have control over ourselves, and the man who has control over his own mind assuredly will have control over every other mind. That is why purity and morality have been always the object of religion; a pure, moral man has control of himself. And all minds are the same, different parts of one Mind. He who knows one lump of clay has known all the clay in the universe. He who knows and controls his own mind knows the secret of every mind and has power over every mind

Now, a good deal of our physical evil we can get rid of, if we have control over the fine parts; a good many worries we can throw off, if we have control over the fine movements; a good many failures can be averted, if we have control over these fine powers. So far, it is utility. Yet beyond, there is something higher.

Now, I shall tell you a theory, which I will not argue, but simply place before you the conclusion. Each man in his childhood runs through the stages through which his race has come up; only the race took thousands of years to do it, while the child takes a few years. The child is first the old savage man—and he crushes a butterfly under his feet. The child is at first like the primitive ancestors of his race. As he grows, he passes through different stages until he reaches the development of his race. Only he does it swiftly and quickly. Now, take the whole of humanity as a race, or take the whole of the animal creation, man and the lower animals, as one whole. There is an end towards which the whole is moving. Let us call it perfection.

Some men and women are born who anticipate the whole progress of mankind. Instead of waiting and being reborn over and over again for ages until the whole human race has attained to that perfection, they, as it were, rush through them in a few short years of their life. And we know that we can hasten these processes, if we be true to ourselves. If a number of men, without any culture, be left to live upon an island, and are given barely enough food, clothing and shelter, they will gradually go on and on, evolving higher and higher stages of civilization. We know also that this growth can be hastened by additional means. We help the growth of trees, do we not? Left to nature they would have grown, only they would have taken a longer time; we help them to grow in a shorter time than they would otherwise have taken. We are doing all the time the same thing, hastening the growth of things by artificial means. Why cannot we hasten the growth of man? We can do that as a race. Why are teachers sent to other countries? Because by these means we can hasten the growth of races. Now, can we not hasten the growth of individuals? We can. Can we put a limit to the hastening? We cannot say how much a man can grow in one life. You have no reason to say that this much a man can do and no more. Circumstances can hasten him wonderfully. Can there be any limit then, till you come to perfection? So, what comes of it?—That a perfect man, that is to say, the type that is to come of this race, perhaps millions of years hence, that man can come today. And this is what the yogis say, that all great incarnations and prophets are such men; that they reached perfection in this one life. We have had such men at all periods of the world's history and at all times. Quite recently, there was such a man who lived the life of the whole human race and reached the end—even in this life. Even this hastening of the growth must be under laws. Suppose we can investigate these laws and understand their secrets and apply them to our own needs; it follows that we grow. We hasten our growth, we hasten our development, and we become perfect, even in this life. This is the higher part of our life, and the science of the study of mind and its powers has this perfection as its real end. Helping others with money and other material things and teaching them how to go on smoothly in their daily life are mere details.

The utility of this science is to bring out the perfect man, and not let him wait and wait for ages, just a plaything in the hands of the physical world, like a log of driftwood carried from wave to wave and tossing about in the ocean. This science wants you to be strong, to take the work in your own hand, instead of leaving it in the hands of nature and get beyond this little life. That is the great idea.

Man is growing in knowledge, in power, in happiness. Continuously, we are growing as a race. We see that is true, perfectly true. Is it true of individuals? To a certain extent, yes. But yet, again comes the question: where do you fix the limit? I can see only at a distance of so many feet. But I have seen a man close his eyes and see what is happening in another room. If you say you do not believe it, perhaps in three weeks that man can make you do the same. It can be taught to anybody. Some persons, in five minutes even, can be made to read what is happening in another man's mind. These facts can be demonstrated.

Now, if these things are true, where can we put a limit? If a man can read what is happening in another's mind in the corner of this room, why not in the next room? Why not anywhere? We cannot say, why not. We dare not say that it is not possible. We can only say we do not know how it happens. Material scientists have no right to say that things like this are not possible; they can only say, 'We do not know.' Science has to collect facts, generalize upon them, deduce principles and state the truth—that is all. But if we begin by denying the facts, how can a science be?

There is no end to the power a man can obtain. This is the peculiarity of the Indian mind, that when anything interests it, it gets absorbed in it and other things are neglected. You know how many sciences had their origin in India. Mathematics began there. You are even today counting one, two, three, etc., to zero, after Sanskrit figures, and you all know that algebra also originated in India, and that gravitation was known to the Indians thousands of years before Newton was born.

You see the peculiarity. At a certain period of Indian history, this one subject of man and his mind absorbed all their interest. And it was so enticing because it seemed the easiest way to achieve their ends. Now, the Indian mind became so thoroughly persuaded that the mind could do anything and everything according to law, that its powers became the great object of study. Charms, magic and other powers, and all that were nothing extraordinary, but a regularly taught science, just as the physical sciences they had taught before that. Such a conviction in these things came upon the race that physical sciences nearly died out. It was the one thing that came before them. Different sects of yogis began to make all sorts of experiments. Some made experiments with light, trying to find out how lights of different colours produced changes in the body. They wore a certain coloured cloth, lived under a certain colour, and ate certain coloured foods. All sorts of experiments were made in this way. Others made experiments in sound by stopping and unstopping their ears. And still others experimented in the sense of smell and so on.

The whole idea was to get at the basis, to reach the fine parts of the thing. And some of them really showed the most marvellous powers. Many of them were trying to float in the air or pass through it. I shall tell you a story which I heard from a great scholar in the West. It was told him by a governor of Ceylon who saw the performance. A girl was brought forward and seated cross-legged upon a stool made of sticks crossed. After she had been seated for a time, the showman began to take out, one after another, these cross-bars; and when all were taken out, the girl was left floating in the air. The governor thought there was some trick, so he drew his sword and violently passed it under the girl; nothing was there. Now, what was this? It was not magic or something extraordinary. That is the peculiarity.

No one in India would tell you that things like this do not exist. To the Hindu it is a matter of course. You know what the Hindus would often say when they have to fight their enemies—'Oh, one of our yogis will come and drive the whole lot out!' It is the extreme belief of the race. What power is there in the hand or the sword? The power is all in the spirit.

If this is true, it is temptation enough for the mind to exert its highest. But as with every other science it is very difficult to make any great achievement, so also with this, nay much more. Yet most people think that these powers can be easily gained. How many are the years you take to make a fortune? Think of that! First, how many years do you take to learn electrical science or engineering? And then you have to work all the rest of your life.

Again, most of the other sciences deal with things that do not move, that are fixed. You can analyse the chair, the chair does not fly from you. But this science deals with the mind, which moves all the time; the moment you want to study it, it slips. Now the mind is in one mood, the next moment, perhaps, it is different, changing, changing all the time. In the midst of all this change it has to be studied, understood, grasped and controlled. How much more difficult, then, is this science! It requires rigorous training. People ask me why I do not give them practical lessons. Why, it is no joke. I stand upon this platform talking to you and you go home and find no benefit, nor do I. Then you say, 'It is all bosh.' It is because you wanted to make a bosh of it. I know very little of this science, but the little that I gained I worked for 30 years of my life, and for six years I have been telling people the little that I know. It took me 30 years to learn it, 30 years of hard struggle. Sometimes, I worked at it 20 hours during the 24; sometimes I slept only one hour in the night; sometimes I worked whole nights; sometimes I lived in places where there was hardly a sound, hardly a breath; sometimes I had to live in caves. Think of that. And yet I know little or nothing; I have barely touched the hem of the garment of this science. But I can understand that it is true and vast and wonderful.

Now, if there is any one amongst you who really wants to study this science, he will have to start with that sort of determination, the same as, nay even more than, that which he puts into any business of life.

And what an amount of attention does business require, and what a rigorous taskmaster it is! Even if the father, the mother, the wife, or the child dies, business cannot stop! Even if the heart is breaking, we still have to go to our place of business, when every hour of work is a pang. That is business, and we think that it is just, that it is right.

This science calls for more application than any business can ever require. Many men can succeed in business; very few in this. Because so much depends upon the particular constitution of the person studying it. As in business all may not make a fortune, but everyone can make something, so in the study of this science each one can get a glimpse which will convince him of its truth and of the fact that there have been men who realized it fully.

This is the outline of the science. It stands upon its own feet and in its own light and challenges in comparison with any other science. There have been charlatans, there have been magicians, there have been cheats, and more here than in any other field. Why? For the same reason, that the more profitable the business, the greater the number of charlatans and cheats. But that is no reason why the business should not be good. And one thing more: it may be good intellectual gymnastics to listen to all the arguments and an intellectual satisfaction to hear of wonderful things. But, if any one of you really wants to learn something beyond that, merely attending lectures will not do. That cannot be taught in lectures, for it is life; and life can only convey life. If there are any amongst you who are really determined to learn it, I shall be very glad to help them.

23

THE GREAT TEACHERS
OF THE WORLD

*Delivered on 3 February 1900, at Shakespeare Club,
Pasadena, California*

The universe, according to the theory of the Hindus, is moving in cycles of wave forms. It rises, reaches its zenith, then falls and remains in the hollow as it were for some time, once more to rise, and so on, in wave after wave and fall after fall. What is true of the universe is true of every part of it. The march of human affairs is like that. The history of nations is like that: they rise and they fall; after the rise comes a fall, again out of the fall comes a rise, with greater power. This motion is always going on. In the religious world, the same movement exists.

In every nation's spiritual life, there is a fall as well as a rise. The nation goes down and everything seems to go to pieces. Then, again, it gains strength, rises; a huge wave comes, sometimes a tidal wave—and always on the topmost crest of the wave is a shining soul, the messenger. Creator and created by turns, he is the impetus that makes the wave rise, the nation rise; at the same time, he is created by the same forces which make the wave, acting and interacting by turns. He puts forth his tremendous power upon society; and society makes him what he is. These are the great world-thinkers. These are the prophets of the world, the messengers of life, the incarnations of God.

Man has an idea that there can be only one religion, that there can be only one prophet and that there can be only one incarnation, but that idea is not true. By studying the lives of all these great messengers, we find that each, as it were, was destined to play a part and a part only; that the harmony consists in the sum total and not in one note. As in the life of races—no race is born to alone enjoy the world. None dare say no. Each race has a part to play in this divine harmony of nations. Each race has its mission to perform, its duty to fulfil. The sum total is the great harmony.

So, not any one of these prophets is born to rule the world forever. None has yet succeeded and none is going to be the ruler forever. Each only contributes a part; as to that part, it is true that in the long run every prophet will govern the world and its destinies.

Most of us are born believers in a personal religion. We talk of principles, we think of theories and that is all right, but every thought and every movement, every one of our actions, shows that we can only understand the principle when it comes to us through a person. We can grasp an idea only when it comes to us through a materialized ideal person. We can understand the precept only through the example. Would to God that all of us were so developed that we would not require any example, would not require any person. But that we are not; and, naturally, the vast majority of mankind has put their souls at the feet of these extraordinary personalities, the prophets, the incarnations of God—incarnations worshipped by the Christians, by the Buddhists and by the Hindus. The Mohammedans from the beginning stood against any such worship. They would have nothing to do with worshipping the prophets or the messengers, or paying any homage to them, but, practically, instead of one prophet, thousands upon thousands of saints are being worshipped. We cannot go against facts! We are bound to worship personalities, and it is good. Remember that word from your great prophet to the query: 'Lord, show us the Father', 'He that hath seen me hath seen the Father.' Which of us can imagine anything except that He is a man? We can only see Him in and through humanity. The vibration of light is everywhere in this room: why cannot we see it everywhere? You have to see it only in that lamp. God is an omnipresent principle—everywhere, but we are so constituted at present that we can see Him, feel Him, only in and through a human God. And when these great lights come, then man realizes God. And they come in a different way from what we come. We come as beggars; they come as emperors. We come here like orphans, as people who have lost their way and do not know it. What are we to do? We do not know what is the meaning of our lives. We cannot realize it. Today we are doing one thing, tomorrow another. We are like little bits of straw rocking to and fro in water, like feathers blown about in a hurricane.

But, in the history of mankind, you will find that there come these messengers, and that from their very birth their mission is found and formed. The whole plan is there, laid down; you see them swerving not one inch from that. Because they come with a mission, they come with a message, they do not want to reason. Did you ever hear or read of these great teachers, or prophets, reasoning out what they taught? No, not one of them did so. They speak direct. Why should they reason? They see the truth. And not only do they see it but they show it! If you ask me, 'Is there any God?' and I say, 'Yes'. You immediately ask my grounds for saying so and poor me has to exercise all his powers to provide you with some reason. If you had come to Christ and said, 'Is there any God?', he would have said, 'Yes'; and if you had asked, 'Is there any proof?', he would have replied, 'Behold the Lord!' And thus, you see, it is a direct perception, and not at all the ratiocination of reason. There is no groping in the dark, but there is the strength of direct vision. I see this table; no amount of reason can take that faith from me. It is a direct perception. Such is their faith—faith in their ideals, faith in their mission, faith in themselves, above all else. The great shining ones believe in themselves as nobody else ever does. The people say, 'Do you believe in God? Do you believe in a future life? Do you believe in this doctrine or that dogma?' But here the base is wanting: this belief in oneself. Ay, the man who cannot believe in himself, how can they expect him to believe in anything else? I am not sure of my own existence. One moment I think that I am existing and nothing can destroy me; the next moment I am quaking in fear of death. One minute I think I am immortal; the next minute, a spook appears and then I don't know what I am, nor where I am. I don't know whether I am living or dead. One moment, I think that I am spiritual, that I am moral, and the next moment, a blow comes and I am thrown flat on my back. And why?—I have lost faith in myself, my moral backbone is broken.

But in these great teachers, you will always find this sign: they have intense faith in themselves. Such intense faith is unique and we cannot understand it. That is why we try to explain away in various ways what these teachers speak of themselves; and people invent 20,000 theories to explain what they say about their realization. We do not think of ourselves in the same way and naturally we cannot understand them.

Then again, when they speak, the world is bound to listen. When they speak, each word is direct; it bursts like a bombshell. What is in the word, unless it has the power behind? What matters it what language you speak, and how you arrange your language? What matters is whether you speak correct grammar or with fine rhetoric? What matters it whether your language is ornamental or not? The question is whether or not you have anything to give. It is a question of giving and taking, and not listening. Have you anything to give?—that is the first question. If you have, then give. Words but convey the gift: it is but one of the many modes. Sometimes we do not speak at all. There is an old Sanskrit verse which says, 'I saw the teacher sitting under a tree. He was a young man of 16, and the disciple was an old man of 80. The preaching of the teacher was silence, and the doubts of the disciple departed.'

Sometimes, they do not speak at all, but yet they convey the truth from mind to mind. They come to give. They command, they are the messengers; you have to receive the command. Do you not remember in your own scriptures the authority with which Jesus speaks? 'Go ye, therefore, and teach all nations...teaching them to observe all things whatsoever I have commanded you.' It runs through all his utterances, that tremendous faith in his own message. That you find in the life of all these great giants whom the world worships as its prophets.

These great teachers are the living gods on this earth. Whom else should we worship? I try to get an idea of God in my mind, and I find what a false little thing I conceive; it would be a sin to worship that God. I open my eyes and look at the actual life of these great ones of the earth. They are higher than any conception of God that I could ever form. For, what conception of mercy could a man like me form who would go after a man if he steals anything from me and send him to jail? And what can be my highest idea of forgiveness? Nothing beyond myself. Which of you can jump out of your own bodies? Which of you can jump out of your own minds? Not one of you. What idea of divine love can you form except what you actually live? What we have never experienced we can form no idea of. So, all my best attempts at forming an idea of God would fail in every case. And here are plain facts, and not idealism—actual facts of love, of mercy, of purity, of which I can have no conception even. What wonder that I should fall at the feet of these men and worship them as God? And what else can anyone do? I should like to see the man who can do anything else, however much he may talk. Talking is not actuality. Talking about God, the impersonal, this and that is all very good, but these man-gods are the real gods of all nations and all races. These divine men have been worshipped and will be worshipped so long as man is man. Therein is our faith, therein is our hope, of a reality. Of what avail is a mere mystical principle!

The purpose and intent of what I have to say to you is this, that I have found it possible in my life to worship all of them, and to be ready for all that are yet to come. A mother recognizes her son in any dress in which he may appear before her; and if one does not do so, I am sure she is not the mother of that man. Now, as regards those of you that think that you understand truth and divinity and god in only one prophet in the world, and not in any other, naturally, the conclusion which I draw is that you do not understand divinity in anybody; you have simply swallowed words and identified yourself with one sect, just as you would in party politics, as a matter of opinion, but that is no religion at all. There are some fools in this world who use brackish water although there is excellent sweet water nearby because, they say, the brackish-water well was dug by their father. Now, in my little experience, I have collected this knowledge—that for all the devilry that religion is, blamed with, religion is not at all in fault: no religion ever persecuted men, no religion ever burnt witches, no religion ever did any of these things. What then incited people to do these things? Politics, but never religion; if such politics takes the name of religion, whose fault is that?

So, when each man stands and says, 'My Prophet is the only true Prophet,' he is not correct—he knows not the alpha of religion. Religion is neither talk, nor theory, nor intellectual consent. It is realization in the heart of our hearts; it is touching God; it is feeling, realizing that I am a spirit in relation with the universal spirit and all its great manifestations. If you have really entered the house of the Father, how can you have seen His children and not known them? And if you do not recognize them, you have not entered the house of the Father. The mother recognizes her child in any dress and knows him however disguised. Recognize all the great, spiritual men and women in every age and country, and see that they are not really at variance with one another. Wherever there has been actual religion—this touch of the divine, the soul coming in direct sense contact with the divine—there has always been a broadening of the mind which enables it to see the light everywhere. Now, some Mohammedans are the crudest in this respect, and the most sectarian. Their watchword is: 'There is one God and Mohammed is His Prophet.' Everything beyond that not only is bad, but must be destroyed forthwith; at a moment's notice, every man or woman who does not exactly believe in that must be killed; everything that does not belong to this worship must be immediately broken; every book that teaches anything else must be burnt. From the Pacific to the Atlantic, for 500 years blood ran all over the world. That is Mohammedanism! Nevertheless, among these Mohammedans, wherever there was a philosophic man, he was sure to protest against these cruelties. In that he showed the touch of the divine and realized a fragment of the truth; he was not playing with his religion; for it was not his father's religion he was talking, but spoke the truth direct like a man.

Side by side with the modern theory of evolution, there is another thing: atavism. There is a tendency in us to revert to old ideas in religion. Let us think something new, even if it be wrong. It is better to do that. Why should you not try to hit the mark? We become wiser through failures. Time is infinite. Look at the wall. Did the wall ever tell a lie? It is always the wall. Man tells a lie—and becomes a god too. It is better to do something; never mind even if it proves to be wrong. It is better than doing nothing. The cow never tells a lie, but she remains a cow all the time. Do something! Think some thought; it doesn't matter whether you are right or wrong. But think something! Because my forefathers did not think this way, shall I sit down quietly and gradually lose my sense of feeling and my own thinking faculties? I may as well be dead! And what is life worth if we have no living ideas, no convictions of our own about religion? There is some hope for the atheists, because though they differ from others, they think for themselves. The people who never think anything for themselves are not yet born into the world of religion; they have a mere jellyfish existence. They will not think; they do not care for religion. But the disbeliever, the atheist cares, and he is struggling. So think something! Struggle Godward! Never mind if you fail, never mind if you get hold of a queer theory. If you are afraid to be called queer, keep it in your own mind—you need not go and preach it to others. But do something! Struggle Godward! Light must come. If a man feeds me every day of my life, in the long run I shall lose the use of my hands. Spiritual death is the result of following each other like a flock of sheep. Death is the result of inaction. Be active; and wherever there is activity, there must be difference. Difference is the sauce of life; it is the beauty, it is the art of everything. Difference makes all beautiful here. It is variety that is the source of life, the sign of life. Why should we be afraid of it?

Now, we are coming into a position to understand about the prophets. Now, we see that the historical evidence is—apart from the jellyfish existence in religion—that where there has been any real thinking, any real love for God, the soul has grown Godwards and has got as it were, a glimpse now and then, has come into direct perception, even for a second, even once in its life. Immediately, 'All doubts vanish forever, all the crookedness of the heart is made straight, all bondages vanish and the results of action and karma fly when He is seen who is the nearest of the near and the farthest of the far.' That is religion, that is all of religion; the rest is mere theory, dogma, so many ways of going to that state of direct perception. Now we are fighting over the basket and the fruits have fallen into the ditch.

If two men quarrel about religion, just ask them the question: 'Have you seen God? Have you seen these things?' One man says that Christ is the only prophet: well, has he seen Christ?

'Has your father seen Him?'

'No, Sir.'

'Has your grandfather seen Him?'

'No, Sir.'

'Have you seen Him?'

'No, Sir.'

'Then what are you quarrelling for? The fruits have fallen into the ditch, and you are quarrelling over the basket!' Sensible men and women should be ashamed to go on quarrelling in that way!

These great messengers and prophets are great and true. Why? Because, each one has come to preach a great idea. Take the prophets of India, for instance. They are the oldest of the founders of religion. We take first, Krishna. You who have read the Gita see all through the book that the one idea is non-attachment. Remain unattached. The heart's love is due to only one. To whom? To Him who never changeth. Who is that One? It is God. Do not make the mistake of giving the heart to anything that is changing because that is misery. You may give it to a man, but if he dies, misery is the result. You may give it to a friend, but he may tomorrow become your enemy. If you give it to your husband, he may one day quarrel with you. You may give it to your wife, and she may die the day after tomorrow. Now, this is the way the world is going on. So says Krishna in the Gita: the Lord is the only one who never changes. His love never fails. Wherever we are and whatever we do, He is ever and ever the same merciful, the same loving heart. He never changes, He is never angry, whatever we do. How can God be angry with us? Your babe does many mischievous things: are you angry with that babe? Does not God know what we are going to be? He knows we are all going to be perfect, sooner or later. He has patience, infinite patience. We must love Him and everyone that lives—only in and through Him. This is the keynote. You must love the wife, but not for the wife's sake. 'Never, O Beloved, is the husband loved on account of the husband, but because the Lord is in the husband.' The Vedanta philosophy says that even in the love of the husband and wife, although the wife is thinking that she is loving the husband, the real attraction is the Lord, who is present there. He is the only attraction, there is no other, but the wife in most cases does not know that it is so. Ignorantly she is doing the right thing, which is loving the Lord. Only, when one does it ignorantly, it may bring pain. If one does it knowingly, that is salvation. This is what our scriptures say. Wherever there is love, wherever there is a spark of joy, know that to be a spark of His presence because He is joy, blessedness and love itself. Without that there cannot be any love.

This is the trend of Krishna's instruction all the time. He has implanted that upon his race, so that when a Hindu does anything, even if he drinks water, he says, 'If there is virtue in it, let it go to the Lord.' The Buddhist says, if he does any good deed, 'Let the merit of the good deed belong to the world; if there is any virtue in what I do, let it go to the world and let the evils of the world come to me.' The Hindu says he is a great believer in God; the Hindu says that God is omnipotent and that He is the soul of every soul everywhere; the Hindu says, 'If I give all my virtues unto Him, that is the greatest sacrifice, and they will go to the whole universe.'

Now, this is one phase; and what is the other message of Krishna? 'Whosoever lives in the midst of the world, and works, and gives up all the fruit of his action unto the Lord, he is never touched with the evils of the world. Just as the lotus, born under the water, rises up and blossoms above the water, even so is the man who is engaged in the activities of the world, giving up all the fruit of his activities unto the Lord.'

Krishna strikes another note as a teacher of intense activity. Work, work, work day and night, says the Gita. You may ask, 'Then, where is peace? If all through life I am to work like a cart horse and die in harness, what am I here for?' Krishna says, 'Yes, you will find peace. Flying from work is never the way to find peace.' Throw off your duties if you can, and go to the top of a mountain; even there the mind is going—whirling, whirling, whirling.

Someone asked a sannyasin, 'Sir, have you found a nice place? How many years have you been travelling in the Himalayas?'

'For 40 years,' replied the sannyasin.

'There are many beautiful spots to select from and to settle down in: why did you not do so?'

'Because for these 40 years, my mind would not allow me to do so. We all say, "Let us find peace", but the mind will not allow us to do so.'

You know the story of the man who caught a Tartar. A soldier was outside the town, and he cried out when he came near the barracks, 'I have caught a Tartar.'

A voice called out, 'Bring him in.'

'He won't come in, sir.'

'Then you come in.'

'He won't let me come in, sir.'

So, in this mind of ours, we have 'caught a Tartar': neither can we tone it down, nor will it let us be toned down. We have all 'caught Tartars'. We all say, be quiet, peaceful and so forth. But every baby can say that and thinks he can do it. However, that is very difficult. I have tried. I threw overboard all my duties and fled to the tops of mountains; I lived in caves and deep forests—but all the same, I 'caught a Tartar' because I had my world with me all the time. The 'Tartar' is what I have in my own mind, so we must not blame poor people outside. 'These circumstances are good, and these are bad,' so we say, while the 'Tartar' is here, within; if we can quiet him down, we shall be all right.

Therefore Krishna teaches us not to shirk our duties, but to take them up manfully, and not think of the result. The servant has no right to question. The soldier has no right to reason. Go forward and do not pay too much attention to the nature of the work you have to do. Ask your mind if you are unselfish. If you are, never mind anything, nothing can resist you! Plunge in! Do the duty at hand. And when you have done this, by degrees you will realize the truth: 'Whosoever in the midst of intense activity finds intense peace, whosoever in the midst of the greatest peace finds the greatest activity, he is a yogi, he is a great soul, he has arrived at perfection.'

Now, you see that the result of this teaching is that all the duties of the world are sanctified. There is no duty in this world which we have any right to call menial; and each man's work is quite as good as that of the emperor on his throne.

Listen to Buddha's message—a tremendous message. It has a place in our heart. Says Buddha, 'Root out selfishness and everything that makes you selfish. Have neither wife, child, nor family. Be not of the world; become perfectly unselfish.' A worldly man thinks he will be unselfish, but when he looks at the face of his wife it makes him selfish. The mother thinks she will be perfectly unselfish, but she looks at her baby and immediately selfishness comes. So is with everything in this world. As soon as selfish desires arise, as soon as some selfish pursuit is followed, immediately the whole man, the real man, is gone: he is like a brute, he is a slave, he forgets his fellow men. No more does he say, 'You first and I afterwards', but it is 'I first and let everyone else look out for himself.'

We find that Krishna's message has also a place for us. Without that message, we cannot move at all. We cannot conscientiously and with peace, joy and happiness take up any duty of our lives without listening to the message of Krishna: 'Be not afraid even if there is evil in your work, for there is no work which has no evil.' 'Leave it unto the Lord and do not look for the results.'

On the other hand, there is a corner in the heart for the other message: time flies; this world is finite and all misery. With your good food, nice clothes and your comfortable home, O sleeping man and woman, do you ever think of the millions that are starving and dying? Think of the great fact that it is all misery, misery, misery! Note the first utterance of the child: when it enters into the world, it weeps. That is the fact—the child weeps. This is a place for weeping! If we listen to the messenger, we should not be selfish.

Behold another messenger, He of Nazareth. He teaches, 'Be ready, for the kingdom of Heaven is at hand.' I have pondered over the message of Krishna and am trying to work without attachment, but sometimes I forget. Then, suddenly, comes to me the message of Buddha: 'Take care, for everything in the world is evanescent, and there is always misery in this life.' I listen to that and I am uncertain which to accept. Then again comes, like a thunderbolt, the message: 'Be ready, for the kingdom of Heaven is at hand.' Do not delay a moment. Leave nothing for tomorrow. Get ready for the final event, which may overtake you immediately, even now. That message also has a place and we acknowledge it. We salute the messenger, we salute the Lord.

And then comes Mohammed, the messenger of equality. You ask, 'What good can there be in his religion?' If there were no good, how could it live? The good alone lives, that alone survives because the good alone is strong, therefore it survives. How long is the life of an impure man, even in this life? Is not the life of the pure man much longer? Without doubt, for purity is strength, goodness is strength. How could Mohammedanism have lived, had there been nothing good in its teaching? There is much good. Mohammed was the prophet of equality, of the brotherhood of man, the brotherhood of all Mussulmans

So we see that each prophet, each messenger, has a particular message. When you first listen to that message and then look at his life, you see his whole life stands explained, radiant.

Now, Ignorant fools start 20,000 theories and put forward,

according to their own mental development, explanations to suit their own ideas and ascribe them to these great teachers. They take their teachings and put their misconstruction upon them. With every great prophet, his life is the only commentary. Look at his life: what he did will bear out the texts. Read the Gita, and you will find that it is exactly borne out by the life of the teacher.

Mohammed by his life showed that amongst Mohammedans there should be perfect equality and brotherhood. There was no question of race, caste, creed, colour, or sex. The Sultan of Turkey may buy a Negro from the mart of Africa, and bring him in chains to Turkey, but should he become a Mohammedan and have sufficient merit and abilities, he might even marry the daughter of the Sultan. Compare this with the way in which the Negroes and the American Indians are treated in this country! And what do Hindus do? If one of your missionaries chance to touch the food of an orthodox person, he would throw it away. Notwithstanding our grand philosophy, you note our weakness in practice; but there you see the greatness of the Mohammedan beyond other races, showing itself in equality, perfect equality regardless of race or colour.

Will other and greater prophets come? Certainly they will come in this world. But do not look forward to that. I should better like that each one of you became a prophet of this real New Testament, which is made up of all the Old Testaments. Take all the old messages, supplement them with your own realizations, and become a prophet unto others. Each one of these teachers has been great; each has left something for us; they have been our gods. We salute them, we are their servants; and, all the same, we salute ourselves; for if they have been prophets and children of God, we also are the same. They reached their perfection, and we are going to attain ours now.

Remember the words of Jesus: 'The kingdom of Heaven is at hand!' This very moment let everyone of us make a staunch resolution: 'I will become a prophet, I will become a messenger of light, I will become a child of God, nay, I will become a God!'

24

MY LIFE AND MISSION

Delivered on 27 January 1900, at Shakespeare Club, Pasadena, California

Now, ladies and gentlemen, the subject for this morning was to have understood the Vedanta philosophy. That subject itself is interesting, but rather dry and very vast.

Meanwhile, I have been asked by your president and some of the ladies and gentlemen here to tell them something about my work and what I have been doing. It may be interesting to some here, but not so much so to me. In fact, I do not quite know how to tell it to you, for this will be the first time in my life that I have spoken on that subject.

Now, to understand what I have been trying to do, in my small way, I will take you, in imagination, to India. We have not time to go into all the details and all the ramifications of the subject, nor is it possible for you to understand all the complexities in a foreign race in this short time. Suffice it to say, I will at least try to give you a little picture of what India is like.

It is like a gigantic building all tumbled down in ruins. At first sight, then, there is little hope. It is a nation gone and ruined. But you wait and study, then you see something beyond that. The truth is that so long as the principle, the ideal, of which the outer man is the expression, is not hurt or destroyed, the man lives, there is hope for that man. If your coat is stolen

20 times, that is no reason why you should be destroyed. You can get a new coat. The coat is unessential. The fact that a rich man is robbed does not hurt the vitality of the man, does not mean death. The man will survive.

Standing on this principle, we look in and we see—what? India is no longer a political power; it is an enslaved race. Indians have no say, no voice in their own government; they are three hundred millions of slaves—nothing more! The average income of a man in India is two shillings a month. The common state of the vast mass of the people is starvation, so that, with the least decrease in income, millions die. A little famine means death. So there, too, when I look on that side of India, I see ruin, hopeless ruin.

But we find that the Indian race never stood for wealth. Although they acquired immense wealth, perhaps more than any other nation ever acquired, yet the nation did not stand for wealth. It was a powerful race for ages, yet we find that that nation never stood for power, never went out of the country to conquer. Quite content within their own boundaries, they never fought anybody. The Indian nation never stood for imperial glory. Wealth and power, then, were not the ideals of the race.

What then? Whether they were wrong or right—that is not the question we discuss—that nation, among all the children of men, has believed and believed intensely that this life is not real. The real is God; and they must cling unto that God through thick and thin. In the midst of their degradation, religion came first. The Hindu man drinks religiously, sleeps religiously, walks religiously, marries religiously, robs religiously.

Did you ever see such a country? If you want to get up a gang of robbers, the leader will have to preach some sort of religion, then formulate some bogus metaphysics and say that this method is the clearest and quickest way to get God. Then he finds a following, otherwise not. That shows that the vitality of the race, the mission of the race is religion; because that has not been touched, therefore that race lives.

See Rome. Rome's mission was imperial power, expansion. And so soon as that was touched, Rome fell to pieces, passed out. The mission of Greece was intellect, as soon as that was touched, why, Greece passed out. So in modern times, Spain and all these modern countries. Each nation has a mission for the world. So long as that mission is not hurt, that nation lives, despite every difficulty. But as soon as its mission is destroyed, the nation collapses.

Now, that vitality of India has not been touched yet. They have not given up that, and it is still strong—in spite of all their superstitions. Hideous superstitions are there, most revolting some of them. Never mind. The national life—current is still there—the mission of the race.

The Indian nation never will be a powerful conquering people—never. They will never be a great political power; that is not their business, that is not the note India has to play in the great harmony of nations. But what has she to play? God and God alone. She clings unto that like grim death. Still there is hope there.

So, then, after your analysis, you come to the conclusion that all these things, all this poverty and misery, are of no consequence—the man is living still and therefore there is hope.

Well! You see religious activities going on all through the country. I do not recall a year that has not given birth to several new sects in India. The stronger the current, the more the whirlpools and eddies. Sects are not signs of decay, they are a sign of life. Let sects multiply, till the time comes when every one of us is a sect, each individual. We need not quarrel about that.

Now, take your country. (I do not mean any criticism). Here the social laws, the political formation—everything is made to facilitate man's journey in this life. He may live very happily so long as he is on this earth. Look at your streets—how clean! Your beautiful cities! And in how many ways a man can make money! How many channels to get enjoyment in this life! But, if a man here should say, 'Now look here, I shall sit down under this tree and meditate; I do not want to work', why, he would have to go to jail. See! There would be no chance for him at all. None. A man can live in this society only if he falls in line. He has to join in this rush for the enjoyment of good in this life, or he dies.

Now let us go back to India. There, if a man says, 'I shall go and sit on the top of that mountain and look at the tip of my nose all the rest of my days', everybody says, 'Go, and Godspeed to you!' He need not speak a word. Somebody brings him a little cloth and he is all right. But if a man says, 'Behold, I am going to enjoy a little of this life', every door is closed to him.

I say that the ideas of both countries are unjust. I see no reason why a man here should not sit down and look at the tip of his nose if he likes. Why should everybody here do just what the majority does? I see no reason.

Nor why, in India, a man should not have the goods of this life and make money. But you see how those vast millions are forced to accept the opposite point of view by tyranny. This is the tyranny of the sages. This is the tyranny of the great, tyranny of the spiritual, tyranny of the intellectual, tyranny of the wise. And the tyranny of the wise, mind you, is much more powerful than the tyranny of the ignorant. The wise, the intellectual, when they take to forcing their opinions upon others, know a hundred thousand ways to make bonds and barriers which it is not in the power of the ignorant to break.

Now, I say that this thing has got to stop. There is no use in sacrificing millions and millions of people to produce one spiritual giant. If it is possible to make a society where the spiritual giant will be produced and all the rest of the people will be happy as well, that is good, but if the millions have to be ground down, that is unjust. Better that the one great man should suffer for the salvation of the world.

In every nation you will have to work through their methods. To every man you will have to speak in his own language. Now, in England or in America, if you want to preach religion to them, you will have to work through political methods—make organizations, societies, with voting, balloting, a president, and so on because that is the language, the method of the Western race. On the other hand, if you want to speak of politics in India, you must speak through the language of religion. You will have to tell them something like this: 'The man who cleans his house every morning will acquire such and such an amount of merit, he will go to heaven, or he comes to God.' Unless you put it that way, they will not listen to you. It is a question of language. The thing done is the same. But with every race, you will have to speak their language in order to reach their hearts. And that is quite just. We need not fret about that.

In the order to which I belong we are called sannyasins. The word means 'a man who has renounced'. This is a very, very, very ancient order. Even Buddha, who was 560 years before Christ, belonged to that order. He was one of the reformers of his order. That was all. So ancient! You find it mentioned away back in the vedas, the oldest book in the world. In old India there was the regulation that every man and woman, towards the end of their lives, must get out of social life altogether and think of nothing except God and their own salvation. This was to get ready for the great event—death. So old people used to become sannyasins in those early days. Later on, young people began to give up the world. And young people are active. They could not sit down under a tree and think all the time of their own death, so they went about preaching and starting sects and so on. Thus, Buddha, being young, started that great reform. Had he been an old man, he would have looked at the tip of his nose and died quietly.

The order is not a church, and the people who join the order are not priests. There is an absolute difference between the priests and the sannyasins. In India, priesthood, like every other business in a social life, is a hereditary profession. A priest's son will become a priest, just as a carpenter's son will be a carpenter, or a blacksmith's son a blacksmith. The priest must always be married. The Hindu does not think a man is complete unless he has a wife. An unmarried man has no right to perform religious ceremonies.

The sannyasins do not possess property and they do not marry. Beyond that there is no organization. The only bond that is there is the bond between the teacher and the taught—and that is peculiar to India. The teacher is not a man who comes just to teach me, and I pay him so much, and there it ends. In India it is really like an adoption. The teacher is more than my own father, and I am truly his child, his son in every respect. I owe him obedience and reverence first, before my own father even because, they say, the father gave me this body, but he showed me the way to salvation, he is greater than father. And we carry this love, this respect for our teacher all our lives. And that is the only organization that exists. I adopt my disciples. Sometimes the teacher will be a young man and the disciple a very old man. But never mind, he is the son and he calls me 'Father', and I have to address him as my son, my daughter and so on.

Now, I happened to get an old man to teach me and he was very peculiar. He did not go much for intellectual scholarship, scarcely studied books, but when he was a boy he was seized with the tremendous idea of getting truth direct. First, he tried by studying his own religion. Then he got the idea that he must get the truth of other religions; and with that idea he joined all the sects, one after another. For the time being he did exactly what they told him to do—lived with the devotees of these different sects in turn, until interpenetrated with the particular ideal of that sect. After a few years he would go to another sect. When he had gone through with all that, he came to the conclusion that they were all good. He had no criticism to offer to any one; they are all so many paths leading to the same goal. And then he said, 'That is a glorious thing, that there should be so many paths, because if there were only one path, perhaps it would suit only an individual man. The more the number of paths, the more the chance for everyone of us to know the truth. If I cannot be taught in one language, I will try another, and so on.' Thus his benediction was for every religion.

Now, all the ideas that I preach are only an attempt to echo his ideas. Nothing is mine originally except the wicked ones, everything I say which is false and wicked. But every word that I have ever uttered which is true and good is simply an attempt to echo his voice. Read his life by Prof. Max Muller—*Ramakrishna: His Life and Sayings*, first published in London in 1896, reprinted in 1951 by Advaita Ashrama.

Well, there at his feet I conceived these ideas—there with some other young men. I was just a boy. I went there when I was about 16. Some of the other boys were still younger, some a little older—about a dozen or more. And together we conceived that this ideal had to be spread. And not only spread, but made practical. That is to say, we must show the spirituality of the Hindus, the mercifulness of the Buddhists, the activity of the Christians, the brotherhood of the Mohammedans, by our practical lives. 'We shall start a universal religion now and here,' we said, 'we will not wait'.

Our teacher was an old man who would never touch a coin with his hands. He took just the little food offered, just so many yards of cotton cloth, no more. He could never be induced to take any other gift. With all these marvellous ideas, he was strict because that made him free. The monk in India is the friend of the prince today, dines with him; and tomorrow he is with the beggar, sleeps under a tree. He must come into contact with everyone, must always move about. As the saying is, 'The rolling stone gathers no moss.' The last 14 years of my life, I have never been for three months at a time in any one place—continually rolling. So do we all.

Now, this handful of boys got hold of these ideas, and all the practical results that sprang out of these ideas. Universal religion, great sympathy for the poor and all that are very good in theory, but one must practice.

Then came the sad day when our old teacher died. We nursed him the best we could. We had no friends. Who would listen to a few boys, with their crank notions? Nobody. At least, in India, boys are nobodies. Just think of it—a dozen boys, telling people vast, big ideas, saying they are determined to work these ideas out in life. Why, everybody laughed. From laughter it became serious; it became persecution. Why, the parents of the boys came to feel like spanking every one of us. And the more we were derided, the more determined we became.

Then came a terrible time—for me personally and for all the other boys as well. But to me came such misfortune! On the one side was my mother, my brothers. My father died at that time and we were left poor. Oh, very poor, almost starving all the time! I was the only hope of the family, the only one who could do anything to help them. I had to stand between my two worlds. On the one hand, I would have to see my mother and brothers starve unto death; on the other, I had believed that this man's ideas were for the good of India and the world, and had to be preached and worked out. And so the fight went on in my mind for days and months. Sometimes I would pray for five or six days and nights together without stopping. Oh, the agony of those days! I was living in hell! The natural affections of my boy's heart drawing me to my family—I could not bear to see those who were the nearest and dearest to me suffering. On the other hand, nobody to sympathize with me. Who would sympathize with the imaginations of a boy—imaginations that caused so much suffering to others? Who would sympathize with me? None—except one.

That one's sympathy brought blessing and hope. She was a woman. Our teacher, this great monk, was married when he was a boy and she a mere child. When he became a young man, and all this religious zeal was upon him, she came to see him. Although they had been married for long, they had not seen very much of each other until they were grown up. Then he said to his wife, 'Behold, I am your husband; you have a right to this body. But I cannot live the sex life, although I am married you. I leave it to your judgment.' And she wept and said, 'Godspeed you! The Lord bless you! Am I the woman to degrade you? If I can, I will help you. Go on in your work.'

That was the woman. The husband went on and became a monk in his own way; and from a distance the wife went on helping as much as she could. And later, when the man had become a great spiritual giant, she came—really, she was the first disciple—and she spent the rest of her life taking care of the body of this man. He never knew whether he was living or dying, or anything. Sometimes, when talking, he would get so excited that if he sat on live charcoals, he did not know it. Live charcoals! Forgetting all about his body, all the time.

Well, that lady, his wife, was the only one who sympathized with the idea of those boys. But she was powerless. She was poorer than we were. Never mind! We plunged into the breach. I believed, as I was living, that these ideas were going to rationalize India and bring better days to many lands and foreign races. With that belief, came the realization that it is better that a few persons suffer than that such ideas should die out of the world. What if a mother or two brothers die? It is a sacrifice. Let it be done. No great thing can be done without sacrifice. The heart must be plucked out and the bleeding heart placed upon the altar. Then great things are done. Is there any other way? None have found it. I appeal to each one of you, to those who have accomplished any great thing. Oh, how much it has cost! What agony! What torture! What terrible suffering is behind every deed of success in every life! You know that, all of you.

And thus we went on, that band of boys. The only thing we got from those around us was a kick and a curse—that was all. Of course, we had to beg from door to door for our food: got hips and haws—the refuse of everything—a piece of bread here and there. We got hold of a broken-down old house, with hissing cobras living underneath, and because that was the cheapest, we went into that house and lived there.

Thus we went on for some years, in the meanwhile making excursions all over India, trying to bring about the idea gradually. Ten years were spent without a ray of light! Ten more years! A thousand times despondency came, but there was one thing always to keep us hopeful—the tremendous faithfulness to each other, the tremendous love between us. I have got a 100 men and women around me; if I become the devil himself tomorrow, they will say, 'Here we are still! We will never give you up!' That is a great blessing. In happiness, in misery, in famine, in pain, in the grave, in heaven, or in hell who never gives me up is my friend. Is such friendship a joke? A man may have salvation through such friendship. That brings salvation if we can love like that. If we have that faithfulness, why, there is the essence of all concentration. You need not worship any gods in the world if you have that faith, that strength, that love. And that was there with us all throughout that hard time. That was there. That made us go from the Himalayas to Cape Comorin, from the Indus to the Brahmaputra.

This band of boys began to travel about. Gradually we began to draw attention: 90 per cent was antagonism, very little of it was helpful. For we had one fault: we were boys—in poverty and with all the roughness of boys. He who has to make his own way in life is a bit rough, he has not much time to be smooth and suave and polite—'my lady and my gentleman' and all that. You have seen that in life, always. He is a rough diamond, he has not much polish, he is a jewel in an indifferent casket.

And there we were. 'No compromise!' was the watchword. 'This is the ideal, and this has got to be carried out. If we meet the king, though we die, we must give him a bit of our minds; if the peasant, the same.' Naturally, we met with antagonism.

But, mind you, this is life's experience; if you really want the good of others, the whole universe may stand against you and cannot hurt you. It must crumble before your power of the Lord Himself in you if you are sincere and really unselfish. And those boys were that. They came as children, pure and fresh from the hands of nature. Said our master: 'I want to offer at the altar of the Lord only those flowers that have not even been smelled, fruits that have not been touched with the fingers.' The words of the great man sustained us all. For he saw through the future life of those boys that he collected from the streets of Calcutta, so to say. People used to laugh at him when he said, 'You will see—this boy, that boy, what he becomes.' His faith was unalterable: 'Mother showed it to me. I may be weak, but when she says this is so—she can never make mistakes—it must be so.'

'So things went on and on for 10 years without any light, but with my health breaking all the time. It tells on the body in the long run: sometimes one meal at nine in the evening, another time a meal at eight in the morning, another after two days, another after three days—and always the poorest and roughest thing. Who is going to give to the beggar the good things he has? And then, they have not much in India. And most of the time walking, climbing snow peaks, sometimes ten miles of hard mountain climbing, just to get a meal. They eat unleavened bread in India, and sometimes they have it stored away for 20 or 30 days, until it is harder than bricks; and then they will give a square of that. I would have to go from house to house to collect sufficient for one meal. And then the bread was so hard, it made my mouth bleed to eat it. Literally, you can break your teeth on that bread. Then I would put it in a pot and pour over it water from the river. For months and months, I existed that way—of course, it was telling on the health.

Then I thought, I have tried India, it is time for me to try another country. At that time your Parliament of the World's Religions was to be held, and someone was to be sent from India. I was just a vagabond, but I said, 'If you send me, I am going. I have not much to lose and I do not care if I lose that.' It was very difficult to find the money, but after a long struggle they got together just enough to pay for my passage—and I came. Came one or two months earlier, so that I found myself drifting about in the streets here, without knowing anybody.

But finally the Parliament of the World's Religions opened and I met kind friends, who helped me right along. I worked a little, collected funds, started two papers and so on. After that, I went over to England and worked there. At the same time, I carried on the work for India in America too.

My plan for India, as it has been developed and centralized, is this: I have told you of our lives as monks there, how we go from door to door, so that religion is brought to everybody without charge, except, perhaps, a broken piece of bread. That is why you see the lowest of the low in India holding the most exalted religious ideas. It is all through the work of these monks.

But ask a man, 'Who are the English?'—he does not know.

He says perhaps, 'They are the children of those giants they speak of in those books, are they not?'

'Who governs you?'

'We do not know.'

'What is the government?' They do not know. But they know philosophy. It is a practical want of intellectual education about life on this earth they suffer from. These millions and millions of people are ready for life beyond this world—is not that enough for them? Certainly not. They must have a better piece of bread and a better piece of rag on their bodies. The great question is: how to get that better bread and better rag for these sunken millions.

First, I must tell you, there is great hope for them because, you see, they are the gentlest people on earth. Not that they are timid. When they want to fight, they fight like demons. The best soldiers the English have are recruited from the peasantry of India. Death is a thing of no importance to them. Their attitude is, 'Twenty times I have died before, and I shall die many times after this. What of that?' They never turn back. They are not given to much emotion, but they make very good fighters.

Their instinct, however, is to plough. If you rob them, murder them, tax them, do anything to them, they will be quiet and gentle, so long as you leave them free to practice their religion. They never interfere with the religion of others. 'Leave us liberty to worship our gods and take everything else!' That is their attitude. When the English touch them there, trouble starts. That was the real cause of the 1857 Mutiny—they would not bear religious repression. The great Mohammedan governments were simply blown up because they touched the Indians' religion.

But aside from that, they are very peaceful, very quiet, very gentle, and, above all, not given to vice. The absence of any strong drink, oh, it makes them infinitely superior to the mobs of any other country. You cannot compare the decency of life among the poor in India with life in the slums here. A slum means poverty, but poverty does not mean sin, indecency and vice in India. In other countries, the opportunities are such that only the indecent and the lazy need be poor. There is no reason for poverty unless one is a fool or a blackguard—the sort who want city life and all its luxuries. They will not go into the country. They say, 'We are here with all the fun and you must give us bread.' But that is not the case in India, where the poor fellows work hard from morning to sunset and somebody else takes the bread out of their hands, and their children go hungry. Notwithstanding the millions of tons of wheat raised in India, scarcely a grain passes the mouth of a peasant. He lives upon the poorest corn, which you would not feed to your canary birds.

Now there is no reason why they should suffer such distress—these people, oh, so pure and good! We hear so much talk about the sunken millions and the degraded women of

India—but none come to our help. What do they say? They say, 'You can only be helped, you can only be good by ceasing to be what you are. It is useless to help Hindus.' These people do not know the history of races. There will be no more India if they change their religion and their institutions because that is the vitality of that race. It will disappear; so, really, you will have nobody to help.

Then there is the other great point to learn: that you can never help really. What can we do for each other? You are growing in your own life, I am growing in my own. It is possible that I can give you a push in your life, knowing that, in the long run, all roads lead to Rome. It is a steady growth. No national civilization is perfect yet. Give that civilization a push and it will arrive at its own goal: do not strive to change it. Take away a nation's institutions, customs, manners and what will be left? They hold the nation together.

But here comes the very learned foreign man and he says, 'Look here; you give up all those institutions and customs of thousands of years and take my tomfool tinpot and be happy.' This is all nonsense.

We will have to help each other, but we have to go one step farther: the first thing is to become unselfish in help. 'If you do just what I tell you to do, I will help you, otherwise not.' Is that help?

And so, if the Hindus want to help you spiritually, there will be no question of limitations: perfect unselfishness. I give and there it ends. It is gone from me. My mind, my powers, my everything that I have to give, is given: given with the idea to give and no more. I have seen many times people who have robbed half the world and they gave $20,000 'to convert the heathen'. What for? For the benefit of the heathen, or for their own souls? Just think of that.

And the Nemesis of crime is working. We men try to hoodwink our own eyes. But inside the heart, He has remained, the real Self. He never forgets. We can never delude Him. His eyes will never be hoodwinked. Whenever there is any impulse of real charity, it tells, though it be at the end of a thousand years. Obstructed, it yet wakens once more to burst like a thunderbolt. And every impulse where the motive is selfish, self-seeking—though it may be launched forth with all the newspapers blazoning, all the mobs standing and cheering—it fails to reach the mark.

I am not taking pride in this. But, mark you, I have told the story of that group of boys. Today there is not a village, not a man, not a woman in India that does not know their work and bless them. There is not a famine in the land where these boys do not plunge in and try to work and rescue as many as they can. And that strikes to the heart. The people come to know it. So help whenever you can, but mind what your motive is. If it is selfish, it will neither benefit those you help, nor yourself. If it is unselfish, it will bring blessings upon them to whom it is given and infinite blessings upon you, sure as you are living. The Lord can never be hoodwinked. The law of karma can never be hoodwinked.

Well then, my plans are, therefore, to reach these masses of India. Suppose you start schools all over India for the poor, still you cannot educate them. How can you? The boy of four years would better go to the plough or to work, than to your school. He cannot go to your school. It is impossible. Self-preservation is the first instinct. But if the mountain does not go to Mohammed, then Mohammed can come to the mountain. Why should not education go from door to door, say I. If a ploughman's boy cannot come to education, why not meet him at the plough, at the factory, just wherever he is? Go along with him, like his shadow. But there are these hundreds and thousands of monks, educating the people on the spiritual plane; why not let these men do the same work on the intellectual plane? Why should they not talk to the masses a little about history—about many things? The ears are the best educators. The best principles in our lives were those which we heard from our mothers through our ears. Books came much later. Book learning is nothing. Through the ears, we get the best formative principles. Then, as they get more and more interested, they may come to your books too. First, let it roll on and on—that is my idea.

Well, I must tell you that I am not a very great believer in monastic systems. They have great merits and also great defects. There should be a perfect balance between the monastics and the householders. But monasticism has absorbed all the power in India. We represent the greatest power. The monk is greater than the prince. There is no reigning sovereign in India who dares to sit down when the 'yellow cloth' is there. He gives up his seat and stands. Now, that is bad, so much power, even in the hands of good men—although these monastics have been the bulwark of the people. They stand between the priestcraft and knowledge. They are the centres of knowledge and reform. They are just what the prophets were among the Jews. The prophets were always preaching against the priests, trying to throw out superstitions. So are they in India. But all the same so much power is not good there, better methods should be worked out. But you can only work in the line of least resistance. The whole national soul there is upon monasticism. You go to India and preach any religion as a householder: the Hindu people will turn back and go out. If you have given up the world, however, they say, 'He is good, he has given up the world. He is a sincere man, he wants to do what he preaches.' What I mean to say is this that it represents a tremendous power. What we can do is just to transform it, give it another form. This tremendous power in the hands of the roving sannyasins of India has got to be transformed and it will raise the masses up.

Now, you see, we have brought the plan down nicely on paper, but I have taken it at the same time from the regions of idealism. So far the plan was loose and idealistic. As years went on, it became more and more condensed and accurate; I began to see by actual working its defects and all that.

What did I discover in its working on the material plane? First, there must be centres to educate these monks in the method of education. For instance, I send one of my men, and he goes about with a camera: he has to be taught in those things himself. In India, you will find every man is quite illiterate and that teaching requires tremendous centres. And what does all that mean? Money. From the idealistic plane you come to everyday work. Well, I have worked hard, four years in your country, and two in England. And I am very thankful that some friends came to the rescue. One who is here today with you is amongst them. There are American friends and English friends who went over with me to India, and there has been a very rude beginning. Some English people came and joined the orders. One poor man worked hard and died in India. There are an Englishman and an Englishwoman who have retired; they have some means of their own and they have started a centre in the Himalayas, educating the children. I have given them one of the papers I have started—a copy you will find there on the table—*The Awakened India*. And there they are instructing and working among the people. I have another centre in Calcutta. Of course, all great movements must proceed from the capital. For what is a capital? It is the heart of a nation. All the blood comes into the heart and thence it is distributed; so all the wealth, all the

My Life and Mission ◆ 291

ideas, all the education, all spirituality will converge towards the capital and spread from it.

I am glad to tell you I have made a rude beginning. But the same work I want to do, on parallel lines, for women. And my principle is: each one helps himself. My help is from a distance. There are Indian women, English women and I hope American women will come to take up the task. As soon as they have begun, I wash my hands of it. No man shall dictate to a woman, nor a woman to a man. Each one is independent. What bondage there may be is only that of love. Women will work out their own destinies—much better, too, than men can ever do for them. All the mischief to women has come because men undertook to shape the destiny of women. And I do not want to start with any initial mistake. One little mistake made then will go on multiplying; and if you succeed, in the long run that mistake will have assumed gigantic proportions and become hard to correct. So, if I made this mistake of employing men to work out this women's part of the work, why, women will never get rid of that—it will have become a custom. But I have got an opportunity. I told you of the lady who was my master's wife. We have all great respect for her. She never dictates to us. So it is quite safe.

That part has to be accomplished.

25

THE SAGES OF INDIA

In speaking of the sages of India, my mind goes back to those periods of which history has no record, and tradition tries in vain to bring the secrets out of the gloom of the past. The sages of India have been almost innumerable, for what has the Hindu nation been doing for thousands of years except producing sages? I will take, therefore, the lives of a few of the most brilliant ones, the epoch-makers, and present them before you, that is to say, my study of them.

In the first place, we have to understand a little about our scriptures. Two ideals of truth are in our scriptures; the one is, what we call the eternal, and the other is not so authoritative, yet binding under particular circumstances, times and places. The eternal relations which deal with the nature of the soul and of God, and the relations between souls and God are embodied in what we call the shrutis, the vedas. The next set of truths is what we call the smritis, as embodied in the words of Manu, Yajnavalkya and other writers and also in the puranas, down to the tantras. The second class of books and teachings is subordinate to the shrutis, inasmuch as whenever any one of these contradicts anything in the Shrutis, the shrutis must prevail. This is the law. The idea is that the framework of the destiny and goal of man has been all delineated in the vedas, the details have been left to be worked out in the smritis and puranas. As for general directions, the shrutis are enough; for spiritual life, nothing more can be said, nothing more can be known. All that is necessary has been known, all the advice that is necessary to lead the soul to perfection has been completed in the shrutis; the details alone were left out, and these the smritis have supplied from time to time.

Another peculiarity is that these shrutis have many sages as the recorders of the truths in them, mostly men, even some women. Very little is known of their personalities, the dates of their birth and so forth, but their best thoughts, their best discoveries, I should say, are preserved there, embodied in the sacred literature of our country, the vedas. In the smritis, on the other hand, personalities are more in evidence. Startling, gigantic, impressive, world-moving persons stand before us, as it were, for the first time, sometimes of more magnitude even than their teachings.

This is a peculiarity which we have to understand—that our religion preaches an impersonal personal God. It preaches any amount of impersonal laws plus any amount of personality, but the very fountain-head of our religion is in the shrutis, the vedas, which are perfectly impersonal; the persons all come in the smritis and puranas—the great avataras, incarnations of God, prophets and so forth. And this ought also to be observed that except our religion every other religion in the world depends upon the life or lives of some personal founder or founders. Christianity is built upon the life of Jesus Christ, Mohammedanism upon Mohammed, Buddhism upon Buddha, Jainism upon the Jinas and so on. It naturally follows that there must be in all these religions a good deal of fight about what they call the historical evidences of these great personalities. If at any time the historical evidences about the existence of these personages in ancient times become weak, the whole building of the religion tumbles down and is broken to pieces. We escaped this fate because our religion is not based upon persons but on principles. That you obey your religion is not because it came through the authority of a sage, no, not even of an incarnation. Krishna is not the authority of the vedas, but the vedas are the authority of Krishna himself. His glory is that he is the greatest preacher of the vedas that ever existed. So with the other incarnations, so with all our sages. Our first principle is that all that is necessary for the perfection of man and for attaining unto freedom is there in the vedas. You cannot find anything new. You cannot go beyond a perfect unity, which is the goal of all knowledge; this has been already reached there and it is impossible to go beyond the unity. Religious knowledge became complete when Tat Twam Asi was discovered and that was in the vedas. What remained was the guidance of people from time to time according to different times and places, according to different circumstances and environments; people had to be guided along the old, old path, and for this these great teachers came, these great sages. Nothing can bear out more clearly this position than the celebrated saying of Shri Krishna in the Gita: 'Whenever virtue subsides and irreligion prevails, I create Myself for the protection of the good; for the destruction of all immorality I am coming from time to time.' This is the idea in India.

What follows? That on the one hand, there are these eternal principles which stand upon their own foundations without depending on any reasoning even, much less on the authority of sages however great, of incarnations however brilliant they may have been. We may remark that as this is the unique position in India, our claim is that the Vedanta only can be the universal religion, that it is already the existing universal religion in the world because it teaches principles and not persons. No religion built upon a person can be taken up as a type by all the races of mankind. In our own country, we find that there have been so many grand characters; in even a small city many persons are taken up as types by the different minds in that one city. How is it possible that one person as Mohammed or Buddha or Christ, can be taken up as the one type for the whole world, nay, that the whole of morality, ethics, spirituality and religion can be true only from the sanction of that one person and one person alone? Now, the Vedantic religion does not require any such personal authority. Its sanction is the eternal nature of man, its ethics are based upon the eternal spiritual solidarity of man, already existing, already attained and not to be attained.

On the other hand, from the very earliest times, our sages have been feeling conscious of this fact that the vast majority of mankind requires a personality. They must have a personal god in some form or other. The very Buddha who declared against the existence of a personal god had not died 50 years before his disciples manufactured a personal god out of him. The personal god is necessary, and at the same time we know that instead of and better than vain imaginations of a personal god, which in 99 cases out of a 100 are unworthy of human worship we have in this world, living and walking in our midst, living Gods, now and then. These are more worthy of worship than any imaginary God, any creation of our imagination, that is to say, any idea of God which we can form. Shri Krishna is much greater than any idea of God you or I can have. Buddha is a much higher idea, a more living and idolized idea, than the ideal you or I can conceive of in our minds; and therefore it is that they always command the worship of mankind even to the exclusion of all imaginary deities.

This our sages knew, and, therefore, left it open to all Indian people to worship such great personages, such incarnations.

Nay, the greatest of these incarnations goes further: 'Wherever an extraordinary spiritual power is manifested by external man, know that I am there, it is from Me that that manifestation comes.' That leaves the door open for the Hindu to worship the incarnations of all the countries in the world. The Hindu can worship any sage and any saint from any country whatsoever, and as a fact we know that we go and worship many times in the churches of the Christians and many, many times in the Mohammedan mosques, and that is good. Why not? Ours, as I have said, is the universal religion. It is inclusive enough, it is broad enough to include all the ideals. All the ideals of religion that already exist in the world can be immediately included and we can patiently wait for all the ideals that are to come in the future to be taken in the same fashion, embraced in the infinite arms of the religion of the Vedanta.

This, more or less, is our position with regard to the great sages, the incarnations of God. There are also secondary characters. We find the word rishi again and again mentioned in the vedas, and it has become a common word at the present time. The rishi is the great authority. We have to understand that idea. The definition is that the rishi is the *mantradrashta*, the seer of thought. What is the proof of religion?—this was asked in very ancient times. There is no proof in the senses was the declaration.

यतो वाचो निवर्तन्ते अप्राप्य मनसा सह

(From whence words reflect back with thought without reaching the goal.)

Upanishads, Verse 1

न तत्र चक्षुर्गच्छति न वाग्गच्छति नो मनः

(There the eyes cannot reach, neither can speech, nor the mind.)

Upanishads, Verse 3

This has been the declaration for ages and ages. Nature outside cannot give us any answer as to the existence of the soul, the existence of God, the eternal life, the goal of man and all that. This mind is continually changing, always in a state of flux; it is finite, it is broken into pieces. How can nature tell of the infinite, the unchangeable, the unbroken, the indivisible, the eternal? It never can. And whenever mankind has striven to get an answer from dull dead matter, history shows how disastrous the results have been. How comes, then, the knowledge which the vedas declare? It comes through being a rishi. This knowledge is not in the senses, but are the senses the be-all and the end-all of the human being? Who dare say that the senses are the all-in-all of man? Even in our lives, in the life of every one of us here, there come moments of calmness, perhaps, when we see before us the death of one we loved, when some shock comes to us, or when extreme blessedness comes to us. Many other occasions there are when the mind, as it were, becomes calm, feels for the moment its real nature and a glimpse of the infinite beyond, where words cannot reach nor the mind go, is revealed to us. This happens in ordinary life, but it has to be heightened, practiced, perfected. Men found out ages ago that the soul is not bound or limited by the senses, no, not even by consciousness. We have to understand that this consciousness is only the name of one link in the infinite chain. Being is not identical with consciousness, but consciousness is only one part of being. Beyond consciousness is where the bold search lies.

Consciousness is bound by the senses. Beyond that, beyond the senses, men must go in order to arrive at truths of the spiritual world, and there are even now persons who succeed in going beyond the bounds of the senses. They are called rishis because they come face to face with spiritual truths.

The proof, therefore, of the vedas is just the same as the proof of this table before me, *pratyaksha*, direct perception. This I see with the senses and the truths of spirituality we also see in a superconscious state of the human soul. This rishi-state is not limited by time or place, by sex or race. Vatsyayana boldly declares that this rishihood is the common property of the descendants of the sage, of the Aryan, of the non-Aryan, of even the Mlechchha. This is the sageship of the vedas and constantly we ought to remember this ideal of religion in India, which I wish other nations of the world would also remember and learn, so that there may be less fight and less quarrel. Religion is not in books, nor in theories, nor in dogmas, nor in talking, not even in reasoning. It is being and becoming. Ay, my friends, until each one of you has become a rishi and come face to face with spiritual facts, religious life has not begun for you. Until the superconscious opens for you, religion is mere talk, it is nothing but preparation. You are talking second-hand, third-hand and here applies that beautiful saying of Buddha when he had a discussion with some Brahmins.

They came discussing about the nature of Brahman and the great sage asked, 'Have you seen Brahman?'

'No,' said the Brahmin.

'Or your father?'

'No, neither has he.'

'Or your grandfather?'

'I don't think even he saw Him.'

'My friend, how can you discuss about a person whom

your father and grandfather never saw and try to put each other down?' That is what the whole world is doing. Let us say in the language of the Vedanta, 'This atman is not to be reached by too much talk, no, not even by the highest intellect, no, not even by the study of the vedas themselves.'

Let us speak to all the nations of the world in the language of the vedas: vain are your fights and your quarrels; have you seen God whom you want to preach? If you have not seen, vain is your preaching; you do not know what you say; and if you have seen God, you will not quarrel, your very face will shine. An ancient sage of the Upanishads sent his son out to learn about Brahman, and the child came back and the father asked, 'What have you learnt?' The child replied he had learnt so many sciences. But the father said, 'That is nothing, go back.' And the son went back, and when he returned again the father asked the same question and the same answer came from the child. Once more he had to go back. And the next time he came, his whole face was shining; and his father stood up and declared, 'Ay, today, my child, your face shines like a knower of Brahman.' When you have known God, your very face will be changed, your voice will be changed, your whole appearance will he changed. You will be a blessing to mankind; none will be able to resist the rishi. This is the rishihood, the ideal in our religion. The rest, all these talks and reasonings and philosophies and dualisms and monisms and even the vedas themselves are but preparations, secondary things. The other is primary. The vedas, grammar, astronomy, etc., all these are secondary; that is supreme knowledge which makes us realize the unchangeable one. Those who realized are the sages whom we find in the vedas; and we understand how this rishi is the name of a type, of a class, which every one of us, as true Hindus, is expected to become at some period of our life, and becoming which, to the Hindu means salvation. Not belief in doctrines, not going to thousands of temples, nor bathing in all the rivers in the world, but becoming the rishi, the mantra-drashta—that is freedom, that is salvation.

Coming down to later times, there have been great world-moving sages, great incarnations of whom there have been many; and according to the Bhagavata, they also are infinite in number, and those that are worshipped most in India are Rama and Krishna. Rama, the ancient idol of the heroic ages, the embodiment of truth, of morality, the ideal son, the ideal husband, the ideal father, and above all, the ideal king, this Rama has been presented before us by the great sage Valmiki. No language can be purer, none chaster, none more beautiful and at the same time simpler than the language in which the great poet has depicted the life of Rama. And what to speak of Sita? You may exhaust the literature of the world that is past, and I may assure you that you will have to exhaust the literature of the world of the future, before finding another Sita. Sita is unique; that character was depicted once and for all. There may have been several Ramas, perhaps, but never more than one Sita! She is the very type of the true Indian woman, for all the Indian ideals of a perfected woman have grown out of that one life of Sita; and here she stands these thousands of years, commanding the worship of every man, woman and child throughout the length and breadth of the land of Aryavarta. There she will always be, this glorious Sita, purer than purity itself, all patience and all suffering. She who suffered that life of suffering without a murmur, she the ever-chaste and ever-pure wife, she the ideal of the people, the ideal of the gods, the great Sita, our national God she must always remain. And every one of us knows her too well to require much delineation. All our mythology may vanish, even our vedas may depart, and our

Sanskrit language may vanish forever, but so long as there will be five Hindus living here, even if only speaking the most vulgar patois, there will be the story of Sita present. Mark my words: Sita has gone into the very vitals of our race. She is there in the blood of every Hindu man and woman; we are all children of Sita. Any attempt to modernize our women, if it tries to take our women away from that ideal of Sita, is immediately a failure, as we see every day. The women of India must grow and develop in the footprints of Sita, and that is the only way.

The next is He who is worshipped in various forms, the favourite ideal of men as well as of women, the ideal of children, as well as of grown-up men. I mean He whom the writer of the Bhagavata was not content to call an incarnation but says, 'The other incarnations were but parts of the Lord. He, Krishna, was the Lord Himself.' And it is not strange that such adjectives are applied to him when we marvel at the many-sidedness of his character. He was the most wonderful sannyasin and the most wonderful householder in one; he had the most wonderful amount of rajas, power and was at the same time living in the midst of the most wonderful renunciation. Krishna can never he understood until you have studied the Gita, for he was the embodiment of his own teaching. Every one of these incarnations came as a living illustration of what they came to preach. Krishna, the preacher of the Gita, was all his life the embodiment of that Song Celestial; he was the great illustration of non-attachment. He gives up his throne and never cares for it. He, the leader of India, at whose word kings come down from their thrones, never wants to be a king. He is the simple Krishna, ever the same Krishna who played with the gopis. Ah, that most marvellous passage of his life, the most difficult to understand and which none ought to attempt to understand until he has become perfectly chaste and pure, that most marvellous expansion of love, allegorized and expressed in that beautiful play at Vrindaban, which none can understand but he who has become mad with love, drunk deep of the cup of love! Who can understand the throes of the lore of the gopis—the very ideal of love, love that wants nothing, love that even does not care for heaven, love that does not care for anything in this world or the world to come? And here, my friends, through this love of the Gopis has been found the only solution of the conflict between the personal and the impersonal god.

We know how the personal god is the highest point of human life; we know that it is philosophical to believe in an Impersonal God immanent in the universe, of whom everything is but a manifestation. At the same time our souls hanker after something concrete, something which we want to grasp, at whose feet we can pour out our soul and so on. The personal god is therefore the highest conception of human nature. Yet reason stands aghast at such an idea. It is the same old, old question which you find discussed in the *Brahma Sutras*, which you find Draupadi discussing with Yudhishthira in the forest: if there is a personal god, all-merciful, all-powerful, why is the hell of an earth here, why did he create this?—He must be a partial God. There was no solution and the only solution that can be found is what you read about the love of the gopis. They hated every adjective that was applied to Krishna; they did not care to know that he was the Lord of creation, they did not care to know that he was almighty, they did not care to know that he was omnipotent and so forth. The only thing they understood was that he was infinite love, that was all. The gopis understood Krishna only as the Krishna of Vrindaban. He, the leader of the hosts, the king of kings, to them was the shepherd and the shepherd forever.

'I do not want wealth, nor many people, nor do I want

learning; no, not even do I want to go to heaven. Let one be born again and again, but Lord, grant me this that I may have love for Thee and that for love's sake.' A great landmark in the history of religion is here, the ideal of love for love's sake, work for work's sake, duty for duty's sake, and it for the first time fell from the lips of the greatest of incarnations, Krishna, and for the first time in the history of humanity, upon the soil of India. The religions of fear and of temptations were gone forever and in spite of the fear of hell and temptation of enjoyment in heaven came the grandest of ideals, love for love's sake, duty for duty's sake, work for work's sake.

And what a love! I have told you just now that it is very difficult to understand the love of the gopis. There are not wanting fools, even in the midst of us, who cannot understand the marvellous significance of that most marvellous of all episodes. There are, let me repeat, impure fools, even born of our blood, who try to shrink from that as if from something impure. To them I have only to say, first make yourselves pure; and you must remember that he who tells the history of the love of the gopis is none else but Shuka Deva. The historian who records this marvellous love of the gopis is one who was born pure, the eternally pure Shuka, the son of Vyasa. So long as there is selfishness in the heart, so long is love of God impossible; it is nothing but shopkeeping: 'I give you something O Lord, you give me something in return'; and says the Lord, 'If you do not do this, I will take good care of you when you die. I will roast you all the rest of your lives, perhaps' and so on. So long as such ideas are in the brain, how can one understand the mad throes of the gopis' love? 'O for one, one kiss of those lips! One who has been kissed by Thee, his thirst for Thee increases for ever, all sorrows vanish and he forgets love for everything else but for Thee and Thee alone.' Ay, forget first the love for gold, name and fame and for this little trumpery world of ours. Then, only then, you will understand the love of the gopis, too holy to be attempted without giving up everything, too sacred to be understood until the soul has become perfectly pure.

People with ideas of sex, of money, of fame, bubbling up every minute in the heart, daring to criticize and understand the love of the gopis! That is the very essence of the Krishna incarnation. Even the Gita, the great philosophy itself, does not compare with that madness, for in the Gita the disciple is taught slowly how to walk towards the goal, but here is the madness of enjoyment, the drunkenness of love, where disciples and teachers and teachings and books and all these things have become one; even the ideas of fear, God, heaven—everything has been thrown away. What remains is the madness of love. It is forgetfulness of everything and the lover sees nothing in the world except that Krishna and Krishna alone, when the face of every being becomes a Krishna, when his own face looks like Krishna, when his own soul has become tinged with the Krishna colour. That was the great Krishna!

Do not waste your time upon little details. Take up the framework, the essence of the life. There may be many historical discrepancies, there may be interpolations in the life of Krishna. All these things may be true, but at the same time, there must have been a basis, a foundation for this new and tremendous departure. Taking the life of any other sage or prophet, we find that that prophet is only the evolution of what had gone before him, we find that that prophet is only preaching the ideas that had been scattered about his own country even in his own times. Great doubts may exist even as to whether that prophet existed or not. But here, I challenge anyone to show whether these things, these ideals—work for work's sake, love for love's sake, duty for duty's sake—were not original ideas with Krishna, and as such, there must have been someone with whom these ideas originated. They could not have been borrowed from anybody else. They were not floating about in the atmosphere when Krishna was born. But the Lord Krishna was the first preacher of this; his disciple Vyasa took it up and preached it unto mankind. This is the highest idea to picture. The highest thing we can get out of him is Gopijanavallabha, the beloved of the gopis of Vrindaban.

When that madness comes in your brain, when you understand the blessed Gopis, then you will understand what love is. When the whole world will vanish, when all other considerations will have died out, when you will become pure-hearted with no other aim, not even the search after truth, then and then alone will come to you the madness of that love, the strength and the power of that infinite love which the gopis had, that love for love's sake. That is the goal. When you have got that, you have got everything.

To come down to the lower stratum—Krishna, the preacher of the Gita. Ay, there is an attempt in India now which is like putting the cart before the horse. Many of our people think that Krishna as the lover of the gopis is something rather uncanny, and the Europeans do not like it much. Dr So-and-so does not like it. Certainly then, the gopis have to go! Without the sanction of Europeans how can Krishna live? He cannot! In the Mahabharata there is no mention of the gopis except in one or two places and those not very remarkable places. In the prayer of Draupadi, there is mention of a Vrindaban life, and in the speech of Shishupala there is again mention of this Vrindaban. All these are interpolations! What the Europeans do not want: must be thrown off. They are interpolations, the mention of the gopis and of Krishna too! Well, with these men, steeped in commercialism, where even the ideal of religion has become commercial, they are all trying to go to heaven by doing something here; the bania wants compound interest, wants to lay by something here and enjoy it there. Certainly the gopis have no place in such a system of thought. From that ideal lover we come down to the lower stratum of Krishna, the preacher of the Gita.

Than the Gita, no better commentary on the Vedas has been written or can be written. The essence of the shrutis, or of the Upanishads, is hard to be understood, seeing that there are so many commentators, each one trying to interpret in his own way. Then the Lord Himself comes, He who is the inspirer of the shrutis, to show us the meaning of them as the preacher of the Gita, and today India wants nothing better, the world wants nothing better than that method of interpretation. It is a wonder that subsequent interpreters of the scriptures, even commenting upon the Gita many times could not catch the meaning, many times could not catch the drift. For what do you find in the Gita and what in modern commentators? One non-dualistic commentator takes up an Upanishad; there are so many dualistic passages and he twists and tortures them into some meaning and wants to bring them all into a meaning of his own. If a dualistic commentator comes, there are so many non-dualistic texts which he begins to torture, to bring them all round to dualistic meaning.

But you find in the Gita there is no attempt at torturing any one of them. They are all right, says the Lord; for slowly and gradually the human soul rises up and up, step after step, from the gross to the fine, from the fine to the finer, until it reaches the absolute, the goal. That is what is in the Gita. Even the 'Karma Kanda' is taken up and it is shown that although it cannot give salvation direct, but only indirectly, yet that is also valid; images are valid indirectly; ceremonies, forms, everything is valid only with one condition, purity of the heart. For worship is valid and leads to the goal if the heart is pure and the heart is sincere; and all these various modes of worship are necessary, else why should they be there? Religions and sects are not the work of hypocrites and wicked people who invented all these to get a little money, as some of our modern men want to think. However reasonable that explanation may seem, it is not true, and they were not invented that way at all. They are the outcome of the necessity of the human soul. They are all here to satisfy the hankering and thirst of different classes of human minds and you need not preach against them. The day when that necessity will cease, they will vanish along with the cessation of that necessity; and so long as that necessity remains, they must be there in spite of your preaching, in spite of your criticism. You may bring the sword or the gun into play, you may deluge the world with human blood, but so long as there is a necessity for idols, they must remain. These forms and all the various steps in religion will remain and we understand from Lord Shri Krishna why they should.

A rather sadder chapter of India's history comes now. In the Gita we already hear the distant sound of the conflicts of sects and the Lord comes in the middle to harmonize them all; He, the great preacher of harmony, the greatest teacher of harmony, Lord Shri Krishna. He says, 'In Me they are all strung like pearls upon a thread.' We already hear the distant sounds, the murmurs of the conflict and possibly there was a period of harmony and calmness, when it broke out anew, not only on religious grounds, but roost possibly on caste grounds, the fight between the two powerful factors in our community, the kings and the priests. And from the topmost crest of the wave that deluged India for nearly a thousand years, we see another glorious figure, and that was our Gautama Shakyamuni. You all know about his teachings and preachings. We worship him as God incarnate, the greatest, the boldest preacher of morality that the world ever saw, the greatest Karma Yogi; as disciple of himself, as it were, the same Krishna came to show how to make his theories practical. There came once again the same voice that in the Gita preached, 'Even the least bit done of this religion saves from great fear.' 'Women, or Vaishyas, or even Shudras, all reach the highest goal.' Breaking the bondages of all, the chains of all, declaring liberty to all to reach the highest goal, come the words of the Gita, rolls like thunder the mighty voice of Krishna: 'Even in this life they have conquered relativity, whose minds are firmly fixed upon the sameness, for God is pure and the same to all, therefore such are said to be living in God.'

'Thus seeing the same Lord equally present everywhere, the sage does not injure the Self by the self, and thus reaches the highest goal.' As it were to give a living example of this preaching, as it were to make at least one part of it practical, the preacher himself came in another form and this was Shakyamuni—the preacher to the poor and the miserable, he who rejected even the language of the gods to speak in the language of the people, so that he might reach the hearts of the people, he who gave up a throne to live with beggars, and the poor, and the downcast, he who pressed the Pariah to his breast like a second Rama.

You all know about his great work, his grand character. But the work had one great defect, for that we are suffering even today. No blame attaches to the Lord. He is pure and glorious, but unfortunately such high ideals could not be well assimilated by the different uncivilized and uncultured races of mankind who flocked within the fold of the Aryans. These races, with varieties of superstition and hideous worship, rushed within the fold of the Aryans and for a time appeared as if they had become civilized, but before a century had passed they brought out their snakes, their ghosts, all the other things their ancestors used to worship, and thus the whole of India became one degraded mass of superstition.

The earlier Buddhists in their rage against the killing of animals had denounced the sacrifices of the vedas; and these sacrifices used to be held in every house. There was a fire burning and that was all the paraphernalia of worship. These sacrifices were obliterated and in their place came gorgeous temples, gorgeous ceremonies and gorgeous priests and all that you see in India in modern times. I smile when I read books written by some modern people who ought to have known better, that the Buddha was the destroyer of Brahminical idolatry. Little do they know that Buddhism created Brahminism and idolatry in India.

There was a book written a year or two ago by a Russian gentleman, who claimed to have found out a very curious life of Jesus Christ, and in one part of the book he says that Christ went to the temple of Jagannath to study with the Brahmins, but became disgusted with their exclusiveness and their idols, and so he went to the Lamas of Tibet instead, became perfect and went home. To any man who knows anything about Indian history, that very statement proves that the whole thing was a fraud because the temple of Jagannath is an old Buddhistic temple. We took this and others over and re-Hinduised them. We shall have to do many things like that yet. That is Jagannath and there was not one Brahmin there then, and yet we are told that Jesus Christ came to study with the Brahmins there. So says our great Russian archaeologist.

Thus, in spite of the preaching of mercy to animals, in spite of the sublime ethical religion, in spite of the hairsplitting discussions about the existence or non-existence of a permanent soul, the whole building of Buddhism tumbled down piecemeal;

and the ruin was simply hideous. I have neither the time nor the inclination to describe to you the hideousness that came in the wake of Buddhism. The most hideous ceremonies, the most horrible, the most obscene books that human hands ever wrote or the human brain ever conceived, the most bestial forms that ever passed under the name of religion, have all been the creation of degraded Buddhism.

But India has to live and the spirit of the Lords descended again. He who declared, 'I will come whenever virtue subsides', came again and this time the manifestation was in the South, and up rose that young Brahmin of whom it has been declared that at the age of 16 he had completed all his writings; the marvellous boy Shankaracharya arose. The writings of this boy of 16 are the wonders of the modern world and so was the boy. He wanted to bring back the Indian world to its pristine purity, but think of the amount of the task before him. I have told you a few points about the state of things that existed in India. All these horrors that you are trying to reform are the outcome of that reign of degradation. The Tartars and the Baluchis and all the hideous races of mankind came to India and became Buddhists, assimilated with us and brought their national customs, and the whole of our national life became a huge page of the most horrible and the most bestial customs. That was the inheritance which that boy got from the Buddhists and from that time to this, the whole work in India is a reconquest of this Buddhistic degradation by the Vedanta. It is still going on, it is not yet finished. Shankara came, a great philosopher, and showed that the real essence of Buddhism and that of the Vedanta are not very different, but that the disciples did not understand the master and have degraded themselves, denied the existence of the soul and of God, and have become atheists. That was what Shankara showed and all the Buddhists began to come back to the old religion. But then they had become accustomed to all these forms; what could be done?

Then came the brilliant Ramanuja. Shankara, with his great intellect, I am afraid, had not as great a heart. Ramanuja's heart was greater. He felt for the downtrodden, he sympathized with them. He took up the ceremonies, the accretions that had gathered, made them pure so far as they could be and instituted new ceremonies, new methods of worship for the people who absolutely required them. At the same time he opened the door to the highest, spiritual worship from the Brahmin to the Pariah. That was Ramanuja's work. That work rolled on, invaded the North, was taken up by some great leaders there, but that was much later during the Mohammedan rule; and the brightest of these prophets of comparatively modern times in the North was Chaitanya.

You may mark one characteristic since the time of Ramanuja—the opening of the door of spirituality to everyone. That has been the watchword of all prophets succeeding Ramanuja, as it had been the watchword of all the prophets before Shankara. I do not know why Shankara should be represented as rather exclusive; I do not find anything in his writings which is exclusive. As in the case of the declarations of the Lord Buddha, this exclusiveness that has been attributed to Shankara's teachings is most possibly not due to his teachings, but to the incapacity of his disciples.

This one great Northern sage, Chaitanya, represented the mad love of the gopis. Himself a Brahmin, born of one of the most rationalistic families of the day, himself a professor of logic fighting and gaining a word-victory, for, this he had learnt from his childhood as the highest ideal of life and yet through the mercy of some sage the whole life of that man became changed; he gave up his fight, his quarrels, his professorship of logic and became one of the greatest teachers of bhakti the world has ever known—mad Chaitanya. His bhakti rolled over the whole land of Bengal, bringing solace to everyone. His love knew no bounds. The saint or the sinner, the Hindu or the Mohammedan, the pure or the impure, the prostitute, the streetwalker—all had a share in his love, all had a share in his mercy: and even to the present day, although greatly degenerated, as everything does become in time, his sect is the refuge of the poor, of the downtrodden, of the outcast, of the weak, of those who have been rejected by all society. But at the same time I must remark for truth's sake that we find this: in the philosophic sect, we find wonderful liberalisms. There is not a man who follows Shankara who will say that all the different sects of India are really different. At the same time he was a tremendous upholder of exclusiveness as regards caste. But with every Vaishnavite preacher we find a wonderful liberalism as to the teaching of caste questions, but exclusiveness as regards religious questions.

The one had a great head, the other a large heart, the time was ripe for one to be born, the embodiment of both this head and heart; the time was ripe for one to be born who in one body would have the brilliant intellect of Shankara and the wonderfully expansive, infinite heart of Chaitanya; one who would see in every sect the same spirit working, the same God; one who would see God in every being, one whose heart would weep for the poor, for the weak, for the outcast, for the downtrodden, for everyone in this world, inside India or outside India; and at the same time whose grand brilliant intellect would conceive of such noble thoughts as would harmonize all conflicting sects, not only in India but outside of India, and bring a marvellous harmony, the universal religion of head and heart into existence. Such a man was born and I had the good fortune to sit at his feet for years. The time was ripe, it was necessary that such a man should be born and he came; and the most wonderful part of it was that his life's work was just near a city which was full of Western thoughts, a city which had run mad after these occidental ideas, a city which had become more Europeanized than any other city in India. There he lived, without any book-learning whatsoever; this great intellect never learnt even to write his own name, but the most graduates of our university found in him an intellectual giant.

He was a strange man, this Shri Ramakrishna Paramahamsa. It is a long, long story and I have no time to tell anything about him tonight. Let me now only mention the great Shri Ramakrishna, the fulfilment of the Indian sages, the sage for the time, one whose teaching is just now, in the present time most beneficial. And mark the divine power working behind the man. The son of a poor priest, born in an out-of-the-way village, unknown and unthought of, today is worshipped literally by thousands in Europe and America and tomorrow will be worshipped by thousands more. Who knows the plans of the Lord!

Now, my brothers, if you do not see the hand, the finger of Providence, it is because you are blind, born blind indeed. If time comes, and another opportunity, I will speak to you more fully about him. Only let me say now that if I have told you one word of truth, it was his and his alone, and if I have told you many things which were not true, which were not correct, which were not beneficial to the human race, they were all mine, and on me is the responsibility.

www.ingramcontent.com/pod-product-compliance
Lightning Source LLC
Chambersburg PA
CBHW031421150426
43191CB00006B/346